The ORIGINAL MOUNTAIN BIKE BOOK

Rob van der Plas and Charles Kelly
with contributions by Philip Keyes
and Jacquie Phelan

BICYCLE BOOKS
FROM

MBI Publishing Company

First published in 1998 by MBI Publishing Company, 729 Prospect Avenue, PO Box 1, Osceola, WI 54020-0001 USA

MBI Publishing Company books are also available at discounts in bulk quantity for industrial or sales-promotional use. For details write to Special Sales Manager at Motorbooks International Wholesalers & Distributors, 729 Prospect Avenue, PO Box 1, Osceola, WI 54020-0001 USA.

Library of Congress Cataloging-in-Publication Data Available
ISBN 0-933201-86-9

On the front cover: Hans-Joerg Rey completing a front-wheel landing after a wicked jump.

On the frontispiece: Emmet Purcel blazes through one of the many streams and water crossings around the Boseman, Montana area.

On the title page: Purcel demonstrates how to attack the gorgeous trails around Bozeman, Montana.

On back cover: This is a dream workshop that every serious mountain biker and technician should have. It is equipped with all the specialty tools, such as pullers and wrenches as well as a abundant selection of general tools. Tierra and Estela Villasenor slicing through the scenic trails around Bozeman, Montana.

Designed by Katie L. Sonmor

Printed in Hong Kong through World Print, Ltd.

Table of Contents

Part IV. Maintenance and Repairs of Your Mountain Bike   121

ABOUT THE AUTHORS

Charles Kelly is the unquestioned father of mountain bike writing. He was one of the early mountain bikers in Marin County, using his mountain bike for every conceivable practical purpose as well as riding up and down Mount Tam—and giving younger road bike riders a run for their money. He was the publisher, with Denise Caramagno, of the sport's first periodical, *The Flat Tire Flyer*, and a partner in MountainBikes, the first commercial mountain bike company. For many years, he could rightly bill himself as the world's greatest expert on the world's smallest subject (mountain biking wasn't considered a big issue at the time). These days, he is billed as "Elder Statesman" in *Dirt Rag*, the off-beat mountain bike magazine where much of his writing appears now. He lives in Fairfax, at the foot of Mount Tamalpais in Marin County.

Rob van der Plas is the author of the first mountain bike book ever published, and has written many other cycling-related books and articles. Having ridden off-road on conventional bikes long before the mountain bike was introduced, he had his first mountain bike built to his own specifications by a frame builder in Germany, where his engineering job had taken him when most of the early development took place. He was the first one to realize that the existing bike books weren't much use if you're interested in mountain biking. So he wrote and published the first book on the subject, *The Mountain Bike Book*, which appeared early in 1984. Today he lives in San Francisco and rides in the Marin Headlands.

Jacquie Phelan is also known as Alice B. Toeclips. An accomplished road bike racer at the time mountain bikes first came out, she lived in the right place to rub shoulders with many of the first mountain bikers, and it wasn't long before she became one of the most eminent women racers and riders. She is the founder of WOMBATS, the Women's Mountain Bike & Tea Society, and devotes much of her time and energy to popularizing mountain biking among women.

Philip Keyes is the Land Access editor for *Dirt Rag* magazine and the president of the New England Mountain Bike Association.

CHAPTER ONE

INTRODUCTION

No doubt about it: mountain biking has come of age. In fact, the mountain bike has taken over. The vast majority of all bicycles sold now fall into the category of mountain bikes and their close relatives, all characterized by fat tires, flat handlebars, and multispeed derailleur gearing.

The mountain bike has also revolutionized cycling. Formerly biking was preserved for smooth asphalt, now you can go almost anywhere on a bike—providing it's a mountain bike. Cyclists have fallen in love with this rugged bike for all seasons.

Indeed, it is hard not to be enthusiastic about this wonderful bicycle. It helps novices become experts in record time, and it allows experienced cyclists to do things they had never before thought possible. The mountain bike is not only agile and rugged enough to go anywhere; it is also safer, more reliable, and more comfortable than any other bike available.

Even though the mountain bike has become the bike for all uses, the machine's real advantage is its off-road performance. There are many ways of riding off-road, depending on the terrain and your own circumstances. Special breeds of mountain bikes have been developed in response to these diverse needs. It makes a difference whether you live in a wooded area with narrow, rutted trails that can only be mastered at modest speeds—referred to as technical trail riding—or near mountainous areas with many fast downhill runs, in a wet and soggy part of the world or in a desert region. We'll show you the appropriate techniques and the best selection of equipment to meet these varied conditions.

ABOUT THIS BOOK

This book is devoted specifically to the mountain bike and the way it is used—all of its uses, not just for riding on trails. Consequently, you will find quite a lot of advice related to propelling your bike in general, although the emphasis will be on specific recommendations for riding off-road.

The book is a collaborative effort. Most of the text was originally written by Rob van der Plas, some chapters by Charles Kelly, and one chapter each by Jacquie Phelan and Philip Keyes.

There are four distinct parts and an appendix. Part I (Chapters 1 through 6), explains the basics, including background information and essential selection criteria, as well as how to get started.

Part II (Chapters 7 through 15) takes you off-road, explaining issues related to how and where to ride and covering special topics such as racing and touring, biking for women, and land access.

Part III (Chapters 16 through 24) deals with the equipment in more detail, explaining the operation of, and the quality criteria for the bike and its various components and the way they work together.

Part IV (Chapters 25 through 34) contains full maintenance instructions for each component and the bike as a whole.

The Appendix contains reference material: a list of addresses, a frame sizing aid, and a gearing table.

Throughout the text, you will encounter references to manufacturers, brands, makes, and models of certain products related to the subject. Some of these terms are protected brand names or registered trademarks, though they are not identified as such in the text. Their use here is for informative purposes only, for which reason these terms are not identified by the registration symbol. Other terms have at times been hotly contested—for example, the term *mountain bike* itself, which has been the subject of several lawsuits.

Another warning concerns the volatility of any kind of information on the subject of mountain bikes. What's here today may be gone tomorrow. Some of the brand names recommended in the previous edition of this book are no longer around, as are some of the types of components. The same may well happen to some of today's hot brands and types of equipment. We tend to take a skeptical stand: we try to steer clear of what is hyped up too much, instead taking as objective a look as possible at what makes sense and what doesn't. As a result, you will find that we shrug off one or two of the things touted vigorously in the mountain biking magazines and we mention some practical items that may be hard to find, but are worth the search.

DEFINING THE MOUNTAIN BIKE

The mountain bike combines some of the best characteristics of several other machines, though it is clearly designed afresh. The fat tires have a tough tread for good traction on dirt, yet they are also light and flexible, and can be inflated to a high pressure, resulting in remarkably little rolling resistance. The handlebars are wide enough to offer firm handling, and flat enough to allow instant access to the brakes. At the same time, they are ergonomically designed, so they don't force you into a posture that is uncomfortable.

The frame is rugged, yet quite light. The wheels are driven via a gearing system (ranging from 18 to 24 speeds) that allows you to take most inclines in your stride. The gears are easy to operate by means of indexed shifters. But this intriguing machine won't merely climb, it will go downhill safely, due to its balanced geometry. And with the help of its special brakes, it can be stopped on a dime. In addition, many models available these days have at least a front suspension, making high-speed riding over rough terrain not only more comfortable but also safer, because it is eassier to remain in control when your hands aren't knocked off the handlebars over every bump.

In subsequent chapters, we shall take a closer look at the characteristic features of the mountain bike and its components. You will learn that there are enough differences within the range of mountain bikes available to make some machines more suitable for certain purposes than others.

Perhaps the greatest positive aspect of the mountain bike is the appeal it has to those who have not previously felt very much at ease on a bike. Turned off by the poor performance and discomfort of the old utility bike, yet not at ease with the drop-handlebar road bike, these are the people whose bikes, if they had them at all, stood rusting away in a corner of the garage for many years. Young and old, men and women—all feel at ease on the mountain bike.

Many of us still cherish our lighter and more agile road bikes with skinny tires for use on paved roads. But the mountain bike has brought a form of equality to cycling. Now even the less skilled can buy a quality bike that matches their riding habits. The mountain bike is the bicycle for everyone.

EVOLUTION OF THE MOUNTAIN BIKE

Although the mountain bike is a recent development, it already has a history that deserves to be told. In fact, its roots can be traced back to 1933. Although balloon-tired bicycles had been around for about five years at the time, that was the year Ignaz Schwinn introduced his most successful version in the United States. It had fat tires but few of the other virtues of the modern mountain bike, except ruggedness and a well-balanced frame geometry. Heavy and indestructible, it soon became the standard for newspaper delivery and other forms of utilitarian cycling. Actually, it was meant to be a gag. Emulating the motorized vehicles of adult Americans, it offered kids the closest approximation to a car possible on two wheels that was muscle-powered.

Half a century later this curious design was to experience an unexpected revival. Cycling in America had gone through fits and starts, ups and downs. The 10-speed boom had come and gone, but at least it had finally allowed self-respecting adults to progress self-propelled, which had been unheard of for many years. Meanwhile, the younger generation's BMX bike had not only become a toy and a means of competition but had also led to some surprisingly sophisticated technology.

The mountain bike is a synthesis of the old utility bike, the 10-speed, and the BMX bike. Popular lore has it that it all started just north of San Francisco, on the slopes of Mount Tamalpais in Marin County, and we'll take a closer look at the various scenarios in the next chapter. Rather, we like to think of "Mount Tam" as only one of several places where this development occurred. What happened there no doubt also happened elsewhere, and the timing couldn't have been too far off.

As it was, people there made a sport of riding motorcycles down the rough slopes of Marin County's highest mountain, which gave them hair-raising thrills. It was horrible in environmental terms, as it not only was noisy but also caused erosion, which disturbed the natural watershed. When the water district authorities, who controlled the land, got wind of it, they restricted motorcycles to paved roads. Some of these riders thought of other ways to get their thrills: they took to riding down the same slopes on bicycles, getting back up the road with their bikes in a pickup truck.

They must have ruined a lot of bicycles that way, not to mention what they did to the environment, even without a motor. It became apparent that the Schwinn Excelsior, built from 1933 until 1941, was the most suitable bike for the purpose.

A few problems remained, though. This bike's coaster brake (back-pedaling brake to our British readers) had a way of overheating on the downhill. After only one descent, the heat would literally boil the grease out of the bearings. You had to repack the bearings with fresh grease after each ride. The most famous stretch of Tamalpais slope is called Repack in its honor. Besides, the idea of riding down only to hitch a ride back up in a truck seemed perverse to the true cyclist. That's how the idea evolved to equip the fat-tire bike with derailleur gearing.

Joe Breeze, a frame builder of some expertise, went a step further. At the request of Charles Kelly, Breeze copied the geometry that seemed to lend the Schwinn Excelsior its superb uphill and downhill qualities onto a frame built of lightweight tubing, resulting in a machine that weighed much less. This was adapted to take the most suitable components available at the time, such as 15-speed derailleur gears, cantilever brakes, and moped handlebars and brake levers. Essentially, the mountain bike was born. It just hadn't come of age yet.

This process was helped along by the various entrepreneurs who started businesses dealing specifically with mountain bikes. This group included both pioneers who had experienced the development hands-on, such as Gary Fisher, Joe Breeze, Steve Potts, and Charles Cunningham, and those who just appeared on the scene, such as Tom Ritchie, who produced a series of Breeze-designed frames for Fisher and his partners, and Mike Sinyard, whose company, Specialized, developed the first mass-produced mountain bike, the original Stumpjumper.

Although Specialized clearly had a head start on them, the big American and Japanese bike manufacturers were not caught napping. They did not waste much time before bringing out their own real or presumed mountain bikes. Some of the Americans merely continued the junk they had been making for the cash-and-carry market in a form that made it look like a mountain bike. Others went into the business seriously. But most soon learned to do things right, especially those who had always been concerned with quality.

Despite the American head start, first Japanese, then Taiwanese manufacturers soon flooded the market with mountain bikes. As early as 1984, only two years after the introduction of the Stumpjumper,

mountain bikes accounted for a third of the adult bicycle sales in the United States. Today, the mountain bike has taken first place, regularly accounting for more than 80 percent of all adult bike sales.

Special components, specifically designed with the mountain bike in mind, soon started to edge out the grab-bag of adapted items from other fields that had served so well in getting the show on the road. Manufacturers such as Shimano, SunTour, SR, and Dia-Compe brought out comprehensive ranges of special mountain bike components. Encouraged by Japanese tax incentives, they kept improving their wares from year to year. Just when everybody thought the perfect mountain bike derailleur was here, they introduced indexed gearing, and as soon as they had progressed from the original 15 to 21 speeds, it became all the rage to install 24-speed systems—and we expect the first 27-speed systems to appear any day now. No sooner had a great brake been found, when the next generation of even better, or cooler, brakes appeared on the market. And just when many of us thought we were comfortable on the mountain bike, the manufacturers proclaimed that what was needed most was a suspension system to soften the ride. We're still improving the mountain bike, but yes, it has come of age.

Simultaneously, an entirely new competitive sport has sprouted up. Off-road or mountain bike racing is now not only a popular participation sport; it also very soon became commercialized, with many of the major and minor manufacturers sponsoring their own teams. California and Colorado led the way, but soon enough other parts of the United States, Canada, and Britain could boast literally dozens of mountain bike competitions and other off-road events each weekend.

Over the last ten years, there's been quite a consolidation in the manufacture and marketing of bikes and components. Whereas in the early days mountain bikes were offered by many different manufacturers, and the components were picked from quite a range of different suppliers, the lion's share of the market is now in far

fewer hands. Of the component manufacturers, Shimano is the only significant one left, although other individual manufacturers still offer specific items, the one making brakes, the other chains, a third one hubs, and so forth. When it comes to complete bikes, the American manufacturer Trek now owns, besides its house brand, bikes carrying logos ranging from that of Gary Fisher to Klein and Bontrager—these latter three being one-time independent mountain bike pioneers.

MOUNTAIN BIKE PERIODICALS

Nowhere can the rapid development of the mountain bike be more clearly traced than in the remarkable increase in periodicals devoted to its use. Back in 1980, Charlie Kelly and Denise Caramagno first brought out their slightly outrageous *Fat Tire Flyer*. Initially, it was no more than a couple of mimeographed sheets of 8 1/2 by 11, folded in the middle, filled largely by the sponsors under various pseudonyms. It saw a rapid rise in readership within a very short time, and succeeded in obtaining enough advertising to pay the bills, despite its frank talk and off-beat editorial style.

Today, there are at least five national magazines in the United States alone specifically devoted to the mountain bike, and there are mountain bike periodicals in many other countries as well, confirming how international this trend has become. The popularity of mountain biking has forced cycling periodicals to devote most of their space to mountain biking, crowding out road biking more and more.

Commerce and industry in general also have taken serious notice of mountain biking. Both in bike magazines and elsewhere, advertisers of all sorts of products like to depict healthy adults grinding uphill or speeding down on mountain bikes to promote items that have little bearing on just what kind of machine you ride—or in fact on whether you ride a bike at all.

Yes, cycling has gone through a revolution: the mountain bike revolution. Clearly, the mountain bike is here to stay. In the rest of the book, we'll show you how to make the most of it.

THE ROOTS AND EVOLUTION OF MOUNTAIN BIKING

I n this chapter, Charles Kelly presents the two sides of the evolution of mountain biking. The first part contains an overview of the origins and development of both the machine and the sport. The second part gives a first-hand account of mountain biking's most hallowed event, the Repack Downhill.

THE ORIGINS

Much of today's bike technology was in place a hundred years ago. Rim brakes, ball bearings, chain drive, pneumatic tires, and the "safety bicycle" configuration were among the most important of the first wave of technical improvements to cycling, and are essentially unchanged today. The mountain bike may be seen as a re-adaptation, as the first bikes had to contend with roads worse than what many "mountain bikers" venture onto today.

Between the turn of the century, when roads had improved in response first to bicycles and then to motor vehicles, and the mid-1970s, when cyclists started to venture off-road in increasing numbers, some important technology came along. First came the balloon tire. Although it had been around since the late 1920s, the most popular incarnation was introduced in 1933 by Ignaz Schwinn as a way of associating bicycles with the new breed of streamlined cars and motorcycles with their fat tires. At that time, bicycle sales had declined a long way from the boom of 35 years earlier, and when other manufacturers followed the Schwinn example with more fat-tire bikes, a new boom took place, which would have conse-

Three California mountain bike pioneers. From left to right: Steve Potts, Gary Fisher, and Charlie Cunningham. This photograph was taken on Mount Tamalpais in 1985. As of this writing, they're all still doing what they like best—riding and building bikes. Steve Potts builds frames and special components for Wilderness Trails Bicycles, in which he and Charlie Cunningham are both partners. Charlie custom-builds probably the finest aluminum frames in existence, and Gary's company is now part of Trek but has retained a strong identity thanks to his personal involvement. *Gordon Bainbridge photograph*

quences four decades later as another generation of cyclists mined heaps of old bikes for usable parts.

Perhaps the other most important development was derailleur gearing. As mountain biking evolved, lightweight tub-ing, indexed shifting, and more effective shock-absorbing technology were added to the list of things the modern rider has over the riders of a hundred years ago.

The basic configuration of a bike with balloon tires and derailleur gears was

Gary Fisher showing off one of the first Joe Breeze-built mountain bikes based on the Schwinn Excelsior frame geometry. This frame weighs about 5 pounds less than that of the original. *Gordon Bainbridge photograph*

developed in a number of places and times. The first that I know of was John Finley Scott's "Woodsy Bike," built in the early 1950s from a Schwinn World frame. Its configuration was very similar to that of the first bikes that would earn the title "mountain bike." Scott's bike had a diamond frame, balloon tires, flat bars, rim brakes, and derailleur gears, a configuration that would not appear in Marin County for another 25 years.

The idea of adapting derailleur gearing to a tough old bike was a natural, and although Scott's Woodsy Bike did not inspire a movement, during the 1970s in various parts of the United States a number of small groups developed the concept that would earn the title "Clunker" in Marin County. The basic conversion involved a

drum brake rear hub from a tandem, which would accept a five-speed cluster, and either a cantilever or drum front brake.

Installing the rear hub was not a process of just bolting it on. The rear drop-out width of an old bike was 4 1/2 inches, or about 114 mm—that's 1/4 inch narrower than the 120-mm standard used on a rear hub with a five-speed freewheel, so some bending of the stays was required. Typical frame bending ("cold setting") involved tying a string to one drop-out, running it around the head tube and tying it to the other drop-out. Sighting down the string and measuring the distance from the seat tube to the string helped the "mechanic" maintain straightness while he used a 4-foot-long two-by-four for leverage to open the drop-out spacing. The 1/4-inch difference does not sound like much, but installing the wheel without spreading the drop-outs was very difficult.

There are no derailleur hangers on a one-speed, which typically has rear-facing "track" drop-outs, so some modification had to be added. Shift levers moved from the down tube to the handlebars, at first with shifters mounted on the stem (which old-time riders called the "goose neck"), then with the same shifters moved to the handlebars, and then with "thumb shifters," which first appeared as original equipment on inexpensive five- and ten-speeds.

All of these developments took place more or less independently in a number of places, although they first appeared in Marin County in 1974 on bikes owned by riders from Cupertino, about 60 miles to the south. By this time these riders had been at it for a few years. In 1975, Marin riders followed this lead, and by 1976 there were several dozen modified "clunkers" in the area, making it the hotbed of an insignificant sport.

Handmade framesets for balloon-tire off-road bikes first appeared in 1976 in California, and by 1979 several garage operations in California were turning out limited productions of what would soon be called mountain bikes. Cost was $1,000 to $1,500, and getting one was a matter of considerable determination; the quality,

next to even a cheap modern bike, was laughable. Every component was originally designed for some other use and adapted for use on the mountain bike. You would find motorcycle handlebars and brake levers from a German company; a touring triple chainring from a French manufacturer; French derailleurs and brakes; Japanese shifters, chain, and rims; English saddle; and American hubs. All these were assembled onto a frame built from straight-gauge tubing in a California bike shop.

It was not until 1982 that standard component groups for mountain bikes appeared on the market, making the sport available to the masses. For reasons that seem obvious in hindsight, all that was required to make mountain biking universal was a supply of bicycles, and since mass production made them available to everyone, they have within a decade removed "traditional" road bicycles from market dominance. Competition among hundreds of mountain bike manufacturers, along with companies large and small that produce every possible mountain bike accessory has been intense. It has driven the development of the technological marvels of cycling machinery to new heights.

To a great extent, mountain biking is driven by racing—and the image of racing. Progressing from the first races on record to an Olympic sport in only two decades, mountain biking has arrived bigger and faster than any cycling sport and certainly is dominant in the United States.

European off-road racing—cyclocross—allowed riders to change equipment, and a case could be made that this prevented the Europeans, with a healthy head start in cycling, from developing the sport of mountain biking.

By contrast, mountain bike racers don't get to change machines. It simplified the events, and it seemed not only more fair but also a more legitimate test of the equipment. This self-sufficiency was the primary rule for mountain bike racing when the first National Off-Road Bicycle Association (NORBA) was formed in California in 1983.

This attitude has paid dividends to the average riders. Not many cyclists have a legitimate use for a Tour de France race bike because the design of the bike assumes a support crew. By contrast, you don't have to be familiar with cycling to realize from looking at it that a mountain bike is obviously built to go the distance.

REPACK REUNION

This had the makings of a great day. Just before hitting the street for Repack, I dug through the old drawer and found the two hand-held digital timers. The last time they were used had been in 1984. Surely the batteries had turned to green dust by now, more than twelve years later. I popped open the back, and the batteries looked OK. When all else fails, try the *on* switch. I did, and was rewarded by bright red LED digits. We had precision timing. But only if we wanted it. This was an informal event, a reunion. No one would want to race. The timers were like your old prize ribbons, a link to the past and only for show. But they worked, and that was nice to know.

I had gotten the word off the street a week or two before the day, and that was strange. A guy said, "Hey, when's the Repack race?"

It was news to me, but if you knew where to listen, it was all over Fairfax. Repack. Happening. But when? I followed the spoor back to Joe Breeze. He called and asked for phone numbers of guys I hadn't thought about for a long time. I asked, "What's the deal?"

He acted innocent and said, "Yeah, October 21, didn't you realize it? It's the twentieth anniversary of the first race. I think some guys are getting together, heading on up there, about ten in the morning." Something like that.

I was at that race in October 1976, and Joe wasn't. I wouldn't have known that date, but Joe had made a thesis out of something we did only 24 times in our lives. No fact is too obscure. He has mined my battered notebooks that hold all the known race results, and built a database that can tell you the day anyone made his or her best run. And though I didn't have any idea what the date of the first race was, I knew Joe was close. Twenty years this October.

When I heard this, I knew I would not want to be anywhere on the planet on October 21, 1996, at 10:00 A.M. except the top of Repack.

I kept running into old friends that morning, cruising the streets on their old bikes, and it took a while to get out of town. I got so far behind schedule that I accepted a pickup truck ride to the top of the paved road. A ride up the hill was more important when the bikes weighed twice as much and had one gear, but being behind schedule was a convenient excuse to avoid half the climbing. We parked at the top of Azalea Hill, and a few more carloads showed up. I knew some of the riders getting out, and they had some old iron to ride, so they showed it off—one-speed with a coaster brake and no front brake, a bike that will not stop on this course in less than a couple of hundred feet, which is about twice as far as you can see most of the time. Guys started orbiting slowly, watching others putting wheels on and getting bikes off racks. I didn't know what the delay was, but when I got tired of waiting for anyone to move toward the dirt road, I took off, and they all followed me. Hmmm. I hoped they didn't think I was in charge of this.

Riding slowly up the last part of the approach, I saw a scene from photos taken long ago. The autumn lighting was the same: low morning sun slanting across a perfectly clear blue sky on a cool fall morning. A time capsule opened in front of me. Instead of the rainbow of bright jerseys and company logos you see at any typical mountain bike event, I saw a single orange Lycra jersey adrift in a sea of blue denim. How did a guy who dresses like that even *hear* about it? Shorts? Helmets? Out of the question. Levis, boots, work shirt, and baseball cap are what you wear to race Repack. If there was a jersey, the only appropriate one was Velo-Club Tamalpais, muted blue and yellow without a dozen manufacturer's logos, worn over a pair of jeans. I see that Ross Parkerson's VCT jersey is worn only for ceremonial occasions now, because it is held together by little more than hope.

About half the assembly of about 60 riders were on the latest high-tech

machinery, and that was only because they no longer had their old bikes. The other half was on the largest collection of retro, original, carefully hoarded, obsolete iron that has ever been assembled, much less raced, in about two decades. There were no in-between bikes. No 1985 Stumpjumpers. It was either primitive, pre-1940 iron with Texas "longhorn" handlebars or new $3,000 Y-frame, full-suspension, 19-pound carbon-fiber machinery. On half a dozen old bikes was the classic clunker tool kit, a pair of Vise-Grips clamped to the seatpost. This took the place of socket sets and screwdrivers for creative trail repairs and provided its own way to attach to the bike.

Otis and Joe brought their original bikes, a pair of Schwinns with coaster brakes, fork braces, steel rims, original paint, and Uniroyal tires. Otis has a Morrow, the most desirable possible downhill unit, and Joe has the lever-shifted Bendix two-speed. Craig Weichel rode his Pro-Cruiser, with no front brake, and Alan Bonds showed up on a perfect specimen of a circa 1976 Schwinn conversion, with a new "Excelsior" spear-point paint job, drum brakes front and rear, and perfect Brooks B-72 saddle. At the other end of the scale, Gary Fisher arrived on a Y-frame Fisher, but suitably attired in jeans, and I had my Ritchey P-21 and I wore the jeans and U.S. Army fatigue shirt that are not only what I wore then but what I have worn most every day since. I would have ridden the old iron if I still had it, but the only one I didn't ride into the ground is in the museum in Crested Butte now.

Because only 200 people ever got to race Repack, it's just something to read about, like reading about climbing Mount Everest, and its importance is questionable for anyone who was never there. It was important to me, and several major mountain bike developers still refer to it as some big deal, which keeps the image alive. Repack changed every part of my life, and it's an era that was so fleeting and so much fun that I've spent a lot of time since then trying to capture it in print.

Repack wasn't the first downhill bike race. There were other guys in Marin having races as early as 1969, and it wouldn't surprise me if it happened in a lot of places. So why do all these elitist guys who got to be there claim that it was such a big deal?

First, Repack is hard enough to ride that riding it at all was originally a challenge for coaster brake riders with far less experience than anyone has now. Ten minutes on Repack was the most condensed lesson in off-road riding you could get in 1976, and you either learned fast or took up tennis instead. A coaster brake will not stop you on a steep hill—it will barely slow you down. You have to start the turn long before you get to it, and you have to get the bike sideways for a while before it grudgingly changes direction. There is no comparison with a light modern bike with great brakes and suspension. A coaster brake requires commitment—top to bottom, blind turns, whatever—because you're gonna ram anything that gets in the way. There was a good reason most people in the 1970s thought we were crazy.

A coaster brake turns kinetic energy into heat, and it keeps it all in a small place. Repack will heat the hub far beyond whatever it is rated to handle. If you don't have a front brake, the coaster brake will be smoking at the bottom, and if you were dumb enough to ride with a New Departure instead of a Morrow or a Bendix or even a Musselman brake, that bogus brake would be ground to dust halfway down and you would be in free-fall.

On that morning in 1976 some of us got together to settle once and for all who was the fastest downhiller on dirt. We decided we would do it as a time trial, to give everyone the same chance, and that may have been the breakthrough that made the race so popular.

It required far more organization to pull off a race like that than just getting a few people together at the top of the hill and yelling, "Go!" We didn't have radio contact between the start and finish lines, so timing had to be done carefully. We started with a Navy chronometer and an alarm clock with sweep second hand, but within a few weeks of the first race, Fred Wolf and I

had each spent $70 to purchase a matched pair of the first digital stopwatches to hit the market. Times given in hundredths of a second give riders confidence that the results are accurately measured, and even if the confidence was only as good as the timer's handling of the clocks, there were no ties and no arguments. No one was so critical of the timing system that they wanted to do it themselves, and it fell to me to handle the timing and keep the records in a beat-up notebook that now has sweat stains on a lot of the pages.

Repack created a standard that no other form of racing could. How long will it take you to get down the hairiest hill we could find? The standard to shoot at was five minutes. If you could get under that time, you joined the top ten percent, about 20 riders; you were an Expert, and you raced against Experts. Until you broke five minutes, you raced in the Novice class.

The field grew slowly over the first three years to about 30 riders who could be counted on to show up, and 5 or 10 more who might. The race felt like it was as fair as anyone could expect it to be. Because the riders started at two-minute intervals in inverse order of their best times, the times would usually get faster with each new rider to arrive at the finish over a period of about an hour. Years later I saw that it often took hours at supposedly organized events to sort out winners, but at Repack, with only a paper system and two timers, no radios and no computers, we gave complete results with any number of riders, in two racing categories, a couple of minutes after the last rider finished.

Far from answering anything with our first race, it turned out that we asked the eternal question, and the answer changed daily. In the first race, Alan Bonds was the only rider who got all the way down without a crash, and it was the winning strategy. It was important to go fast, but it was more important to stay on the bike. That didn't sit right with guys who had figured they would win and then would never have to defend the title. No one had figured he was going to crash, but there's a

difference between just riding the hill and racing the hill. OK, Alan, you got lucky. Think you'll be lucky in a week? Be here.

That's how it started. Everyone wanted a shot at the title. Joe Breeze showed up from Mill Valley for the third race, along with some of the Larkspur guys who called themselves the Canyon Gang, riders who shredded their side of the mountain and had been at it longer than we had. Gary Fisher raced in the fifth event. After that the word got to the riders from the Berkeley Trailers Union (BTU) across the bay, guys remarkably like us in their equipment and attitudes, and the arms race was on. The race was so hard on equipment that just having a bike that would go the distance was an advantage where the attrition rate was over half of the riders either crashing or damaging their bikes.

Even though some of the races were won by coaster-brake riders, the repairs that were necessary afterward and gave the hill its name made it a hassle for all but the most dedicated kick-back people. Front and rear drum brakes had become the choice by 1976 because they allowed for gears and hand-operated brakes on the bike. Amazingly, the coaster-brake group included Joe Breeze, who won the most events, until he had made his own frame in 1977. Part of the impetus for building that frame was my pressure on him to make a bike for me that would give me a competitive advantage that my modest skills didn't. Joe did, but he kept the first one, and by the time he had finished his own bike, there were eight more people who wanted one of those bikes. Hardly anyone ever asks me, but if I had to pick the day mountain biking started, it was the day in September 1977 that Joe rolled out his first Breezer, inspired by Repack.

Aside from creating a need for improved equipment and a place to test it, Repack did one more thing that made it important to mountain biking, and it was something that people noticed. The organized but informal underground competition was wacky and harmless, and Very California. It surfaced in "Clunker Bikes," an article in the spring 1978

CoEvolution Quarterly that mentioned the Repack race and a place in Colorado called Crested Butte as the homes of the sport. A year later I made my first writing sale, to *Bicycling*, with a story about Repack, and followed with another on mountain biking in a national outdoor magazine, and suddenly I had another career. I wrote for magazines. The only thing I was expert enough to write about was mountain bikes, and because hardly anyone else knew enough to write about them I found that I could keep selling articles.

In 1979 a camera crew from a San Francisco television station talked me into putting on a race for them to film. It didn't take much reason to do a race, and that was as good as any, and we had a great turnout. The film had everything, including Matthew Seiler's bike sailing directly over the cameraman's head, long-haired rider diving down a bank to retrieve it, remounting, straightening his bars, and riding off. Interviews with riders still pumping adrenaline were wide-eyed, hyperventilated, and funny. The piece was broadcast locally, then later on a national program, and the old footage is a priceless documentary of a Day in the Life. Mountain bikes had been noticed, and Repack was the reason.

Back to the hill, present time. I pulled out the timers, and no one seemed surprised that I had brought them or that they worked. It was as though I was expected to bring them. Each timer had a 20-year-old bottle cap taped over the reset switch to prevent accidents. Once the clocks were started (by banging together the start buttons), they could not be shut off or reset without removing the tape.

It was time for me to get out of there and beat the rush. Riding the hill that changed my life, and by extension a lot of other lives, is a spiritual experience for me. I don't go there that often, probably two or three times a year now, even though it is within five miles of my house, but you never forget the road, and I don't have any problem knowing what is around every turn. All the long-time riders have it memorized, because knowing every rock and rut and the radius of blind turns was a

cheaper advantage than technology. People worked hard to memorize it. One day I walked down from the top with a friend who took a photograph every fifty feet, converting the results to slides that we could project in sequence as a memory aid. Joe made detailed maps, with all landmarks noted, for his own study.

The number of regulars who ride here is enough that the "groove" is easily visible, 6 inches wide, polished of loose rocks that are everywhere else on the road, and snaking from side to side across the ruts. When bicycle suspension systems arrived on Repack, the character of the braking ripples into the switchbacks changed. The distance between ripples went from a couple of inches to a foot or so. I usually follow the groove on the road, but Joe says it's wrong in a lot of places, and he is as good an authority as anyone, with the second-fastest time recorded. One thing about Repack, you never have any idea how anyone else does it. All you can know is how you do it, and you wonder how anyone can do it so much faster.

I guess people use the word "technical" now to mean gnarly. Even with modern brakes and suspension, you can't stop on the steepest partwhich is a section near the top made up of loose gravel and deep dust scattered over what feels like a cliff about 50 yards long. Your best hope is to control your out-of-controlness and try to drift under maximum braking to the right part of the off-camber surface, to line up with the road when it opens up, and you can let go of the brakes so your tires suddenly get traction back, and you accelerate so fast you can feel the G-forces slapping you in the back. Gotta ride in the weeds on the left side of the road on the next turn, stay out of the parallel ruts in the middle. How did I ever *do* this with just a coaster brake?

I had only one really bad crash on Repack. Nothing in my life ever hit me as hard as this road hit me in the chest, right here at the steepest part, on a fall day in 1979. I was so stunned I had no idea if I was all right and just couldn't feel anything, or if I was dying. I lay there with-

out moving for a minute or so, because I wanted to put off finding out how injured I really was. At a Repack race you didn't see anyone for most of the length of the course, because people only gathered at the bottom, and the top had no one. There was no sympathy anywhere to be found. I thought, Bob Burrowes would be getting off the starting line in about 30 seconds, and when he came around that curve he would ride between my legs at 35 miles per hour, and he would not be happy if I spoiled his run by causing him to crash. It was not a good time or place to lie in the road. I found that I could move, and that the skateboarder's gloves, knee pads, and elbow pads I was wearing had kept me from being battered at the contact points. I was more alive than I had ever been. I heard the sound of Repack, Bob's tires ricocheting off the rocks above me, and grunts when he scared himself. I dragged my bike to the side of the trail in time for him to rocket past with a good line.

You hated to crash and spoil someone else's run, because if you did, you were going to hear about it from the other rider. No one got a lot of shots at the Repack title, and it was an effort just to get to the start. Wasting a run because of another rider's mistake was the worst thing that could happen, and you would have to look pretty badly injured before another racer would blow his run by stopping to help you.

I think these thoughts in the two seconds it takes to pass the spot. Repack is fast and slow at the same time. It's like listening to your favorite song. You know exactly what is going to happen.

Halfway down I see trucks on the road, and I slow down to touring speed. The rangers are nice enough to be where you can see them a long way off. It doesn't matter if I go by slowly, and it feels good that it doesn't. I can cruise past these guys, and as soon as I get around the turn, I'm gone.

I don't miss the old equipment. If there is one thing you remember from a 50-pound bike with drum brakes, it is the grip it took to operate the brakes.

An unidentified mountain bike pioneer on a home-built machine. The outfit is representative of what the pioneers were wearing on a cool day in the late 1970s and early 1980s. No, he's not wearing a helmet—safety equipment didn't make any serious inroads until the mid-1980s. *Gordon Bainbridge photograph*

Drum brakes fade as they heat up, and as you went down Repack it took more and more grip on the longest motorcycle levers you could get. By the time you got to the bottom you had to practically pry your fingers off the handlebars. It was painful during the ride, and for the next half-hour your forearms would burn from the effort.

Joe Breeze has named every part of Repack. There's Yellow Face, Upper and Lower Dipper, Danger X, and so on. Here's the spot we call "Vendetti's Face." Marc Vendetti went down here in the second or third Repack, and he left a good portion of his face on the road. We knew something was wrong, because his time was too long. Anyone who wasn't down in five minutes was not having a good run. If it was over six, you knew there was trouble, but no one cared to trudge up the hill to see what it was unless it went up to an hour or so. Marc arrived at the finish stunned, blood running down his face, and Ray Flores caught it on film. It was classic, I tell ya.

Through the switchbacks, then Camera Corner—a hard left that is featured in all the old photo collections. Over the off-camber rock that years ago Alan Bonds and I spent an afternoon attacking with a pick to see if we could create a better line on the turn. It's a hard rock, and even the road grader that scrapes the road every couple of years has given up, as we did. The hump remains, and I have the same thought I always had when I went over it: if you could cut just a little channel through the left side of the rock, you could line up on this corner perfectly and take two seconds off your time. I was talking with Joe Breeze, and we commiserated that there is no good way to get over this rock and set up for the turn. It always feels as though you did it wrong, and if there's a right way you can just never find it.

When I got to the bottom, I was one of the first there. The racers were waiting for casuals like me to clear the course, and Joe Breeze had mentioned while we were at the top that he had stashed a couple of kegs of beer at the bottom, which got things rolling. By the time the first racers got down the hill, there was a party going on.

The Repack finish line is a lonely rock that sticks up out of a level piece of ground, a rough, dome-shaped monument about three feet high, about three feet across, and uncomfortable as hell to sit on. It has no name; it's just the rock. I have spent a lot of time sitting on it writing race results while the sharp angles stabbed my butt, and standing on top of it addressing small gatherings of people like the one I'm looking at today.

The finish is not a straightaway: it's a blind left turn to the rock, which marks the actual line, and you can't see the rock until you are about 30 feet from it. Everyone tries a flashy sideways stop. If you didn't try to finish sideways, everyone would say, "What's wrong with *him?*" So everyone is out of control at the finish, because the turn tightens up, and the rock is a good perch, because when the sideways riders hit it, it doesn't move.

A couple of the old bikes come in with coaster brakes in the classic condition, a stinking cloud of petroleum smoke pouring off the hub, burned grease running down the spokes, and the hub shell so hot that someone always spits on it to see it boil away and hear the sizzle.

The party around the rock is like old times—so many conversations going on at once that it sounds like a schoolyard during recess, a "bike pile" growing as riders fling one-speeds on top to show how much they don't worry about 50 pounds of indestructible iron that has been stripped of anything nonessential. After some calculation by Chris on his envelope, the winners are announced. They high-five each other, and that is that. We've used it all up, whatever it was. The beer runs out, and people start to drift off.

I don't know when the next event will be, but I never knew that in 1979 either. When the sun and moon and stars line up, it will happen again.

SELECTING AND SETTING UP YOUR MOUNTAIN BIKE

No, we can't tell you just which make and model of mountain bike to choose, but in this chapter, we'll help you establish what you need and how to select what best suits your needs. The three major criteria are type, size, and price.

Before we go into details, though, please take a minute to check out the illustration, which shows the parts of the mountain bike and their names. It shows a fairly generic machine without suspension; various other models are depicted in the photographs in this chapter. The components in the illustration are labeled with the names we'll be using throughout this book.

In mountain bike circles, there are only a small number of manufacturers who provide most of the components. Collectively all the moving parts (hubs, pedals, crankset, derailleurs, chain, headset bearings) are referred to as a component "gruppo" in the United States or "groupset" in Great Britain.

Shimano leads the component market. Their derailleurs, hubs, pedals, cranks, chains, and other components can be found on bikes in any price category. None of the other manufacturers makes as many different parts as Shimano does. Campagnolo, the main European manufacturer of road bike components, gave up the production of mountain bike components, but another European company, Sachs, has become a serious contender.

Of course, the Shimano parts found on the $169 bike bought at a department store are not of the same quality as those

More and more mountain bikes are sold with at least front suspension, usually some form of telescoping fork. The drawback is that these suspension forks are sensitive to abuse and dirt penetration, requiring frequent overhauling. The relatively simple models found on $600 to $800 bikes, like this one, actually require less maintenance.

The parts of the mountain bike. This illustration shows the names of the most important components that are common on all mountain bikes. Not shown here are suspension components and accessories.

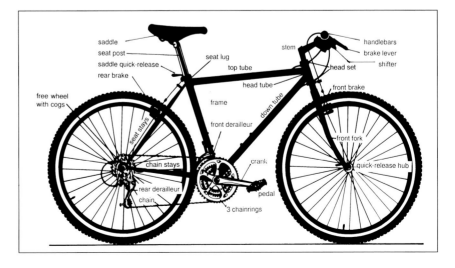

A modern conventional mountain bike without suspension. Although most bikes in this price category (about $600) come with suspension these days, non-suspension bikes like this are an excellent choice for general off-road use. This Gary Fisher Aquila is equipped with Grip Shift derailleur controls.

From Europe comes the variant known as city bike—this one is made by the American company Trek for the European market, although it is also available in the United States. Equipped with somewhat narrower tires and complete with lights, luggage racks, and often fenders, they're most suitable as a general means of transport, for paved and unpaved roads—but not for really rough terrain.

on an $800 or $3,000 machine. So seeing a bike advertised as being "Shimano-equipped" doesn't tell you much about its quality. The question is, which Shimano gruppo? The three most expensive categories don't really differ in quality very much, except that the most expensive one, XTR, is lighter than the next one down, XT, which in turn is slightly lighter and more nicely finished than the next one down, LX. Below these three, materials, finish, durability, and adjustability begin to suffer. By the time you reach the items installed on the cheapest bikes, you've got stuff that works OK when new, but is not very durable and is a pain to adjust when it starts to wear out.

MOUNTAIN BIKE TYPES

The most important thing is to decide what type of mountain bike you need, based on the kind of riding you intend to do. Roughly, mountain bikes these days can be divided into the following categories:

Bikes without suspension.

Bikes with front suspension only.

Full-suspension bikes.

Even within these three categories, there are many variations. One bike may be set up for a sportier ride, meaning generally that it'll be lighter and have nimbler handling but also that it'll be less forgiving and often more fragile than another model. And in addition to single bikes, off-road tandems are now widely available—in fact tandeming has gone through a major resurgence due to the availability of off-road tandems.

Hybrids are "multi-use" bikes with slightly narrower tires, higher gearing, and a more upright riding position. They're most suitable for riding on smooth trails and in city traffic.

Suspension seems like a good idea, and comes on most mountain bikes sold in the price category above $500 ($700 in Canada, £300 in Britain). Suspension is good for downhill racing, because it allows you to keep your hands on the handlebars and your butt on the saddle. But you may find that when riding on the level or when climbing, a non-suspension bike is easier to

handle. Although a good front suspension can be of benefit in rough terrain, a full-suspension bike can be overkill.

Suspension adds to the bike's complexity, and your bike will spend less time in the workshop if it doesn't have this additional complexity. Even if you like the idea of suspension, consider the data the manufacturers provide: many suspension forks have maintenance intervals of 20 hours, and even the most durable types need to be overhauled after 100 hours of use. Twenty hours—that's what some of us ride every week. So if you want a trouble-free machine, don't try to go all out on suspension. In Chapter 23 we'll cover suspension systems and their relative merits and drawbacks in greater detail.

If you plan to use your bike for fast downhill rides on really rough terrain—whether you're an experienced rider or not—you'll find a full-suspension bike a real boon. Just how soft your suspension should be is less important than how much travel (that is, the distance between fully extended and fully compressed conditions) the system has. The other criteria are the quality of damping (which prevents the bike from bouncing up and down) and above all just how accurately the various moving components fit.

VALUE FOR MONEY

Mountain bikes and machines that look just like them are available in prices that run the gamut from cash-and-carry junk to expensively crafted works of engineering art. Although almost every price has its justification in terms of the work and materials that went into the finished product, the most expensive will not always be the best for every purpose. We know people who have had trouble with the most exclusive equipment they could (or could not really) afford, whereas others have been perfectly satisfied with bargain-basement machines.

Our subjective evaluation of the mountain bike buying habits of the general populace indicates there are three approaches:

What is the best?

What is the cheapest?

What will be the most suitable?

A full-suspension mountain bike—this is (or rather was, as it's no longer made) the Sonoma Crosstrac. Bikes like this are used for fast downhill work, but they're not necessarily more suitable for most riding than bikes with only a front suspension, or even those without suspension altogether. After a while, even the best ones start to show serious signs of wear and require lots of maintenance. *Photo courtesy Richard R. Ries, from his book* Building Your Perfect Bike, *also published by MBI Publishing Company*

Those who ask the first question, though probably wealthier, are not really any more sophisticated or smarter than those who try to find the answer to the second. It is our aim in this book to bring you into the category of the informed, those who ask—and attempt to answer—the third question: What's the most suitable mountain bike for your use? Only then will you be likely to finish up with a bike that is best *for you.*

If you just want to ride around without any competitive intentions or interest in riding in difficult terrain, you may be well served with a cheap to medium-priced machine. If you want to cycle faster than the next person and if you have developed your riding skills, you may want the very lightest and most sophisticated.

Most people who buy their first mountain bike, and quite a number of those who have had such machines before, don't do so in order to compete with the gonzos who make a living blazing their trail up and down the steepest mountains. They want a bike they are at ease with. It should be the right size, comfortable enough to ride for hours, light and agile enough to be handled easily, and priced somewhere within their financial possibilities. Yes, it can be done, so let's see how to go about it.

SIZING YOUR BIKE

Whatever the make, model, type, color, or price, your bike should be of the right size to match your physique. If it's the wrong size, even the highest-quality bike is worse to ride than an otherwise inferior model of the right size. Here you will find guidelines for making sure you get a bike that fits.

Bicycle sizes are generally quoted as the length of the seat tube, between the center of the bottom bracket and some point at the top. Traditionally, in the English-speaking world this upper point has been defined as the top of the seat lug, that's where the seatpost sticks out of the frame. Nowadays, most manufacturers of mountain bikes refer to the more logical location represented by the centerline of the top tube. Some quote the "straddle height," the distance of the top tube above the ground.

The correct frame size will be a function of the length of your legs. As a guideline, you can refer to Table 1 in the Appendix. It gives suggested nominal frame sizes as a function of the inseam leg length, as measured in the accompanying illustration.

A good way to find the right size is by trying out some bikes. If you intend to use the mountain bike for its original purpose, to ride off-road, the frame should be on the small side. Straddle some bikes in the shop and select one on which you retain up to 7.5 cm (3 inches) of crotch clearance when your feet are flat on the ground.

While straddling the bike, raise the front end. On the right-size bike, you should be able to lift the front wheel about 15 cm (6 inches) off the ground without discomfort.

The bike should also fit when you ride it. To establish this height, you should be able to sit comfortably and pedal backwards with the heel of the foot on the pedals. (Don't pedal it that way when cycling, though; instead, keep the front of the foot centered on the pedal, rather than the heel.)

Once you have established the right saddle height, mark the seatpost with a piece of adhesive tape where it protrudes from the seat tube. Then undo the binder bolt and pull it out to check its length. To be safe, there should be at least 65 mm (2 1/2 inches) of the seatpost below the point you just marked. If there isn't, you either need a different bike or a longer seatpost.

LENGTH OF THE BIKE

Next, consider the length of the bike. Measure the distance from the saddle to the handlebars and the distance between the wheels. Customarily, the length is quoted as the top-tube length, measured between the centerlines of head tube and seat tube. Most manufacturers offer a fixed relationship between seat-tube length and top-tube length. The critical dimension is also affected by the size of the handlebar stem extension and the relative forward position of the saddle with respect to the seatpost.

To find a bike of the right length, start off with the saddle placed in the middle position relative to the seatpost, and the handlebars at the same height as the saddle. Seated on the bike, you should be able to sit relaxed, dividing your weight between handlebars and saddle. You should not feel uncomfortably strained. The other extreme, with the hands too close to the body, rarely occurs, as most bikes seem to be on the long side. Just the same, it's possible, for example, if your upper body or arms are long relative to your leg length.

MOUNTAIN BIKES FOR HIM AND HER

With respect to the way bicycles fit their riders, there are some differences between the typical female and male physiques. In Chapter 14, "Mountain Biking for Women," Jacquie Phelan gives a comprehensive account of what's different for women when it comes to mountain biking, but here are some basic suggestions concerning bike fit. We suggest you also read through Chapter 14 before you walk into a bike shop with the intent of buying a new bike.

For any given total body height, the average woman is presumed to have proportionally longer legs, shorter arms, and a shorter torso than an average male of the same overall height. Applied to bicycle sizing terms, that would translate into a shorter top-tube for the same size frame. Replacing the handlebar stem with a longer or shorter one is often all it takes to improve the bike's fit.

There are a number of special components on the market to suit the particular needs of women. These include wider saddles, narrower and smaller-diameter handlebars, and shorter-reach brake levers. Some manufacturers offer special women's versions, or at least proportional component sizing based on the frame size. This is often only done for more expensive models. Even for cheaper bikes, you can get individual parts replaced by better-fitting ones.

Some men will do better with one or more of the features more typically intended for women, and vice versa. For example, some men have a pelvis that is as wide as that of some women, and for them the wider women's saddle is comfortable. Evaluate your own physical characteristics critically before buying a bike, so you know what to look out for. Then try out several different models, and don't rush into buying something before you are sure it fits and suits you.

WHEEL SIZE

Virtually all regular mountain bikes are equipped with what is referred to as 26-inch wheels. That's the approximate overall outside diameter with inflated tire. There are 26-inch tires in numerous widths. On mountain bikes, they may vary from 42 to 59 mm (1.6 to 2.2 inches). Hybrids roll on 700 mm wheels with tires that are typically 35 to 40 mm wide.

Fitting the bike to the rider. This one really has a frame that's at least an inch too big for the rider. When you straddle the top tube in front of the saddle, you should be able to raise the front wheel about five inches off the ground.

Not everybody needs the widest tires. If you ride on roads most of the time, rarely getting into loose dirt, sharp boulders, mud, or snow, you may be perfectly happy with 40 mm wide tires. The wider tires are the solution for rough terrain or loose dirt, mud, and snow. Generally, bikes are designed with a particular tire size in mind, so it is wise to select a bike that is equipped the way you want it, rather than modifying it later.

Since a different tire width can be installed on the rim, it is often possible to replace narrow tires with wider models for no more than the cost of the tires. That only works if the frame clearances are adequate.

THE RIGHT BIKE FOR YOUR PURPOSE

The first mountain bikes were designed to descend down steep hillsides. That was mainly achieved by keeping the wheelbase long. Since then, different geometries have been introduced.

Today's suspension bikes have returned to the downhill philosophy. If you want a good bike for purely downhill riding at high speeds, full suspension is a treat. However, for cross-country touring and good control, your best bet is probably still a "hardback" bike, whereas the models with only front suspension are perhaps the best suited for mixed use at speed on rough terrain.

CHAINSTAY LENGTH

Short chainstays—on which the distance between the centerlines of the bottom bracket and the rear wheel is 430 mm (17 inches) or less—are reputed to give a bike magic climbing ability. Don't believe it, although these short chainstays do avoid sway of the rear end when applying force to the pedals. That's good if you grind your way up in a gear that is too high. The disadvantage of this design is that it places your weight far back, assuming a given angle of the seat tube relative to the horizontal plane. This actually makes it harder to climb very steep inclines sitting down, as the front end will tend to lift off, so you'll need to get up out of the saddle and balance your weight over the bike.

THE WAY YOU RIDE

If you're a beginner, look for a bike that is built more for comfort than for speed. That means one with relatively shallow frame angles: the head tube should be at an angle of 68–71 degrees relative to the horizontal. Due to some geometric relationships, that also means the bike's frame will be a little on the long side. It will not respond as directly to your steering and accelerating efforts. On the other hand, it won't be quite as scary to ride either. Even though these "comfortable" bikes have a long wheelbase, you will probably sit less stretched out, because these bikes are typically equipped with a short-reach, high-rise handlebar stem.

If you're a more experienced rider, you may want a shorter and steeper-angled machine. Frame angles of 72 degrees or more are not unusual in this category. These fast and agile bikes will have a wheelbase of less than 106 cm (42 inches), compared to about 110 cm (43 to 44

Check the relative position of the controls to make sure they're comfortable to reach without having to move your hands from the handgrips.

inches) for a novice bike. The distance between saddle and handlebars on the sporty machines is increased by a stem that places the handlebars low and far forward.

The shorter and steeper bikes are agile but less comfortable to ride if you rest on the saddle with all your weight. Instead, distribute your weight between pedals, handlebars, and saddle.

Typically, mountain bikes that are designed for hard riding are built of larger-diameter tubing than that which is used for average-use bikes. This applies especially to the downtube, the chainstays, and the fork. Taking a look at various models and asking specific questions in the bike shop will usually allow you to get a machine that matches your kind of riding. There's no need to buy a bike that's lighter, or conversely more rugged, than what you need. Choose what's best for your kind of riding.

CARRYING A LOAD

If you will be carrying luggage at some time, whether on long tours, to deliver newspapers, or to do the grocery shopping, you will need a bike that lends itself to that purpose. It should have racks installed or have the appropriate attachment bosses and eyelets, so you can install the racks at a later time.

If your bike has bosses front and rear, you'll be well prepared to install just about any manufacturer's racks. It is also possible to attach racks with the aid of provisional clamps. Usually, suspension bikes are not suitable for loaded touring.

GEARING CHOICES

All mountain bikes sold these days have indexed gearing systems with fixed positions for the various gears. Except for racing, we suggest being satisfied with an 18- or 21-speed model in preference to one with 24 speeds. This applies especially if you will be cycling with a loaded bike and do not want to spend a lot of time straightening out your rear wheel.

MATERIALS AND CONSTRUCTION

Many bikes are made with aluminum frames. These are generally light and can be of excellent quality—but so can steel bikes. One disadvantage of aluminum bike frames is the fact that some standard components may not fit on them as easily as they do on a steel frame. The reason lies in the need to use larger-diameter tubing, as explained in Chapter 16. Attaching standard components to such an oversize tube may be tricky. Although the manufacturers get components to fit their frame, finding a fitting replacement part may be difficult.

There are also frames made of titanium and carbon fiber. These tend to be light and expensive. Titanium frames are almost invariably excellent, but we would not recommend them to a beginner: wait until you are ready for the ultimate bike. Carbon fiber was first introduced on very light and expensive machines and is gradually making its way to the more affordable range.

FINE-TUNING YOUR POSITION

When it comes to actually riding the bike, you'll need to adjust it for optimum comfort. It's not really a process to master in a day. Instead, expect to spend the first few weeks working on your posture, adjusting the position of the saddle, handlebars, and brake levers until you are comfortable. And if you're a beginner, you may well find that you need to readjust things again after a few months of practice because you've now developed handling skills that make a slightly more forward-leaning position more comfortable than it seemed at first. The rest of this chapter is devoted to the mechanics of carrying out these adjustments.

SEAT ADJUSTMENTS

To carry out the actual mechanical adjustment on the saddle, first take a close look at the way it is installed on the bike. The saddle height is easy to adjust on a typical mountain bike. Loosen the quick-release binder bolt behind the seat lug, raise or lower the saddle with the attached seatpost in a twisting motion, and tighten the quick-release again when the saddle is at the correct height, making sure it is aligned straight.

To change the saddle's forward position, undo the adjustment bolt (two bolts on some models) on the seatpost. This bolt is usually accessible from below or from the side, but sometimes from under the saddle cover. Some older mountain bike seatposts also have a quick-release here. Once loosened, push the saddle forward or backward until the desired position is reached, then tighten the bolts, making sure the saddle is held at the desired angle relative to the horizontal plane.

HANDLEBAR ADJUSTMENTS

If your bike is equipped with a conventional, or threaded, headset, you can adjust the height of the handlebars within the range allowed by the handlebar stem following the instructions in Chapter 31. (If it has a threadless headset, the handlebar height can be varied only by installing a different stem.)

To change the angle of the handlebars with respect to the horizontal plane, undo the binder bolt that clamps the handlebars in the front of the stem. Twist the

If the bike is not equipped with clipless pedals, there should at least be toeclips to keep your feet in place. Initially, you may feel most comfortable if you don't tighten the straps. If, on the other hand, your bike has clipless pedals, get the matching plates installed on the (special) shoes.

handlebars until they are at the desired angle, and then tighten the binder bolt again, holding the bars centered. To install a longer stem, a different handlebar design, or to install bar-ends, you are referred to the instructions in Chapter 31 or to your friendly bike store.

The correct handlebar position often puts more strain on the hands than beginning cyclists find comfortable, especially when rough surfaces cause vibrations. Minimize this problem by keeping your arms slightly bent, never holding them in a cramped position. If you still experience discomfort, replace the handgrips with cushioned foam models. Wearing gloves will also relieve the strain and damage to the nerves in the palms of your hands.

If your bike comes with bar-ends installed, make sure they both point up and

forward at the same angle and that they can be comfortably reached without straining your wrists. If not, see Chapter 31 for instructions on adjusting their position.

OTHER EQUIPMENT

In addition to the bike itself, you'll need a few other items as well. Get a helmet to protect your skull in case of a fall. (Even the best riders occasionally fall when riding off-road.)

If the bike has clipless pedals, get matching shoes with the appropriate connecting plates installed. If not, almost any kind of comfortable shoes will do, although sturdy shoes with a firm but relatively thin sole will make riding more comfortable. Safest are models with Velcro closures, rather than shoelaces, which might get caught in the chain.

You can get a whole range of special bike clothing—pants, jersey, gloves, socks, jacket, the works. If you wear long slacks, tuck them in to avoid catching the cuffs on the front derailleur or the chain.

You will also need a pump, a water bottle, and some basic tools. More about these and other accessories in Chapter 24.

PRE-RIDE CHECK

Before taking your bike out for a ride, carry out a 3-minute checkup. Here, we'll only explain what to check and how things should be; the actual work is explained in detail under "Daily Inspection" in Chapter 25. To resolve any problems, you are referred to the appropriate sections of the maintenance instruction in the pertinent chapters of Part IV.

Seat Position

Make sure the seat is firmly tight at the right height, pointing straight forward, with the top horizontal. If not, loosen the quick-release lever, put it right, and tighten the lever while holding it in the right place.

Handlebar Position

Check to make sure the handlebars are firmly in place at the right height, and straight. Straddle the front wheel, clamping it between your legs, and try to twist the handlebars. If they turn easily, tighten the expander bolt holding the handlebar stem.

Tire Pressure

Check the tire pressure, preferably with a tire gauge: 4 bar, or 60 psi, for hard smooth surfaces; 3 bar, or 45 psi, for rough but regular surfaces; 2 bar, or 30 psi, for rough and irregular surfaces; even less for loose sand or mud. If you don't have a tire gauge, apply firm pressure of the thumb while steadying your grip from the inside of the rim. If the tire is under inadequate pressure, inflate it with your pump.

Brakes

Check to make sure that both wheels can be stopped fully by pulling the appropriate brake lever.

Gearing

Lift the rear wheel and check whether each of the gears can be engaged by shifting into the various different positions while turning the cranks.

Other Items

Visually inspect the bike to make sure nothing is loose or missing.

Make sure you have at least the essential tools with you—a pump, a patch kit, and a cloth.

If your ride may take you into darkness, make sure you have working lights, front and rear.

If the ride will be longer than an hour, make sure you carry a full water bottle.

CHAPTER FOUR

PLACES TO RIDE

This chapter contains advice on how to find the kind of terrain where the mountain bike can display its strengths most impressively. That doesn't have to be in the mountains; in fact the mountain bike has proven itself on all sorts of terrain, ranging from frozen tundra to rocky deserts and from soggy marshland to forested hillside trails.

Your bike is most efficient, and therefore most enjoyable, when ridden on hard, dry, smooth, and level ground. That may contradict what you've heard about the mountain bike before, but it's useful to keep in mind.

Avoid going off the beaten path to minimize damage to the terrain. Chapters 8, "Riding with Nature," and 15, "Access and Advocacy," describe the relevant issues in some detail.

Riding nowhere special—in most areas, there's enough undeveloped land with little-used trails within easy reach. *Bob Allen Photography*

GETTING OUT THERE

Your mountain bike need not be transported to the trail head in the back of a pickup truck or on the roof of a car. Any bike, including your fat-tired machine, is a means of transportation. If you can, ride it all the way from home.

What's nice about riding off-road is not a function of the roughness, the dirt, or any of the other characteristics of the terrain. Instead, what you'll relish most is the remoteness, the solitude, the experience of nature, and the lack of traffic. Without these, even a mountain bike is not more enjoyable on rough roads than on smooth ones. So, unless you go for the challenge, select the most direct, smoothest, hardest,

driest, and most level surface that can be used to get you from point A to point B.

Keeping that in mind, we can now concentrate on the kind of terrain for which your mountain bike is more suitable than any other machine known to man. The thickest tires and the strongest forks don't detract from your riding pleasure on paved roads as much as they benefit you off-road.

UPHILL-DOWNHILL RIDING

In most parts of the United States and Canada, and perhaps even more so in the rest of the world, there is suitable terrain for real off-road riding within easy cycling reach, wherever you live. Open hillsides or those with rough trails dropping down

steeply can be found in many areas. The mountain bike's characteristics definitely lend it superbly to this kind of use. In fact, that's how the mountain bike was born. The first mountain bike riders did little more (or less) with their machines than ride them down steep, unpaved hillsides at a murderous pace, only to struggle their way up again to start all over.

This kind of uphill-downhill riding is most enjoyable as a group activity. If you have ever tried it alone, you'll probably find it about as interesting as counting sheep, whereas the company, the mutual encouragement, the fun of it all, makes it more exciting. In addition, it is more educational. You may never learn the proper control over

A rock face like this is a great place to practice basic steep-terrain handling and climbing skills. *Bob Allen Photograph*

TRAIL RIDING

If you are more interested in peace and solitude, cycling on unpaved roads and trails is the more mind-expanding experience. There is a distinct thrill to relaxed riding where there is no bustle and roar of cars to interrupt the tranquillity and where all the obstacles are of God's creation, rather than man's.

Although many people prefer to cycle alone or with only one companion, this activity is not the exclusive domain of recluses and hermits. In fact, some of the major organized off-road events, with hundreds of participants, are of this kind. To find the right terrain for non-organized trail biking, the best tool is the topographical map, referred to as the Geological Survey in the United States or Ordnance Survey in Britain.

This kind of map shows all trails, paths, and roads; a road map will show you which of these are paved and used for motor traffic. The difference is your exclusive domain, apart from any right-of-way restrictions you may have to contend with. In fact, access and right of way are the two intangibles in trail cycling these days. The sport is getting too popular too fast, and in defense, or out of fear, authorities have banned cyclists from many potentially suitable areas, an issue that will be addressed in Chapter 15.

You will probably use Forest Service or fire roads and trails used by hikers most of the time. Don't stray off these trails, as this may cause damage, both to the environment and to our reputation. As long as you stay on the trails and do it with a modicum of consideration for others, you have nothing to fear and should not risk being banned from them by public agencies.

In many areas, a distinction is made between single-track trails and wider ones. Single-tracks are often considered off-limits to mountain bikers, although in many areas there are not enough hikers and other trail users to worry about. You'll probably find that hostility against mountain biking on single-track trails increases with its popularity: if you're the only one doing it, nobody minds, but when hordes of bikers start doing it, you'll all get banned off these trails.

your bike and its movements unless you can gauge your own progress with that of others.

Consider the environmental impact and the legality of what you are doing, though. If there is an ordinance against it, chances are it's not merely to spoil your fun but rather to prevent you from doing damage to the natural environment. What some of this riding does to the watershed characteristics of the terrain can be quite serious. Though mountain biking is hardly the direct, or even a significantly contributing, cause of the California mudslides of recent years, authorities will be quick to claim it is. It is better to avoid potential problem areas altogether than to get the blame for something that can't be proven either way.

Downhill riding is fun, but it is truly challenging only if you pay your dues; ride up to the summit before plunging downhill in a rush of speed. For those who don't believe in that philosophy, many ski resorts offer downhill riding with ski lifts for the upward-bound part of the tour.

If you are new to the sport, the best places to do downhill riding are probably known to others who ride mountain bikes. You'll be surprised in what unlikely places you can find quite acceptable slopes, even in otherwise flat country. It needn't be a 1,000-foot drop; riding down the embankment of a high bridge ramp or a pile of soil next to a building site may do the trick for fun and practice.

Another thing to keep in mind is the way you interact with your companions. Among American males in their mating years, there is often a tendency to talk loudly and assertively. Out in the country they can be outright inconsiderate. Subjecting others to your accounts of the performance of your stock or your dating successes from across a canyon is highly improper and can distract severely from everybody's enjoyment of the sport and the outdoors in general. Spend some time saying nothing occasionally, and if you hear others, realize that they would hear your conversation as clearly as you hear theirs. Keep it down, and you, your companions, and others will enjoy nature much more while riding.

SHARED USE

We're not the only people, nor usually the first, to leave the main roads and explore the open terrain. Hikers and equestrians have equally legitimate claims.

Unfortunately, in many areas equestrians have proven to be the most serious enemies of mountain biking. Considering that their steeds can do more damage than mountain bikes do, these horsey people seem to have decided that the best defense is in the attack. We'll have to learn to deal with that attitude, and it will be best to show that you're not the enemy. Look for contact with equestrians and show them that you're just as responsible as they are. Once you're on friendly terms, differences are easier to iron out than when each side sees the other only in negative terms.

We share the trails with hikers too. Those on foot have a justified claim to the most comprehensive access, and cyclists would do well to do all they can to defer to them. We have witnessed both ridiculous pedestrian fear of anything on wheels or hooves, and totally brutal disregard of the rights of those on foot on the part of some mountain bikers. Be considerate, and team up with others to sway both the public and the authorities against instituting or enforcing unwarranted restrictive access rules.

Government authorities and public representatives at all levels are supposed to be accountable to all the people, including you and your mountain biking friends. If you have the right arguments and present them reasonably, chances are pretty good you'll be able to secure or retain access in most cases where you and your bike don't represent a serious threat to the environment.

Join forces with other potential users of the same terrain. Try to emphasize that mountain bike riders are normal, responsible, mature adults who eat lots of apple pie and watch fireworks, rather than some weird bunch of outlaws. It also helps to be a member of some recognized, dignified outdoor or conservation organization and to point this out whenever you present your case in public. Yes, we know that right now many of these organizations are not well disposed toward bikers, but if you can't beat them, you have every right to join them: become active on your own behalf in their organizations, as long as you feel their charter is not intrinsically contradictory to your aims.

FRINGE AREAS

Out here in California where we live, there's rather a lot of publicly accessible nature. But things are different elsewhere. In large parts of the United States, there isn't a national or state forest or park, wilderness area, you name it, within a day's motoring distance. And in some countries the concept of public access is different altogether. In South Africa, we found out that just about every piece of publicly administered land, including

Avoid terrain with features that are likely to cause damage to your equipment. That can include anything from thorny bushes to broken glass. *Bob Allen Photography*

sanctioned mountain bike trails, is only accessible if you first apply for a permit and pay a (albeit modest) fee.

This is only one extreme example. The other extreme is most of Scandinavia, where public access is taken for granted, even on privately owned land. The real message is, find out what the conditions are and select your type of riding accordingly.

Generally, in areas lacking specific facilities that seem to be almost designed for mountain biking, or where there are peculiar problems associated with securing access to them, remember that you can ride on any kind of unpaved road, or for that matter on roughly paved roads, such as the cobblestone roads in many parts of Europe and the potholed major highways in much of the third world, without worrying about such controversial terrain.

Even on the fringes of just about every city and suburb, there are areas where paved roads are anything from sparse to nonexistent. Such areas may not always be the most idyllic, but they are usually quite suitable for your kind of use. If they don't give you the solitude of nature, instead constantly reminding you of man's encroaching action upon God's work, at least they offer a superb training ground for more romantic rides when you do get the chance to ride out in the woods.

Their advantage is that such areas are invariably easily accessible, both in terms of distance and in the way the paved roads allow you to get out there in little time. Use the maps mentioned in this chapter and make the most of the information that can be learned from them. Consult Chapter 12 for an explanation of the most effective ways of using the maps.

With your mountain bike, you can take on the hills, going up, down, and around them. You can go where other road users would not care to travel. These are the advantages of your particular mode of transport. Exploit them. Making the most of these advantages, fearing neither sweat nor agony, the true mountain bike rider quickly discovers enjoyable, scenic, sometimes even spectacular, routes away from regular roads. Get out there and enjoy them to the full.

CHAPTER FIVE

BASIC RIDING SKILLS

Riding off-road requires some practice. You can accelerate this learning process once you know how the bike behaves in response to your actions. Of course, you can learn simply by practicing, and some people have become experts that way in a small amount of time. However, the vast majority of riders can compress their learning curve dramatically by following the advice given in this chapter. It won't make you an expert at handling every conceivable situation—more about that in the next two chapters—but it will increase your sense of accomplishment and the enjoyment you get out of the sport.

The main issue at hand is that of balance, because balance is what you use to control the bike, whether going in a straight line or in a curve, going downhill or up, accelerating or stopping. And to achieve the right balance, you need to get familiar with several things:

Seating position.
Body lean.
Distribution of weight.
Steering angle.
Traction.
Braking.

There's also the issue of gearing, which will be treated separately in Chapter 6. In this chapter, we'll look at the concepts listed here as they affect riding—not one by one, but in conjunction with methods that combine all these factors in your learning process.

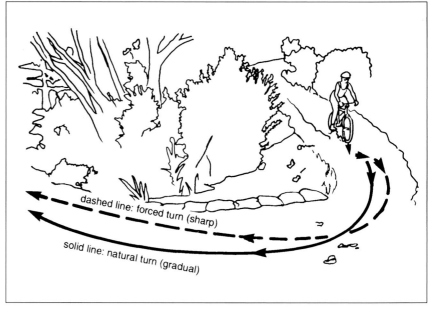

Comparison between the natural turn (solid line) and the forced turn (dashed line). The natural turn requires a large turning radius, whereas the forced turn makes a very sudden deviation possible.

FITTING THE BIKE TO THE RIDER

In this section, we will help you fine-tune the adjustments of the bike so that it serves you best. To do this effectively, you should have selected a bike of the right size, as described in Chapter 3, and set it up preliminarily according to the advice in the same chapter. The correct setup and the initial riding posture will be explained here, which will allow you to reap maximum benefit from the advice contained in this chapter and in Chapter 7, which goes into more detail about off-road techniques.

RIDING POSTURE

Whereas bicycle racers have long known that they are most comfortable in a relatively low, crouched position, most beginning cyclists, whatever kind of bike they ride, sit upright. That may be fine if you travel only short distances on urban streets or make minor excursions at low speed in easy terrain. However, you can learn something about posture from more experienced riders. The fact that you will probably have difficult terrain to handle makes this even more important.

An easy way to convince you how to sit is by checking out some other riders. Look how they sit on their bike and rate them by how gracefully and comfortably they seem to move. Do you agree that the ones who lean forward, somewhat stretched out and with a relatively high saddle and low handlebars seem to be moving with some ease and grace, even uphill? That's the posture to strive for.

In the lower position, the rider's weight is divided more evenly over handlebars, saddle, and pedals. This reduces the pressure on the buttocks and allows the relaxed fast pedaling technique so essential for long-duration power output, as will be explained in Chapter 6, and it enables you to bring more force to bear on the pedals when needed. Finally, it can reduce the wind resistance, which is a major factor in cycling, especially when traveling fast or against the wind.

You'll have more endurance and better control of the bike if you learn to ride in the lower and more stretched-out position early on. Get accustomed to the right posture early in your cycling career, and you'll be a more effective cyclist, one who gets less frustration and more pleasure out of the pursuit.

The following sections describe just how the saddle and the handlebars should be adjusted to achieve the basic relaxed position. Unlike the person riding a bike with drop handlebars, the mountain bike rider cannot provide much variation by holding the handlebars at different points. Instead, he has to bend or straighten his arms to get lower or higher. This may be required to apply more force to the pedals or to reduce the wind resistance by lowering the front, or to get a better view by raising the front a little.

SADDLE HEIGHT

The height of the saddle, or rather the distance of its top relative to the pedals, is the most critical variable for effective cycling. Although it is varied to adapt to the terrain off-road, it should also be set for cycling on normal roads and relatively level ground. The saddle should be adjusted so that your leg can be almost stretched without

straining your knee, which would cause excessive force and rotation at the joint. With the pedal in the highest position, the distance between the pedal and the saddle must be such that the knee is not bent excessively. Once the saddle is at the right height, the correct crank length ensures that the knee does not get bent too much—you may need longer than usual cranks if your legs are unusually long, shorter ones if they are on the short side. Standard cranks are 175 mm long, but they're also available in lengths of 165, 170, and 180 mm.

You may have to do some fine-tuning to achieve long-term comfort. Riders with disproportionately small feet may want to place the saddle a little lower; those with big feet perhaps slightly higher. Raise or lower the seat in steps of 6 mm (1/4 inch) at a time and try to get used to any position by riding perhaps a hundred miles, or several days, before attempting any change, which again must be about 6 mm to make any real difference.

SADDLE POSITION AND ANGLE

The normal saddle position is such that the seatpost is roughly in the middle of the saddle. For optimum pedaling efficiency, adjust the saddle forward or backward after it has been set to the correct height. On any regular mountain bike, when you are sitting on the bike with the front of the foot on the pedal and the crank placed horizontally, the center of the knee joint should be vertically aligned with the spindle of the forward pedal. You can locate the center of the knee joint at the bony protrusion just behind the knee cap.

The angle of the saddle relative to the horizontal plane should initially be set so as to keep level the line that connects the highest points at the front and the back. It may be necessary to modify this angle to prevent slipping forward or backwards once the handlebars have been set to the correct height. This may not become apparent until after some miles of cycling. Adjusting procedures for both forward position and angle are outlined below. To carry out the actual

Even very basic skills, such as getting on and off on the fly, are worth practicing. They'll help you control the bike better once you're riding off-road. *Gene Anthony photograph*

mechanical adjustment on the saddle, refer to the relevant sections of Chapter 3 (or, for a more thorough treatment, Chapters 31 and 32).

HANDLEBAR HEIGHT AND POSITION

Even on a mountain bike, the highest point of the handlebars should be no higher than the top of the saddle to ride efficiently. Just how low the right position is will be determined by the shape of the handlebars and the rider's experience and physique. This depends on the relative distribution of body weight and height, as well as the upper and lower arm length. Only by experimenting can you determine what will work best for you. Here we'll simply tell you how to determine the position for a relaxed initial riding style. After a few weeks of riding, you will have developed enough sensitivity to fine-tune the handlebar height and stem length to match your needs perfectly.

To set the handlebars for a relaxed riding posture, proceed as follows. First set the top of the bars about 3 cm (1 1/4 inches) lower than the saddle. Sit on the bike and reach forward for the handgrips, as though ready to grab the brake handles. In this position, your arms and upper body should form an isosceles triangle, that is, you should neither sit upright with your arms stretched forward nor lean forward too far. The arms should feel neither stretched nor heavily loaded and should not project sideways from the shoulder width too much.

If your hands are much farther apart than the shoulders, the handlebars are too wide. They can either be replaced or cut off at the ends. We have never yet seen the opposite phenomenon on any mountain bike, namely that the handlebars were too narrow. Typically, bikes with an "aggressive" geometry tend to be too stretched out between saddle and handlebars if you are new to the sport. You may have to twist the handlebars a little in the stem, or replace the stem with a shorter model to find the most comfortable position. If your bike comes with bar-ends, make sure they are firmly attached and at such an angle that you can easily hold them without unduly twisting your wrist.

If you have long legs and a short torso, you may not be comfortable even with a short stem. In that case, a smaller frame, which generally also has a shorter top tube, may be in order, with a long seatpost installed to get the right seat height. If no bike can be found with the right top-tube length, you may need a custom-built frame with the desired dimensions of seat tube and top tube. This would be the ultimate solution, although the problem is rarely so critical that you can't make do with a stock frame.

Once you start riding off-road, especially in mountainous terrain, you may want to lower the saddle or move it further back for cycling down a steep incline. Because the variations in geometry from one make and model to the next are quite significant, you may have to do a bit of experimenting to find the best positions for such special uses.

MOUNTING AND DISMOUNTING

Before starting off, make sure your shoelaces are tied and tucked in, or are short enough not to run the risk of getting caught in the chain. Select a low to intermediate gear, with the chain on the middle chainring and an intermediate or big

Practice descending to help get a feel for the bike's shift of balance and traction in steep terrain. *Bob Allen Photography*

sprocket. Start off at the side of the road or trail, after having checked to make sure no one is following closely behind.

Look behind you to make sure you're not in someone else's way, then establish the course you want to follow. If there are obstacles in your path, don't look at them too much; instead look at the path you need to follow to avoid them. (It's miraculous how obstacles start to work like magnets once you fix your sights on them.)

To slow down, whether just to stop or to get off the bike, first look behind you, to make sure you are not getting in the way of following cyclists or motorists. Aim for the place where you want to stop. Change into a lower gear, appropriate for starting off again later. Slow down by braking gently, using mainly the front brake to stop. Just before you come to a standstill, lean in the direction you want to dismount. Place the foot on the ground, moving forward off the saddle to straddle the seat tube. Now you are in the right position to either dismount or start again.

THE STEERING PRINCIPLE

The most effective way to steer a bicycle is not by merely turning the handlebars and following the front wheel, as is the case for any two-track vehicle, such as a car. Although bicycles and other single-track vehicles indeed follow the front wheel, they also require you to lean the vehicle into the curve to balance it at the same time, so it doesn't topple over to the outside of the curve due to the centrifugal force.

If you turned the handlebars while staying upright, the lower part of the bike would start running away from its previous course in the direction in which the front wheel is pointed. Meanwhile, your mass, perched high up on the bike, would continue following the original course due to inertia. Thus, the center of gravity would not be in line with the point of contact between the bike and the ground, and consequently you would come crashing to the ground. Due to the effect of centrifugal force, the tendency to throw you off toward the outside of the curve increases with higher speeds, requiring a more pronounced lean into the curve the faster you are going.

The most effective technique for riding a curve at speed is to place the bike at the appropriate angle under which the centrifugal force is offset by a shift of your weight to the inside, *before* turning. Two methods may be used, depending on the time and space available to carry out the maneuver. These two methods are referred to as the *natural* and the *forced* turn. To understand these techniques, we should first take a look at the intricacies of balancing the bike when riding a straight line, after which the differences between the two methods of turning can be explained.

PHYSICS OF BIKING

What keeps a bicycle or any other single-track vehicle going without falling over is the inertia of its moving mass. Rolling a narrow hoop, such as a bicycle rim, will show that it has an unstable balance. Once the thing starts to lean either left or right, it will go further and further down, until it hits the ground. This is because the mass is no longer supported vertically in line with the force. Try it with a bicycle wheel if you like. If the bike's front wheel could not be steered, and you couldn't move sideways, you'd very soon come down the same way.

On the bike, you notice when the vehicle starts to lean over. Theoretically, there are two ways out of the predicament. Either move your body back over the center of the bike, or move the bike back under your body. In practice, the latter method is used most effectively, especially at higher speeds. When the bike begins leaning to the side, oversteer the front wheel a little in the same direction, which restores the balance. In fact, this balance point will be passed, so the bike starts leaning the other way, and so on—forever.

This entire sequence of movements is easiest to observe when you are cycling slowly. When you try to stand still (also known as a "track stand"), the balancing motions become so extreme that only a highly skilled cyclist can keep control. The faster the bicycle, the less perceptible

(and therefore harder to master) are the steering corrections required to retain balance. To get an understanding of this whole process, try to practice riding a straight line at a low speed. Then do it at a higher speed, and see whether you agree with the explanation.

THE NATURAL TURN

Under normal circumstances, you'll know well ahead of time where to turn, and there is usually enough room to follow a wide curve. This is the situation in a natural turn, shown in the solid line path in the illustration. It makes use of the lean that results from normal straight-path steering corrections. To turn to the right, you simply wait until the bike is leaning that way; the left turn is initiated when the bike is leaning to the left.

Instead of turning the handlebars to that same side, as you would do to get back in balance when trying to ride a straight line, you leave the handlebars alone. This causes the bike to lean further and further in the direction of the turn. Only when the lean is quite significant do you steer in the same direction, but not as abruptly as you would to straighten up. Instead, you fine-tune the ratio of lean and steering to ride out the curve.

You will still be leaning in the same direction when the turn is completed, and you would ride a circle without some corrective action on your part. To get back on a straight course, you steer further into the curve than the amount of lean demanded to maintain your balance. This allows you to resume the slightly curving course with which you approximate the straight line.

Unconsciously, you probably learned to do this when you were a kid, but never realized what was going on. You could perhaps continue to ride a bicycle forever without understanding the theory. However, to keep control over the bike in demanding situations encountered while riding off-road, you will be better off if you have the theoretical knowledge and have learned to ride a calculated course, making use of this information. Get a feel for it by riding around an empty parking lot or any other level area many times,

leaning this way and that, following straight lines and making turns, until it is second nature on the one hand, but also something you understand consciously.

While you are practicing this technique, as well as when riding at other times, note that speed, curve radius, and lean are all closely correlated. A sharper turn requires more lean at any given speed. At a higher speed, any given curve requires greater lean angles than the same curve radius at a lower speed. As you practice this technique, learn to judge which are the appropriate combinations and limitations under different circumstances.

THE FORCED TURN

Especially off-road, you will often be confronted with situations in which you can't wait until you are leaning the right way to make a natural turn. Obstacles, other trail users, or irregularities in the surface may force you into a narrow predetermined path, with only a few inches to spare. Or you may have to get around a curve that is too sharp to be taken naturally at your current riding speed.

These situations require the second method of turning, that is the forced turn, represented by the dashed line in the illustration. In this case, the turn must be initiated quickly, regardless of which way the bike happens to be leaning at the time. You have to coerce the bike to lean in the appropriate direction and at an adequate angle just at the right time. And it has to be done quickly.

Do that by sharply steering *away* from the turn just before you get there. You and the bike will immediately start to lean in the direction of the turn. You would risk a disastrous crash, as your bike moves away from the mass center, if you were to continue in a straight line. You have quickly achieved a considerable lean angle in the direction of the turn. Compensate for this by steering abruptly in the same direction. As this is the direction of the turn, you are set up just right to make a sharp turn. Once completed, steer into the turn a little further to regain the approximately straight course, as explained for the natural turn.

Hans-Joerg Rey demonstrates how to get the front wheel up in the air—more on this in Chapter 7—but in short, the trick is to first put force onto the front end and then suddenly throw back your weight, pulling up the front end with the handlebars. *Bob Allen Photography*

Practice the forced-turn technique often. The beginning cyclist has to overcome all sorts of reasonable inhibitions and to practice a lot before he can initiate a *left* turn by steering *right*. Take your bike to a level, grassy area or an empty parking lot a few days in a row, wearing protective clothing in case you fall: helmet, gloves, jacket, and long pants.

BRAKING TECHNIQUE

When mountain biking, you often have to use the brakes, though not always to make a panic stop. In fact, once you have become a skilled and sensitive cyclist, you'll hardly ever have to brake to a standstill. Instead, you will use the brakes to regulate your speed. Effective braking means that you can ride fast up close to the turn or the obstacle that requires the reduced speed, brake to reach the lower speed quickly, and accelerate immediately afterwards.

You will be using the brakes to get down in speed from 20 to 10 miles per hour to take a turn, or from 20 to 18 miles per hour to avoid running into the rider ahead of you. Or you may have to get down from 30 to 10 miles per hour to

handle a switchback, or to avoid a tree, or miss a rock on a steep descent.

Although at times you may have to reduce your speed quickly, you should also develop a feel for gradual speed reduction to prevent skidding and loss of control. In fact, most cyclists are more often in danger due to braking too vigorously than due to insufficient stopping power.

The modern mountain bike has remarkably effective brakes—provided it's not raining. A modest force on the brake handle can cause a deceleration of about 4.5 m/sec^2 with just one brake. Applying both brakes, the effect is even more dramatic, enabling you to slow down from 30 to 15 miles per hour within one second. There are some limitations to braking that have to be considered, though.

In the first place, moisture has a negative effect on the rim brake's performance, as the buildup of water on the rims drastically reduces the friction between brake pad and rim. This applies especially if ordinary rubber brake pads are used. We have measured a deterioration from 4.5 to 1.5 m/sec^2 for a given hand-lever force for rubber brake pads on aluminum rims (and only about 0.7 m/sec^2 for bicycles with

chrome-plated steel rims, typically found on department-store bikes). Lately, special brake-block materials have been introduced that are less sensitive to rain.

The second limitation is associated with a change in the distribution of weight between the wheels as a result of braking. Because the mass center of the rider is quite high above the ground, and its horizontal distance to the front wheel axle comparatively small, the bicycle has a tendency to tip forward in response to deceleration. Weight is transferred from the rear to the front of the bike. When the deceleration reaches about 3.5 m/sec^2, the weight on the rear wheel is no longer enough to provide traction. Trying to brake harder than that with the rear brake makes the rear wheel skid, resulting in loss of control instead of faster stopping.

In a typical riding posture, the rear wheel is unloaded enough for the bike to tip forward when a deceleration of about 6.5 m/sec^2 is reached. Consequently, no conventional bicycle can ever be controlled when trying to brake harder than this, regardless of the type, number, and quality of the brakes used.

This is a very high deceleration, which you should not often reach, but it is good to realize there is such a limit and that it cannot be avoided by using the rear brake alone or in addition to the front brake, but only by braking less vigorously. During a sudden speed reduction, or panic stop, such high deceleration may be reached. The effect will be even more pronounced on a downslope, as it raises you even higher relative to the front wheel. In all such cases, you can reduce the toppling-over effect by shifting your body weight back and down as much as possible: sit far back and hold the upper body horizontally.

Because twice as great a deceleration is possible with the front brake as with the rear, the former should be used under most conditions—as long as you're going in a straight line. But when you're leaning over in a curve it's easier to maintain your bike on track using the rear brake. Better yet, try to brake *before* you get to the curve, using primarily the front brake.

Making the bike hop. This is one way of controlling your mountain bike that can help you master off-road riding. The principle is to use the springiness of the compressed air in your tires to bounce—first each wheel separately, later both together—up in the air. The arrows represent the relative movement of your body as you go through the procedure.

Most braking is not done abruptly. Gradual deceleration, particularly when the road is slick, in curves, or when others are following closely behind, is vitally important. You must be able to control the braking force within narrow limits. Practice all the various forms and conditions of braking. Pay the utmost attention to the complex relationship between initial speed, curve radius, brake-lever force, and deceleration, to become fully competent at handling the bike when slowing down under all conceivable circumstances.

On a steep downhill, the slope not only increases the tendency to tip you forward, it also induces an accelerating effect, which must be overcome by the brakes merely to keep the speed constant. A 20-percent slope, which is not a rare phenomenon off-road, results in an acceleration of about 2 m/sec^2. Obviously, you will encounter big problems in wet weather on such a downhill stretch if you don't keep your speed down from the start. Reduce the speed by gradual, intermittent braking. This will help wipe most of the water from the rims, retaining braking efficiency a little better. This way, the brakes are not overtaxed when you do have to reduce speed suddenly, as may be required to handle an unexpected obstacle or a sharp turn.

Practice effective braking to achieve complete control of the bicycle under normal and difficult cycling conditions. The dramatic difference in the bike's behavior between braking on the straight and in a curve must be experienced to be appreciated. Again, this is a matter for practice in a place without traffic. Include braking in your regular exercises during the first weeks of cycling preparation. Even after you have been riding for some time, you will be well advised to repeat from time to time the practice sessions for steering and braking control.

TRACTION

To increase forward traction, accelerate more gradually on loose ground and keep your weight back as much as possible when first moving off. The steeper the incline of the slope, the more likely you are to slip, so the more important the countermeasures. After a couple of hours worth of conscious practice, you'll know just how to handle different situations.

To improve sideways traction when steering, don't divert too suddenly and don't divert without making sure your body is leaning into the curve. This too is more likely to be a problem on loose ground, and the worst case is on ice. To handle the latter situation, you actually have to unload the front wheel by sitting back as much as possible (even increase the height of your handlebars, and accept that this is the time to ride in the dork posture).

To secure adequate braking traction, don't brake too suddenly, and use mainly the front brake. As you brake, your mass is transferred forward, tending to unload the rear wheel, making it skid easily. When braking in the front, make sure you're not leaning into a curve at the same time, because that will tend to make you skid sideways and lose control.

OTHER RIDING SKILLS

Riding a mountain bike with total confidence requires hands-on experience, but most of the associated skills can be learned faster and more thoroughly when you understand the underlying principles. Building on the information about posture, gearing, steering, and braking provided in the preceding sections, you will be shown here what to do under various typical riding situations. The many miles of experience will come soon enough when you start riding. However, you will gain the handling practice more effectively by applying these techniques.

GETTING UP TO SPEED

Although you may not be into mountain biking for speed alone, you should learn to get up to speed quickly. The idea is to waste as little time and energy as possible during this process. Tricky, because acceleration demands disproportionately high levels of power output. And the faster it's done, the more demanding it is.

You have to strike a balance. Accelerating faster than necessary wastes energy that may be sorely needed later. Done too slowly, it may become a plodding affair, especially if your speed remains inadequate to overcome steep sections or soft ground. You will have to find the right balance between speed and effort, but the way to reach it is easy to describe: start in a low gear and increase speed gradually but rapidly.

There are two methods: Either increase your pedaling speed in the low gear, changing up only as you reach a significant speed, or apply a surge of hard work, standing on the pedals, throwing your weight from one side to the other. As soon as you're up to speed, sit on the saddle and select a good gear for spinning at a comfortable but high pedaling rate.

ACCELERATING

However efficient a constant speed may be, sometimes you want to accelerate to a higher speed. This may be necessary to catch up with other riders or to avoid getting left behind. Sometimes, you'll need to accelerate to get out of the way of a bike crossing your path or a mad dog chasing you.

You will find accelerating by increasing pedaling speed more effective than by increasing pedal force in a higher gear. In other words, as long as you can spin faster, it is best to shift down into a slightly lower gear and increase the pedaling rate vigorously. Once you gather momentum and are approaching your maximum spinning speed, shift up and continue to gain speed in the slightly higher gear.

Traction plays a big role. You need to keep enough weight on the rear wheel to stop it from slipping, so you may have to transfer some of your weight farther back. In addition to that, increasing speed gradually will allow you to keep traction under control much better than will any sudden surge of force.

RIDING AGAINST THE WIND

At higher speeds or whenever there is a strong headwind, the effect of air drag on the power needed to cycle is quite noticeable. This may not always seem very significant off-road, but air drag certainly matters quite a bit when you are traveling on regular roads and whenever you are in open, level terrain. Economize your efforts by minimizing the wind resistance as much as possible.

To achieve that, keep your profile low when cycling against the wind. When riding alone, try to seek out the sheltered parts of the trail wherever possible.

HILL CLIMBING

With some conscious effort, everybody's climbing skills can be improved up to a point, even though some riders are born climbers, whereas others may have to go uphill slowly all their lives. It is an ability that you can learn and develop well enough to handle all the hills you encounter.

A regular pedaling motion is most efficient, and that is best mastered by staying seated in a low gear. Mountain bikes are invariably equipped with gears that are low enough to allow you to get up almost any incline while staying in the saddle. What's lacking is a true understanding of gear selection by many riders. Only too often do you see people plodding up at very low pedaling rates in too high a gear or, conversely, using very low gears when the terrain doesn't call for it. Refer to Chapter 6 for advice on selecting the right gears.

CLIMBING WHILE STANDING

On very steep sections, where even the lowest available gear is too high to allow a smoothly spinning leg motion, it is time to apply another technique, standing up while riding. This is known as "honking" in England and used to be almost unknown in the United States until the advent of mountain biking. Now it's considered cool to stand up, although few people know they're using an old-fashioned technique that makes use of their body weight to push down the pedals.

When honking, the weight of the whole body is pulled up quickly after each stroke. In this mode, the muscle work is done each time the body is raised, rather than when pushing the pedal down and around. To do it effectively, you can either take quick snappy steps, or throw your weight from side to side in a swinging motion.

THE GEAR SYSTEM

CHAPTER SIX

Your mountain bike is equipped with a sophisticated derailleur system for multiple-speed gearing. To change gears, the chain is shifted onto another combination of chainring and cog with the aid of two derailleur mechanisms. Systems with 21 or 24 gears are generally used, and some old 15- and 18-speed mountain bikes are still around.

The derailleur method of gearing allows minute adjustments of the gear ratio to the cyclist's potential, on the one hand, and to the terrain, wind resistance, and surface conditions on the other. Learning to select the right gear may well provide the biggest single step toward improved cycling speed and endurance.

PARTS OF THE SYSTEM

The mechanical components of the derailleur system as used on the mountain bike are the front and rear derailleurs, the handlebar-mounted shifters, and the cables that connect them. The chain is guided by the front derailleur to run over one of three chainrings mounted on the right-hand crank and by the rear derailleur over any one of six, seven, or eight cogs mounted on a freewheel on the rear wheel hub. Providing you are pedaling forward, the chain can be moved from one chainring to the other by means of the front derailleur, or changer (as it is called in Britain), and from one cog to another by means of the rear derailleur.

The various chainrings and cogs have different numbers of teeth. Consequently, the ratio between pedaling speed and the speed with which the rear wheel is driven

Maxium and minimum chain tension. Try to avoid using these gear combinations that combine the largest front chainring with the largest rear cog (top) and the one with the smallest front chainring with smallest rear cog. (bottom) However, you should be able to reach these combinations as a test to make sure the chain is long enough and not too loose. The reason to avoid them is that they cause chain cross-over, resulting in chain resistance and wear due to the chain's angle.

changes whenever a different combination is selected. Bigger chainrings in the front and smaller cogs in the rear result in higher gears, whereas smaller chainrings and bigger cogs give lower gears. Higher gears are selected when the cycling is easy, so the available output allows a high riding speed. Select a

lower gear when higher resistances must be overcome, such as when riding uphill, against a head wind, or on soft ground, but also when starting off from a standstill.

On the mountain bike, each derailleur is controlled by means of a shift lever that is mounted on the handlebars, within easy reach without taking the hands off the grips. The most popular type of shifter control these days is the twistgrip, best known as Grip Shift. Other bikes have either double-lever (push-push) shifters mounted under the handlebars or single-lever shifters mounted on top of the handlebars.

The front derailleur simply shoves the cage through which the chain runs to the right or the left, placing the chain onto a larger or smaller chainring, respectively. Turning the twistgrip shifter clockwise, or pulling the top-mounted lever back, engages a larger chainring for a higher gear range on most models; shifted the other way, it engages a smaller chainring, obtaining a lower gearing range.

The rear derailleur is more complicated, with a set of little wheels over which the chain runs, but it has the same effect: it moves the chain onto a larger cog (lower gear) or to a smaller one (higher gear) as you move the shifter.

The front derailleur is used to move from one range of gears to another; the rear derailleur for in-between steps. All the gears in the high range are reached by shifting the rear derailleur while the front derailleur remains set for the chain on the largest chainring. The intermediate gears are all reached while the front derailleur is

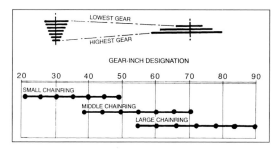

Gearing combinations. The upper detail shows what combinations of chainring and cog result in the highest and lowest gear. The lower detail is a diagrammatic representation of the gearing ranges available with each of the chainrings.

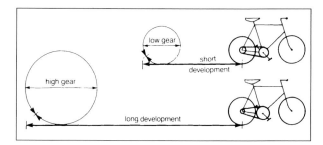

Gear and development designations explained. The gear number, always measured in inches, represents the equivalent wheel diameter of a directly driven wheel for a given gear ratio. The development figure represents the distance in meters traveled per crank revolution for a given gear.

set to engage the intermediate chainring. All the gears in the low range are selected with the front derailleur in the position to put the chain on the smallest chainring.

Although it is possible to select chainring and cog sizes in such a way that intermediate gears between rear derailleur shifts are reached with a front changer shift, the above method simplifies the gear selection procedure considerably. This is certainly advantageous for the typical mountain bike setup, where you often have to change quickly under difficult conditions.

The rear derailleur is controlled by means of the right-hand shifter; the front derailleur with the left-hand shifter. Under-the-bar shifters use one lever to shift up, the other to shift down. In the case of top-mounted shifters, move the lever clockwise to shift up, counterclockwise to shift down. Twistgrips are shifted in opposite directions for the front and the rear. Whatever type of shifter is installed, the one mounted on the right always controls the rear derailleur (used for most shifts), the one on the left the front derailleur.

Older models may not be indexed (meaning you don't shift in steps but you have to fine-tune the position of the lever), and believe it or not, it is quite possible to shift these delicate devices just as accurately—it just takes more practice and sensitivity.

GEARING THEORY

Gearing enables you to pedal at an efficient rate with comfortable force under a wide range of conditions and riding speeds. To visualize the benefits of this, consider two extreme cases of doing a given amount of physical work.

To climb a hill means effectively raising your own weight, and that of the bike, over the difference in elevation between the bottom and the top of the incline.

If the combination of chainring and cog size were fixed, as it is on the single-speed bicycle, any given pedaling speed would invariably correspond to a certain riding speed. Gearing allows you to divide the load over a larger or smaller number of pedal revolutions. The lower the gear, the lighter the load, but the more times you turn the cranks. The higher the gear, the higher your speed at the same pedaling rate, but the harder you have to push the pedals.

The derailleur gearing system allows you to choose the combination of chainring and cog sizes that enables you to operate effectively at your chosen pedaling speed with optimum performance. You may of course also vary the pedaling rate, which would appear to have the same effect as selecting another gear. Indeed, with any given gear, pedaling slower reduces riding speed and therefore demands less power, whereas a higher pedaling rate increases road speed, requiring more power.

However, power output is not the sole, nor indeed the most important, criterion. Performing at the same power output may tax the body differently, depending on the associated force and speed of movement. It has been found that to cycle long distances effectively, without tiring or hurting excessively, the pedal force must be kept down by pedaling at a rate well above what seems natural to the beginning cyclist.

Efficient long-duration cycling requires a pedaling rate of 80 rpm or more. Racers generally pedal even faster, whether riding off-road or not. This skill doesn't come

overnight—you first have to learn to move your legs that fast—but it is an essential requirement for efficient mountain biking. Much of your early cycling practice should therefore be aimed at mastering the art of fast pedaling, referred to as *spinning*.

GEARING PRACTICE

Once you know that high gears mean big chainrings and small cogs, it's time to get some practice riding in high and low gears. First do it "dry": with the bike upside-down or supported with the rear wheel off the ground. Turn the cranks by hand and use the shift levers to change up and down, front and rear, until you have developed a good idea of the combinations reached in all conceivable shifter positions.

Listen for rubbing and crunching noises as you shift, realizing that the shift has not been executed properly until the noises have subdued. Generally, noises come from the front, as the indexing takes care of such problems in the rear. You may have to move the shifter for the front derailleur if you discern a noise after a rear derailleur shift, because the chain—now running at a different angle—may be rubbing against the front derailleur cage.

Now take to the road or any other level terrain. Select a place where you can experiment with your gears without the risk of being run over by a closely following vehicle or of getting in the way of other cyclists.

When shifting, reduce the pedal force, still pedaling forward. The front derailleur in particular will not shift as smoothly as it did when the cranks were turned by hand. You will notice that the noises become more severe and that shifts don't always take place as you intended. To execute a correct front change with a non-indexed top-mounted shifter (or an indexed one that is switched to the friction mode), you may have to overshift slightly first. Push the lever a little beyond the correct position to effect a definite change, then back up until the chain is quiet again. Practice shifting until it goes smoothly.

All this can be learned if you give it some time and attention. All it takes to become an expert very quickly is half an hour of intensive practice each day during one week, and the continued attention required to do it right during regular riding afterwards.

GEAR DESIGNATION

Just how high or low any given gear is may be expressed by quoting the respective chainring and cog size engaged in the particular gear. However, this is not a very good measure.

Changing gear the modern way, with a twistgrip shifter. To date, that usually means Grip Shift, the system's primary manufacturer. Sachs also has its own twistgrip shifter, while until recently, Shimano could not bring its own version into the United States due to a patent and licensing dispute with the maker of Grip Shift.

Changing gear the conventional way—without twistgrip shifters: and under-the-bar shifters.

To allow a direct comparison between the gearing effects of different gears and bikes, two methods are in use, referred to as gear number and development, respectively, as defined in the illustration. The gear number is determined by multiplying the quotient of chainring and cog sizes by the wheel diameter in inches. Thus, combining a 34-tooth chainring with a 17-tooth cog and a 26-inch wheel gives you a gear of 26x(34/17)=52 inches.

Outside the United States, gears are normally expresses in terms of *development*. That is the distance in meters covered by the bike with one crank revolution. To convert a development figure into gear inches, multiply it by 12.5. Refer to the tables in the Appendix.

For off-road purposes, gear ranges tend to be lower than they are on other bikes. Low gears in terms of gear number are in the low to mid twenties (around 1.90 to 2.20 meters in terms of development). The highest gears are those above 80 inches (development of more than 6.40 meters).

GEAR SELECTION

Possibly the biggest problem for the beginning mountain biker is to select the right gear. Choose whichever gear allows you to maximize your pedaling rate without diminishing your capacity to work effectively.

Perhaps you are initially able to pedal no faster than 60 rpm. That will be too low once you have had some riding practice, but for now that may be your limit. So the right gear is the one in which you can reach that rate at any time, preferably exceeding it. Use either an electronic speedometer with a pedaling rate function or count it out with the aid of a wrist watch until you develop a feel for your pedaling speed. If you find yourself pedaling slower, change down into a slightly lower gear to increase the pedaling rate at the same riding speed. If you're pedaling faster, keep it up until you feel you are indeed spinning too lightly, and then change to a slightly higher gear to increase road speed while maintaining the same pedaling rate.

Gradually, you will develop the capacity to pedal faster. As this happens, increase the pedaling rate along with your ability, moving up from 60 to 70, 80, and eventually even higher. When riding with others, don't be guided by their gear selection. They may be stronger or weaker or may have developed their pedaling speed more or less than you have.

It should not take long before you can judge in advance the correct gear, without the need to count out the pedal revolutions. You'll know when to change down into a lower gear as the direction of the road changes, exposing you to a head wind, or when you reach an incline. You will also learn to judge just how far to change down and up again when the conditions become more favorable. Change gears consciously and frequently in small steps, and you will soon master the trick.

BASIC DERAILLEUR CARE

For optimum operation of the derailleur system, several things should be regularly checked and corrected if necessary. The derailleurs themselves, as well as the chain and the various cogs, chainrings, and control cables, must be kept clean and lightly lubricated with oil or grease. Twistgrip shifters and under-the-bar shifters comprise lots of plastic parts, which need special lubricants, because petroleum-based oil and grease tend to either dissolve or age the plastic parts prematurely. This type of grease is available from the shifter manufacturer. The cables must be just taut when the shifters are pushed forward and the derailleurs engage the appropriate gear. The tension screws on top-mounted shifters must be kept tightened to give positive shifting without excessive tightness or slack.

When the chain is shifted beyond the biggest or smallest chainring or cog, or when certain combinations cannot be reached, the derailleurs themselves must be adjusted. They are equipped with set-stop screws, which can be adjusted with a small screwdriver. Instructions for this and all other derailleur maintenance work can be found in Chapter 29.

PART II
THE ART OF MOUNTAIN BIKING

CHAPTER SEVEN
OFF-ROAD RIDING SKILLS

This second part of the book is devoted to the special skills and knowledge required for competent off-road cycling. In this chapter we'll expand on the material introduced in Chapters 5 and 6 to develop specific off-road riding skills. Although the underlying techniques are the same, the particular applications and their circumstances are different enough to justify special treatment. Just the same, we'll start with what may seem to be the simplest feats possible, gradually expanding our practice to some of the really difficult maneuvers that only experienced off-road cyclists have mastered.

BALANCING PRACTICE

The most important aspect of cycling in general, but even more so of mountain biking on rough terrain, is balance. In all the techniques and exercises described here, think about the ways to balance the bike with the movement of your body—sideways, back, forward, up, and down.

One effective form of practice is what is referred to in biking circles as the track stand: keeping the bike stationary while balancing on top of it. To do this, ride the bike over a short distance in a straight line, then slow down gradually until the bike is at a standstill while you are raised off the seat with your feet on the pedals with the cranks horizontal (the 9:15 or 3:45 position). The first few times you do it, choose a stretch of trail or road with a slight incline. Once you can do it there, move on to level ground, and finally to a downhill stretch.

Try to stay upright on the bike with the front brake engaged. Don't try to keep the handlebars straight, but turn them into the direction of your lean one way or the other to maintain your balance, and perhaps disengage the brake just a tiny bit when a slight forward movement is needed to stay upright. When you feel you're leaning to the right, turn the handlebars in that same direction and move your upper body to balance. Use tiny movements of the cranks back and forth, in conjunction with brief releases and reapplications of the brake if necessary.

WALKING AND RUNNING WITH THE BIKE

Although bicycles are meant to be ridden, your mountain bike may occasionally have to be walked or even carried, and when you're in a hurry, as in a race or when keeping up with others, you must master the skill of keeping a gradual motion while running with the bike. It may not seem difficult to walk or run, whether with or without your bike, but it helps to master the distinct skill that allows you to do it effectively. In off-road situations, you may have to dismount suddenly to walk or even carry the bike part of the way, over obstacles or through a muddy or sandy patch.

Simply walking the bike is usually done while holding it by the handlebars and the saddle. On a downhill stretch it is sometimes more convenient to hold just the handlebars while balancing the bike vertically on the rear wheel. Your bike

Mastering balance at Laguna Beach, demonstrated by Hans-Joerg Rey, longtime trials champion of the world and one of the most effective popularizers of the sport. *Bob Allen Photography*

takes up less space using the latter technique. This technique is therefore recommended in terrain with closely spaced obstacles—at home, this is the way to maneuver your bike out from the back of the garage or the garden shed.

Once you have traversed the difficult section, you should be able to get back on without undue loss of time and energy. Doing this skillfully is particularly important in off-road racing, but can also help you enjoy recreational off-road riding. Estimate ahead of time where you will have to get off, and shift down to a low gear. Move forward off the saddle and transfer your weight to the pedal on the side on which you want to get off—usually the left.

Slow down as appropriate for the situation; when you get down to a modest speed, swing the leg over the side opposite to where you'll be getting off, holding it just behind the other leg. Fix your eyes on the point where you are going to stop, and slow down to a trotting speed when you are ready to dismount. Now swing the free leg forward between the leg that's still on the pedal and the bike and take a sizable step forward, moving away from

the bike sideways, far enough to avoid the pedal from overtaking you in a painful manner, and take the other foot off the pedal as well. Keep trotting or slow down to a walking pace, holding the bike either by the handlebar ends or by the handlebars and the saddle.

Now you can either walk or carry the bike. In case you have to carry it to overcome serious obstacles, let the hand on the far side slide down from the handlebars along the downtube, grabbing it a little below the middle, while still trotting or walking. At this point, raise the bike up on your shoulder, letting it slip into place at the point where seat tube and top tube come together. Installing a padded strap there will help protect your shoulder. Grab the handlebars near the middle with the arm that goes through the frame, keeping the other hand free.

After you have carried the bike over the obstacle, you may either want to walk by the side of the bike or get back on. Either way, lower the bike off your shoulder and grab the handlebars at both ends. To walk the bike, just continue this way. To get back on quickly, keep trotting and remount as described above.

AVOIDING OBSTACLES

Off-road, you will often be confronted with obstacles that would be small enough to avoid—if they were not right in your path. This may be anything from a pothole or a broken branch to a crashed cyclist just in front of you. Depending on how much time and space you have available, use either the natural or the forced-turn technique. At speed it is hard to go anywhere except where you are actually looking. Don't look at the obstacle but at the point where you want to pass it, steering to do so in a natural way.

To cycle around an obstacle that appears suddenly, you can develop a technique based on the forced turn. This maneuver is shown in the illustration. As soon as you perceive the obstacle ahead of you, decide whether to pass it to the left or the right. Ride straight up to it and then, before you reach it, briefly but decisively steer in the direction opposite to the obstacle (to the right if you want to pass it on the left). This makes the bike lean over toward the other side. Now steer in that direction just as quickly, which will result in a very sharp forced turn, and then make the correction needed to stay upright. As soon as you've passed the obstacle, oversteer a little more, causing a lean that helps put the bike back on its proper course.

You can practice this technique on an empty parking lot or any other level area, wearing a helmet, gloves, and protective clothing. Mark phony obstacles with chalk or put down foam pads or sponges. Practice passing them gradually and abruptly on both sides, until you've mastered the trick. Only then should you try doing the same in more difficult terrain.

OFF-ROAD BRAKING

Using the brakes to come to a complete standstill, or more typically to reduce your speed to a controllable level on a fast downhill stretch, is a tricky matter under off-road conditions. The slope may be so steep that you tend to topple forward easily, while at the same time you have to deal with the inevitable accelerating effect caused by the downslope. The less predictable

Practice balance like this. It is easiest if you start off on a slight uphill, so that you can keep the chain under tension, applying just enough force to prevent yourself from rolling back.

road surface may greatly reduce the traction between the tires and the ground. Finally, you may have to brake while at the same time making a steering correction to avoid an obstacle.

Before going downhill, get ready for it. If it's a steep decent, put your seat about 1-1/2 inches lower than normal. Sit far back on the seat and hold back, keeping a low profile, the pedals horizontal. The most frequently made mistake among novices is to let one or even both legs dangle, with the pedals either spinning freely or in top-and-bottom position.

Get a feel for how much braking force is needed. While going straight down, you can use both brakes, but on a very long slope you may want to use them intermittently, to keep both of them effective. As long as the slope is not too steep, you can probably get by applying only one brake. Try to brake just enough *before* you get to the curve that you don't need to do so while leaning.

Try to stay relaxed, rather than tensing up in a cramped position, so you follow the bike and its movements. This way you will soon learn to balance the amount of braking necessary with the accompanying weight shifts needed to keep control over the bike. Don't feel you have to be braking all the time: just keep down to a speed that is low enough to give you control in critical locations. That may mean braking rather vigorously on certain sections where the surface is good and the route straight, letting the bike gather momentum again up to the next controllable stretch.

RIDING UPHILL

There are of course many ways of riding uphill, ranging from spinning fast in a relatively low gear for the slope to standing on the pedals honking uphill in a relatively high gear for that slope. When cycling off-road, another factor has to be considered. In addition to otherwise unheard-of grades, the surface is often rough and irregular.

Although your mountain bike probably has the kind of rubber on its wheels that provides as much traction as you can get, the conditions riding up steep slopes are a little tricky. This is due to the combined effect of loose or unpredictable surfaces and the extreme steepness of the grade. As you go uphill, your center of gravity shifts back on the bike. While this does improve traction by increasing the load on the rear wheel, it also reduces the load on the front wheel to such an extent that your steering becomes less predictable.

When you stand on the pedals on a steep uphill stretch, your weight is relatively far back, and that may unload the front wheel so much that the bike gets out of control, beginning to lift off or shift sideways. With the first trace of this, lean a little farther forward, bending the arms a little to lean on the handlebars. Not too far though, keeping enough weight on the rear

wheel to ensure traction. It all becomes a subtle play, balancing your weight by minute shifts forward and backward to keep the front wheel on the ground while retaining traction in the back.

To climb efficiently off-road, you'll need to plan ahead and maintain a certain balance. Before you even get to the uphill stretch, visually scan the path ahead. Size up not only the steepness of the various stretches but also the other terrain conditions—the type of surface, relative unevenness, curves, and lateral slope. All these factors will go into the equation on how to handle the ride. Confusing perhaps at first, but not once you learn to handle each of these elements separately. For your first practice sessions, try to find different stretches with one particular kind of problem, and learn to master each of these separately. Then start combining the various elements until you've mastered the art of climbing under all conceivable conditions, both separately and in combination. We'll start with the easiest case, and then you'll be on your own exploring the various special cases.

Because the case of starting out on an uphill slope was explained before, we'll assume you approach the climb at some speed. Look ahead and size up the situation. Plan ahead where you will need which gear. Generally, if it's steep terrain, start off by selecting the smallest chainring in the front but initially with one of the smaller cogs in the back, as long as you haven't hit the actual climb yet.

Plan which path to take. Look for the least rutted sections of the path (and look where you want to ride, rather then focusing on the spots you want to avoid). Get a good start with the help of your momentum by approaching the hill at some speed, pedaling rather fast in an intermediate gear. You'll get up quite far this way before you even realize you're climbing; but shift down when your momentum starts running out.

Shift down in good time, otherwise before you do shift down you'll have reached a point where your effort is quite high and you'll be pulling on the handlebars to keep going. That's a bad time to shift for two reasons:

1. Even with the smooth operation of modern shifting mechanisms, you still have to release pressure on the pedals when shifting.
2. You can lose your balance when pulling on the handlebars and shifting at the same time.

In the following list, we have summarized the other points to consider when going uphill:

1. Develop a smooth rhythm, balancing your output with your breathing, and avoiding sudden bursts of power, for which you may be punished by getting too tired to handle the rest of the climb.
2. When the traction is secure, ride with your weight equally distributed over the two wheels. But when you reach an obstacle, shift your weight back as the front wheel gets there. Once the front wheel has cleared, shift to a neutral balance again and pedal the rear wheel over it.
3. Keep a moderate grip on the handlebars or bar-ends. Grabbing on too tightly actually reduces control over the bike's steering, and when going uphill, you are often going so slow that steering

becomes quite critical for your balance. Relax as much as possible.
4. Make sure your seat is in a comfortable position, placing your body in a position from which it is easiest to gain traction when needed with a minor shift.
5. Don't lunge from side to side, even when honking (as described in Chapter 5), because the lateral movement can cause a loss of traction and diminish your control over steering and balancing.
6. Look ahead, but don't get intimidated by the amount of climbing ahead of you. If the climb is very long, look at it a piece at a time.

RIDING DOWNHILL

Here, too, looking ahead and balancing are the most important criteria. Control the bike with your weight more on the pedals than on the saddle. The steeper the slope, the more you want to move your body back and your mass center down. Lowering the seat may be necessary on really steep sections. Old mountain bikes were actually designed more with that shift of balance in mind than are today's much shorter bike designs, but you can still shift your weight even on the newer designs—it just takes more conscious effort.

Before you start out, and continually as you're descending, scan the path ahead of you for different conditions and obstacles, while visualizing the path you want to follow. Some of the terrain problems, such as gullies crossing your path, may not be so clearly visible straight ahead as they are when at an angle; use your peripheral vision to detect such items and estimate how they cross your path. To get across such obstacles, unload the front wheel as you reach them by leaning back to get over them gracefully rather than hammering the front of the bike into them. (The section *Jumping the Bike* provides a more advanced treatment of hopping to help you with this technique.) Choose your path so that you cross such obstacles as perpendicularly as possible, certainly if they are narrow and abrupt enough to divert your front wheel.

On rippled, or "washboard," surfaces, you may find that the biggest problem is caused by vibrations. They not only limit your control over the handlebars but may cause you not to see properly, especially if you wear glasses. This is where suspension really pays off, and interestingly enough the simplest suspension tends to do best here: the flexible stem dampens this kind of shock to the rider more effectively than any other form of suspension. True, on very rough terrain a full-suspension bike can allow you speed and control not otherwise obtainable. However, where most mountain bike riding is done, both in the United States and abroad, we've found short ripples in the road to be most common, and these are best absorbed by a flexible stem.

Even if you don't have suspension, you can handle these situations. For about ten years, mountain bikes without suspension were the norm even in high-speed downhill races, and the riders just learned to deal with it. First, use the tires as shock absorbers, by reducing the pressure. (You did remember to bring a pump or a CO_2 inflator to pressure them back up again afterwards, didn't you?) Relax, take the weight off your seat, hold the seat between your legs, and use your arms and legs as shock absorbers. If you start losing

Carrying the bike to cross obstacles is easiest when holding it so that your shoulder nestles at the point where seat tube and top tube meet, while you hold the handlebar from the other side with the arm that goes through the frame.

Bunny hop: Hans-Joerg Rey demonstrating how you jump the bike. This is nothing more than an advanced course in hopping the bike. *Bob Allen Photography*

vision or control, gradually slow down until you've got down to a speed at which you can handle the situation again.

DOWNHILL SWITCHBACKS

Often in off-road situations, you will somehow have to get down slopes that seem too steep and too rough to ride straight down. For the time being they probably are, but there are ways around this problem. Instead of roaring straight down the shortest way, you can use the same technique applied in downhill skiing, shifting your weight from side to side, following what is essentially a switchback course.

The same can be done on a bike. You ride along the contour of the grade, dropping elevation only slightly, deviating from the straight-line path to your eventual destination. Then you shift your weight in a very sharp forced turn toward the opposite side and go down the same way in the new direction. This way, you never reach the murderous speed induced by a straight downhill course. This maneuver is tricky, so you'd better practice it. As your confidence develops, you will be able to handle higher and higher speeds, requiring fewer and fewer turns to get down the hill.

Start this kind of practice on a relatively wide-open downhill stretch, where you have plenty of room to deviate one way or the other. Point your bike down only slightly at an angle, so you are riding along the side of the hill, rather than straight down. Sometime before your speed gets too high, but while still going straight, apply the front and rear brakes together briefly, immediately followed by the steering action and the necessary shift of weight to the uphill side, to induce a forced turn toward the downhill side.

Repeat this maneuver in the opposite direction, again shifting your weight to the uphill side. This way, you make another sharp turn, back the same direction as at first. Continue crisscrossing down the hillside until you get down. It will take you a long time, compared to what it would have taken to roll straight down, and perhaps you picked a slope you could have handled straight down. However, you'll have gained a lot of practice, and once you can do it

down a gentle slope, you will feel confident trying it down a steeper one. With a few days' deliberate practice, you'll have learned to do this so well that you can get down quite steep slopes.

JUMPING THE BIKE

Another useful skill for off-road cycling situations is making first the front, then the rear wheel, jump over an obstacle. You may have to do this when there is an unavoidable obstacle ahead of you. Some obstacles can be overcome by lifting yourself and the bike over them while riding. That's the way it feels when you can do it. To the observer it seems more like flying.

On the move, it's a matter of shifting your weight back and forth to lift the appropriate wheel off the ground. Before you jump up, go forward and down in the arms, and then suddenly throw your weight backwards, while pulling up on the handlebars to lift the front wheel. At the same time accelerate vigorously by pushing hard on the forward pedal.

You'll be using the energy stored in the compressed air in the tires. The basic requirement is a tire pressure that's just high enough to protect the tube yet low enough for your weight when it comes hard down on the rear wheel to go down by about 3/4 to 1 inch. The energy released when this much air is compressed is enough to lift bike and rider up several feet.

Start practicing on a hard, level surface (it won't work at all on soft ground because the energy, instead of being stored by the compressed air in the tire, goes into deforming the soil, which isn't going to spring back). Balance the bike standing still with the cranks horizontal—you just learned how to do that, so we hope you've been practicing. Pounce down with all your weight toward the rear of the bike to compress the rear tire in a short, snappy movement, and then just as snappily transfer your weight forward again. If all is well, the rear wheel will come off the ground.

The first few times you do this, it may seem unspectacular. Keep at it, interrupted by some riding to release the tension that is built up in your nerves more than in the tires. A couple of 15-minute practice sessions two

or three days in a row should pay off with quite spectacular results. You have mastered one third of the trick, and it is time to get on with the next third: raising the front wheel off the ground.

Raising the front wheel is normally referred to as doing a *wheelie*. Do this by merely shifting your weight backward quickly to unload the front wheel and to briefly bring your mass center behind the rear wheel. That's worth practicing, because it will be used in other stunts too. From a low speed or even at a standstill, balance the bike, now that you can do that, and keep your weight low and forward. Then throw your weight back with a decisive jolt, loading the rear wheel and releasing the front while pulling the handlebars up with you. Again, it may take some practice to perfect it, but this particular move is quite easy to learn.

To get both wheels off the ground, you want to do things that are a little more sophisticated than this, though. Because you have to combine it with the raising of the rear wheel eventually, the thing to do is to put an explosive charge under the front wheel, again in the form of tire compression, just as was done to get the rear wheel to come up. So don't just throw your weight back, but first pounce on the front end of the bike. Quickly push down with your body weight on the handlebars, then immediately release it and throw your weight back as in a conventional wheelie.

Finally, it will be time to combine the two movements of lifting the front and the rear wheels. Your first step will be to achieve both lifting movements consecutively, first the front and then the rear. While balancing at a standstill, push down hard on the front end and immediately release it, transferring the weight to the rear and compressing the rear tire quickly; then immediately release the tire by shifting your weight forward again. That was written as one long sentence because it should indeed be one continuous movement that cannot be broken up into steps. Do it as though you're reading and following the sentence as fast as possible.

Suddenly, after a few days with two or three short practice sessions each, you can

Introduction to doing a wheelie—the first step in clearing obstacles while moving forward. Unload the front end by pulling on the handlebars while throwing your weight back until the front wheel lifts high enough to clear the obstacle. Once you've cleared the obstacle with the front end, come out of the saddle and move your body forward to reduce the weight on the rear wheel, enabling it to follow over the obstacle. *Bob Allen Photography*

A rear wheelie, shown here, should only be regarded as a check on your ability to balance. By itself, it's not a useful skill for handling terrain situations. *Bob Allen Photography*

Taking obstacles in your stride. This sequence shows how to make first the rear wheel and then the rear wheel go over an obstacle. The arrows show the relative redistribution of your body weight needed to coax the bike across.

do it, and you wonder why it ever seemed so difficult. Notice how you graduated from putting one wheel up after the other to getting both of them up at the same time, without anyone telling you how it's done? It's nothing but the logical extension of what you were doing, and as you got better at it, those wheels started spending more time up in the air simultaneously.

After some practice you can get both wheels to lift off at the same time while riding along at speed. That's done by distributing your body weight over the front and the rear of the bike while pouncing down and at the same time compressing your body like a spring. When you raise your body just as suddenly by straightening your legs, arms, and back, the whole unit of you and your bike starts to defy gravity and comes straight up. Or so they say. But if

you are at all hesitant, you'll want to make sure nobody is watching as you clown around frustrated without getting any air. On the other hand, if you are at all agile, coordinated, and determined, you will probably master this trick pretty soon, too.

JUMPING OVER OBSTACLES

The hopping routine described in the preceding section is as much a lesson in general bike handling as a practical device in itself. In the fine art of observed trials competition, it is an absolute prerequisite, but in everyday use you'll benefit more from the sense of bike control and balance derived from it than from the actual skill itself. In the real world things happen when you're moving forward, not when you're standing still.

The first step is to learn to go up a step, even if only to practice for bigger and

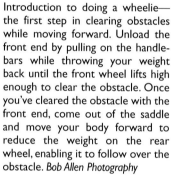

better things. Find an area with a step that is about 6 inches high and learn to approach it, lift the front wheel just before you get there, then hop onto it with the rear wheel and keep riding. Perhaps you even want to practice it on an imaginary ridge: a chalk line drawn on an empty parking lot.

Approach the ridge by riding parallel to it and then hop onto it sideways. That's the approach for obstacles that are almost parallel to your path rather than straight across your path. First briefly steer away from the ridge and then immediately and snappily correct the lean by steering back. You'll shoot across the ridge with the front wheel almost perpendicular to it, before continuing in your original direction.

Whether jumping up a perpendicular or parallel ridge, once the front wheel is over, you have to unload the back by shifting your weight to the front end of the bike and lifting the rear wheel. You'll be surprised how easily it follows.

Your next step toward obstacle-running mastery will be jumping across things like tree trunks. Start off with something a little smaller, like a broomstick. You'll really notice if you don't clear it with either wheel, but it is less intimidating and easier to place just where and how you want it. Front wheel up, rear wheel up, and go. Practice during a few 15-minute sessions, and quite soon you will feel like graduating to tree trunks, boulders, and the like. As soon as you can do it, start applying each skill in your everyday riding so you reach perfect mastery gradually while enjoying what you do, rather than as a conscious exercise.

RIDING THROUGH AND JUMPING OVER A DITCH

Actually, these skills can be used for any hole in the ground. Ditches can be seen as inverted obstacles. Only very wide ones can be ridden through; smaller ones must be handled by jumping over them.

To ride through a wide ditch, select your path so that it is as gradual as possible, then ride through it at an angle. Shift your weight as you go through so that you don't get bogged down at the bottom of the pit. Just before you reach the lowest point, transfer your weight back so the front wheel gets

unloaded. This way you gain badly needed traction on the way up and protect your bike as well as yourself (you might go over the handlebars if the bike suddenly comes to a stop as it bogs down). Transfer the weight back toward the front again as you climb out.

To clear a narrow trench or hole in the ground, you have to do very much the same as when clearing an obstacle projecting from the ground. The reason is that, unless you lift the wheels to make the bike go up at least a little, they'll just fall into the hole. So gain some speed and then, just before you get there, lift the front wheel as you learned to do in the last section. As soon as the front wheel has come left ground, transfer the weight forward to get the rear wheel off the ground and start heading for safe ground with the front wheel, keeping the weight forward until the rear wheel has also cleared the ditch.

Practice this technique as you go on your regular rides, and you'll be surprised how much easier it will become. In effect, once you get this far, you'll find you spend much less time in the saddle than you ever thought you would want to. And even if you are in the saddle, you are always alert and always have your weight distributed over pedals, handlebars, and seat, with your limbs slightly bent but tense enough to act as shock absorbers at all times. This way, obstacles are easy to overcome.

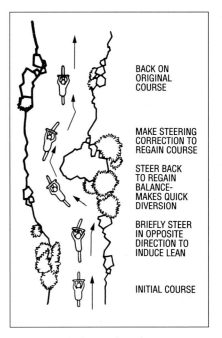

BACK ON ORIGINAL COURSE

MAKE STEERING CORRECTION TO REGAIN COURSE

STEER BACK TO REGAIN BALANCE- MAKES QUICK DIVERSION

BRIEFLY STEER IN OPPOSITE DIRECTION TO INDUCE LEAN

INITIAL COURSE

How to dodge an obstacle on a narrow trail. Focus your sight on the path you want to take. Just before you get to the obstacle, steer into the opposite direction to induce the bike lean needed to do a quick forced turn around the obstacle.

The one-point turn, demonstrated here on a steep downhill to ride a zig-zag, is usually done with one foot on the ground, but if you practice the forced turn properly, you'll eventually learn to make such a sharp forced curve that you can keep both feet on the pedals while doing this. *Andreas Schlueter photograph*

CHAPTER EIGHT RIDING WITH NATURE

For the purpose of this chapter, we'll define nature in a very broad sense. Although we'll mainly concentrate on what's usually understood to be the natural environment, we will also cover the other aspects of what goes on around you. Thus, you will not only learn how best to deal with your natural surroundings but also how to deal with the other people and their animals—horses and dogs—with whom you'll be sharing this natural environment.

ENVIRONMENTAL IMPACT

The biggest arguments involving mountain biking have centered on the question of how environmentally responsible it is. Anything you do out in nature is to some extent damaging, but the questions should be whether it is acceptable and how it compares with other activities. Everything in nature damages the environment to some extent—the deer trampling across the hillside near our Marin County homes have probably done more damage than mountain bikers have. Hikers, and especially equestrians, often leave nasty marks because they put much more pressure, and with much more sudden impact, on a small area when they step than your mountain bike does as it rolls along the trail.

There will always be some kind of erosion, and it is outright dishonest to blame the mountain bike for most of it, even in the worst places. Look at the battle over access to the Marin Headlands—part of the Golden Gate National Recreational Area (GGNRA). Some of us rode there

Take it easy. Although lush terrain like this may seem to be quite rugged, young sprouts, and even the root structure of more mature growth can easily be damaged if they see too much traffic.

long before the mountain bike as such was introduced, and even longer before these lands became part of the GGNRA.

In the late 1980s, hikers and equestrians started urging the GGNRA administrators to restrict mountain biking, and the district responded by ordering a survey of mountain biking and erosion. Not, as you might expect, comparing erosion effects of mountain biking with those of other trail uses, nor even just erosion caused by mountain bikes. Instead, the person who compiled the study finished up showing slides showing trails with erosion caused by anything ranging from the very existence of a trail to heavy equestrian use, and telling us whether it was used by mountain bikers or not. The recommendation was simply to prohibit mountain biking wherever there was erosion—regardless of whether the mountain bike had been the cause of the erosion or not.

We'll get into this subject in more depth in Chapter 15, "Access and Advocacy." Meanwhile, in this chapter, we'll merely suggest ways for you to ride so that you do as little damage as possible.

Yes, this is a staged setting, but the message is simple: learn to deal with dogs without provoking them. The text explains how to go about it.
Bob Allen Photography

The first thing to be aware of is that what's OK today may not be so tomorrow. It often depends on the weather. Terrain that is perfectly stable in dry weather may be too fragile after prolonged rainfall, and other areas may become more vulnerable after snowfall, high winds, protracted dry spells, what have you.

Whether it's OK to ride somewhere can also depend on the time of year, even the time of day. There are lots of areas with nocturnal wildlife, and that may make a ban on nighttime riding quite reasonable in those areas, whereas there is no sensible justification to ban nighttime mountain biking in other areas. And as for time of year, certain terrain may be too sensitive for use in early spring after snowmelt has caused it to become very moist and soft, and when many plants are barely sprouting up but not yet strong enough to survive pressure on the roots. In foothill areas, this may apply not only to the meadows but also to the trails running through them.

EROSION

Erosion is nothing but accelerated damage to the terrain, usually due to water drainage. Take a look at a picture of the Grand Canyon, and you'll see what kind of swath a stream of water can cut into the terrain if you let it do so long enough. Although few would argue that the Grand Canyon is an eyesore, we don't want little canyons, created by water running along your tire tracks, all over the place either. Erosion is at its most severe where there is no vegetation with a root structure that holds the soil together, and for that reason all vegetation should be protected. Even such innocent-seeming events as falling off your bike onto vegetation by the side of the trail should be avoided for nature's sake as much as for your own.

Most erosion is caused by the removal of things—soil, rocks, branches, and so on. To visualize the effect, try taking a single twig away from a wet hillside in the rain. You'll see the water that was previously diverted by the twig suddenly taking a different course and cutting a little gully through the dirt. Multiply that onto some grand scale, and you'll see the

potential for real damage if too much material gets disturbed.

When riding, try to avoid anything that is likely to accelerate the erosive process. Obviously on solid, level ground, there's not much at risk. Neither your tires nor a pair of boots, nor even a horse's hooves, are going to scrape much off a solid rock. But when the soil is softer, your tires will leave tracks, and the more aggressively and thoughtlessly you ride, the more damage they'll do. Take the case of rocky terrain with softer soil filling in between: when you remove some of that soft ground, you'll be changing things quite drastically.

So what constitutes responsible riding? Gradual acceleration, gradual braking, gradual steering. Usually, you're most likely to do damage if you brake abruptly enough with the rear brake to block the rear wheel, cutting a swath into the ground, and likewise when you steer or accelerate abruptly. But there is much more to it than that. At least as important is selecting just where on the trail, or out in the open terrain, you cut your path.

Always try to choose the harder ground over the softer stuff, and especially avoid riding on the edge between hard and soft ground, where it is most likely to become unstable. If it's unavoidable to go where stability of soil is questionable, take it gingerly. There are cases where you'll want to get off the bike, but that's not likely to reduce your ecological impact, because your footprints are probably more damaging than your tires.

TRAIL DISCIPLINE

By and large, the heaviest erosion is caused by the presence of the path or trail itself. That's where the water will start running, and that's where soil will get washed away. Wherever you go will become a trail. Trails are nothing more than footprints multiplied, and if you cut a new path, that will be a miniature trail once it bears your tire tracks, and a full-blown erosion gutter by the time others start following your example. Keep to the trails that are already there and avoid making new ones.

This is especially important on hillsides. Notice that most trails don't go

straight up and down? Instead they meander in a tightly curving path—the steeper the terrain, the tighter the curves, forming actual switchbacks when the slope of the terrain is quite steep, yet the path goes up at a near-constant slope of perhaps only about 10 percent. That's not only done to make it easier for us to climb up and ride down but also because that's the way these trails do the least damage. A straight path going up and down would turn into a veritable torrent during rain, and the damage would be considerable.

You may actually help preserve a trail by discouraging others from taking a shortcut. For that reason, you may want to get involved in trail maintenance programs if these are operated in the area. A little bit of additional vegetation and a repositioned boulder is often all it takes to discourage improper use of a potential shortcut. Don't start doing that kind of work on your own, but if there's a volunteer program, join it, and if there isn't, help organize one that works under professional guidance with the authority in charge of the land.

CROSS-COUNTRY DESCENTS

Although off-road cycling has really come to mean cycling on unpaved roads, there are still some types of terrain where you could be riding without any road or trail. Only too often, there is still some kind of vegetation, usually quite fragile, even in places like that. Don't just take a cursory look and conclude nothing's growing there anyway. Get down on your hands and knees, and verify just what kind of terrain you are about to disturb. If it's consistently hard and any vegetation is obviously rugged, go right ahead as long as it's legal.

Generally, it's much less damaging if you don't go straight down. Instead, try to follow the contours of the terrain on a more gradual drop. The steep descent would create a little channel for water to flow down in the next rain, and on this steep course it would rush down forcefully enough to do serious damage. If you are riding in a group in anything but rock-solid terrain, don't all follow the same route. Instead, fan out so that each rider takes a different route far enough away from the others to spread the

Sometimes it's not what you do to harm nature but nature's little ways of spoiling your fun. Be careful around cacti and thorny vegetation to avoid repeated punctures. *Bob Allen Photography*

load. This fanning out does much less damage than when all riders follow the same course, which would quickly create a new trail where there wasn't one before.

When descending on a zig-zag course, execute your switchback maneuvers in locations where there is a larger level area, preferably on hard ground. And don't drive down following obvious valleys, because that's where water has previously flowed, the ground will be softest, and the most fragile vegetation will be affected by your tires.

We've all seen the spectacular pictures of early mountain bikers coming down steep slopes throwing up a cloud of dust as they brake into a curve. Don't. Instead, slow down gradually—not only do you do much less damage when your rear tire is not skidding on the ground, but you actually slow down much more effectively and predictably when your tires are rolling than you do once they start skidding with a locked brake.

WATERBARS

On many trails that run uphill and downhill, water bars have been installed. These are wooden boards that run across the path, and their purpose is to guide the water as it runs downhill along the path. This is not done to protect nature on a grand scale, but simply to prevent excessive water damage to the trail itself.

The idea is to force the water along the edge of the trail rather than allowing it

to dig an ever deepening gully along the middle of the trail. To the mountain biker, these waterbars may seem a hindrance, causing a sudden drop or rise in your path, making the trail more like a staircase. Yet they're there to preserve that very trail against turning into a dry creek most of the year and a raging torrent in wet weather.

So when riding on trails with these waterbars, don't try to avoid them by riding around them at the edge of the trail, because that would create a channel for the water to flow around the waterbars, creating the very gullies that should be avoided.

Besides, the effect will be that you're effectively widening the trail, requiring more and more maintenance. In the long run, this may increase the likelihood that someone will decide that indeed mountain biking has turned a hillside with an innocuous trail into an ugly wasteland.

Waterbars should be spaced and constructed so that they are nowhere higher than about five inches, and that's a step you should be able to take with your bike even going uphill. Once the steps get significantly bigger, there's a need for trail maintenance, either filling in the low spots in the trail with solid rock materials or installing additional waterbars. If the area is operated and maintained by an enlightened authority, they will welcome your input as to where maintenance is required, so rather than do more damage, consider actually reporting such situations.

DEALING WITH OTHER USERS

When you meet others on the trail, greet them and show that you recognize their presence. Slow down, look at them, get out of their way. Although often easiest to do on a one-by-one basis, it becomes even more important when you're in groups. It can be intimidating for a reserved, elderly hiker to run into a bunch of noisy machos on mountain bikes. Interrupt your group interaction and acknowledge the others on the trail.

DEALING WITH HORSES

Equestrians have a legitimate concern about the reactions of their steeds. Take the trouble to talk to equestrians (here too, not in passing, but after stopping and getting off the bike) and find out from them what you can do to make their horses more comfortable around bikers. Although we can give you some general advice here, it's better to make personal contacts with real live equestrians in your own area.

When approaching a horse head on, it's generally recommended to get off the bike, greet the rider, and perhaps even talk to the horse as you walk past. When approaching a horse from behind, gently call out to the rider that you're behind him and would like to pass. Walk your bike if possible and as you pass, greet the rider and acknowledge the courtesy.

DEALING WITH DOGS

Dogs come in three types: your own, other people's, and loose ones. The most predictable is your own dog, but that's no reason to be carefree about riding with a dog. For a start, realize that however well a dog can run for a short distance, your biking speed is so much higher than when walking that you can quickly exhaust the dog. Go slower and take some rest stops to check on the dog's fitness level—you don't want the poor animal to collapse from exhaustion. Take an extra water bottle for the dog, and let him drink something at regular intervals. Also keep your dog under tight control, and don't allow him to chase wild animals, other mountain bikers, or other trail users. The biggest challenge may come when you encounter other dogs, whether stray ones or those that are accompanying other trail users.

Whether or not you have a dog with you, other people's dogs should be treated with some caution. First let the owner know you're approaching, hoping that the dog owner knows the animal well enough to put it on a leash if it has a tendency to snap at spinning legs. If the dog or the owner seems intimidating, get off your bike and handle the situation on foot, keeping your bike between the dog and yourself if possible. If there is a problem, ask the owner to keep the dog under control with a leash.

Loose dogs offer the greatest potential for trouble. Many of them seem to love chasing anything that moves, and the combination of your forward motion and the spinning motion of your legs makes you a real treat. Don't try to outrun the dog but get off, look the animal in the eyes, and try to keep your bike between for protection. After a while even the most stubborn stray dog will wander off to new adventures, upon which you can get back on board.

OTHER GUIDELINES

Here are some general guidelines, adapted from Jim Zarka's book *All Terrain Biking*. These are conservation practices that help relieve human impact on the land and its inhabitants.

1. If you can choose your time, go into the backcountry when use levels are low, either off-season or during the week. Don't travel when the land can be rapidly degraded. For example, fat tires can do an incredible amount of damage when the trails are muddy from rain or snowmelt.

2. Avoid using both high-impact areas that need a rest and undisturbed places that perhaps should remain left alone altogether. Have the respect and the awareness to be able to say, "Not here, not today."

3. Wildlife not only needs to have undisturbed territory, but the creatures themselves need to remain undisturbed. Never feed birds or other animals, even though they may be inquisitive or obviously used to handouts. Feeding wildlife can upset feeding habits, migration patterns, and reproduction levels. This can ultimately effect behavior, population structure, and species composition.

4. If you stop to photograph or observe birds or other wildlife, stay downwind, avoid sudden movements, and respect their space by not harassing them. Stay away from birthing or nesting sites, feeding grounds, and watering holes. Disturbance in these areas particularly stresses individual animals, and could affect their survival, especially during winter.

5. Traveling quietly and in small groups (four is the optimal number) will allow you to appreciate the environment more and will disturb wildlife and other visitors less. If you are with a large group, split up into smaller groups when you're biking, meeting back together later. Find the right balance between safety and minimum-impact travel.

6. When traveling on existing trails, ride single-file on the designated path. Often there are several parallel trails. These are caused by hikers and bikers who move outside the original trail to avoid mud puddles, rocks, tree roots, or just in order to travel side-by-side. With a mountain bike you should be able to pop over those tree roots and splash through those puddles (after checking them out first). If it doesn't look safe, get off your bike and walk over or through those obstacles. Do your part to keep the trail from becoming as wide as an expressway. If a trail is impassable, pick the best route around the problem area, trying to stay on hard surfaces such as rock, snowpack or sand—and let the agency responsible for the area know that it should get their crew out there to maintain the trail. Don't shortcut trail switchbacks. This causes erosion and gullying.

7. Cross-country travel is only acceptable when group size is small, when fragile areas can be avoided, and when wildlife will remain relatively undisturbed. Stay away from areas where undesignated trail systems are developing.

8. When moving across land with no trail systems, it is usually better not to ride single file. By spreading out, you will reduce the impact on vegetation. Extremely fragile areas, such as cryptogram soils in the desert, should really be avoided altogether.

9. In some areas there is the possibility of meeting livestock on the trail. Horses and other stock are easily frightened; their comprehension is very limited when it comes to seeing the monster we call a bike with rider. In such cases, get off your bike slowly, get way off the trail, and give the animal plenty of room. If anyone is with the animals, let him or her be in charge of the situation. It is best to get on the downhill side of the trail, because when animals spook they usually jump uphill, and they are less frightened when you are below rather than above them. Sometimes it is recommended to talk in a low voice to give the animals advance notice of your whereabouts.

10. When taking a break along the trail, move off to one side, far enough for the visual impact you create to be lessened. This way you and other parties can enjoy more solitude and more of the natural surroundings. Again, find areas to rest that are not fragile—areas without vegetation, such as rock outcroppings or snow patches, are preferable. On the other hand, some vegetation is actually very durable, so use your judgment.

11. Pack out litter—your own as well as others'—and dispose of it properly. This is easy enough to do on your way out, when your day pack or panniers are lighter.

12. What is naturally found in the wilderness must be left there, whether it be organic or inorganic. Allow others the same chance of enjoying something unique and beautiful; let them have that same sense of discovery. At the same time, realize nature's intrinsic right to hold its own, without every visitor laying claim to one thing or another. This holds especially true for archaeological finds in the southwestern areas of the United States, including arrowheads, pottery shards, and other remnants of history. Look at them, take pictures, feel their significance, and then leave them for professionals to use in putting together that area's past culture. You may want to mark the spot on your map and inform the appropriate agency, or you may want to leave it the way you found it, hoping it remains undisturbed.

CHAPTER NINE
COPING WITH THE WEATHER

Mountain biking need not be only a fair-weather game. In fact, the mountain bike is far less weather-sensitive than the traditional road bike. The brakes installed on mountain bikes are so much more effective than those on road bikes that they are adequate in wet weather, though not as good as when it's dry. The main reason why road biking is avoided by many is that handling a bike with narrow tires is tricky in the rain.

It can get pretty messy on a mountain bike in the outback in bad weather. But after all, you're not trying to look fit for society, you're out to have fun in the wilds. And it's not only wet weather (the worst that ever seems to happen in our part of the country) that requires special attention; there are various other weather conditions that will be addressed in this chapter.

DRESS FOR THE WEATHER

Mountain biking in inclement weather will be a lot more comfortable if you are wearing appropriate clothing. Whatever the weather, you're more likely to fall and scrape your skin riding off-road than you are in road biking, but in cold and wet weather your skin becomes much more sensitive. Therefore it's especially important to dress not only for comfort while riding, but also to some extent for protection—against the elements and against getting hurt.

When it's just cold, and not wet, wear a helmet without vent holes (or a wool cap under the helmet), full-finger gloves, wool

socks, firm shoes, long cycling pants, a long-sleeve jersey, and either a wool sweater with a light windproof jacket or a lined jacket. Wearing several layers of clothing rather than just one has two advantages. You can strip off one layer when you get warm, and you are much better protected in case of a fall, when the top layer of clothing slips over the second layer rather than cutting into your skin.

Whatever has been said to promote various high-tech fibers, by far the most suitable one for cold weather is wool. Cotton, other than being less itchy, is actually quite unsuitable (even more so than most synthetic fibers) because it soaks up too much moisture without giving it off to the environment.

Wind is usually a significant cooling factor, even if it's only the airflow generated by your own riding speed. For that reason, we recommend wearing very tightly woven outer shells in weather below about 8 degrees Celsius (46 degrees Fahrenheit), especially when it is windy as well. In freezing weather, this becomes mandatory.

When it's just wet, but not cold, you can follow one of two philosophies: accept getting wet or try to stay dry. We've found the second approach to be extremely difficult, and therefore many experienced cyclists, after initially trying to stay dry, give up and accept that they'll just have to get wet.

No, it's not true that you're likely to catch a cold, flu, or pneumonia from riding in the rain with wet clothing. As long as you are moving, you'll stay warm

enough to avoid exposure. What is important, though, is not to allow your body to cool off too suddenly with everything wet. So keep riding vigorously enough to keep warm until you have reached home or some other place of shelter.

When temperatures get below freezing, you may want to add another layer, and that's the time to look into tights and a long-sleeved undershirt. Look for light, knitted materials made either of polyester or polypropylene. Both those materials are hydrophobic (meaning they are afraid of water), which helps them wick any moisture resulting from perspiration away from your body. Besides, they are light and flexible enough not to hinder your movements.

If it's wet and cold, things get a lot trickier because the wet clothing does not adequately insulate your body. So under these conditions your goal should indeed be to keep dry as well as warm. Dress right for cold weather, and then top it all off with some really waterproof outer shells, such as a rubberized or plastic-coated nylon jacket or poncho (cape) and rainpants. But the coldest, and as it seems wettest, parts of your body will be your hands, feet, and head, so what do you do about them?

Tacky though they seem, one good kind of glove for these conditions are those cheap ones made of fleece-lined imitation leather. Mittens will be even better, although they make shifting and braking a little harder, but much less so on modern bikes with twistgrip shifters and effective brakes than on older models with long brake

Riding singletrack in the snow near Queenstown, on New Zealand's South Island. The man on the bike is Hans-Joerg Rey, best known as the popularizer of trick and trials riding techniques. *Bob Allen Photography*

Getting serious on ice. A participant in the annual Iditabike tour in Alaska. *Renner photograph*

cold weather is to select one without—and those models tend to be quite a bit cheaper, too. Feel free to follow the fashion when it's warm, but in winter it's more important to be physically comfortable.

If you can't find suitable clothing in bike stores, look around in the cross-country clothing section of a ski shop. A lot of cross-country ski wear comes pretty close to what you'll need in cold weather. However, some of our problems are not addressed there. It doesn't usually protect against rain, and your hands and feet need much better protection when riding a bike than when cross-country skiing. For the rest of your clothing, consider gear developed for hiking and fishing—but make sure you get something light and flexible enough to allow free movement that will not get caught in the bike's moving parts.

RIDING IN THE RAIN

In addition to water drops falling down, three other things change for the biker if it's raining. Water and dirt are thrown up by the tires, the brakes become less effective, and your vision deteriorates (especially if you wear glasses). There are a few things you can do to partially compensate for these problems. In the first place, ride more slowly and cautiously. That will tend to minimize the stuff sprayed off the wheels, minimize the need for sudden heavy braking, and allow safe reaction times even with impaired vision.

Mounting fenders, or mudguards, on the bike is of only limited practical use—and whether it makes any sense at all depends on the terrain. Fenders work fine on asphalt, gravel trails, and rocky surfaces; but don't bother in really muddy terrain, because the mud will settle on the inside of the fenders and quickly block rotation of the wheels. The only kind that will be of any benefit under those circumstances is the one that mounts very high in the back, keeping the worst spray off the rear wheel from hitting you in the back.

RIDING IN THE SNOW AND ICE

Bikes often develop more mechanical problems in ice and snow. To minimize them, keep your bike clean, dry, and

levers and shift levers mounted above or under the handlebars.

For the feet, you can either get weatherproof overbooties or follow the low-budget approach: wear plastic bags over your wool socks, *inside* your shoes. You'll get bags like this every time you buy anything in the produce department of a supermarket, and this is a great way to recycle them.

We haven't found something effective to keep your nose warm yet, but the rest of your head will benefit from a little extra care beyond the helmet. You can wear either a balaclava or a relatively light wool skiing cap under your helmet. And however fashionable all those racing-car-inspired fresh-air scoops are on helmets, the only way to keep warm and dry in

Wet weather makes for muddy dirt. You can leave your face unwashed for a while to prove where you've been, but don't forget to clean your bike right away so that it's ready for the next trip. *Photographs by Bob Allen* (left) *and Hans Smolik* (right)

well-lubricated. Clean and lubricate it immediately after any ride in the snow.

Soft snow rides like loose sand. The bike will dig deeply into it, and the resistance becomes disproportionally high. There are a few things you can do. Let some air out of the tires, bringing the pressure down to about 1.5 bar (22 psi), which will increase the tire's footprint and thus prevent it from digging into the snow too far.

Select a low gear, pedal at a normal rate, and accept that progress will be slow in the snow.

Keep the load off the front wheel as much as possible. Raise the handlebars and sit farther back, with most of your weight resting on the rear wheel. This prevents loss of balance when steering and improves traction.

When riding on ice, your traction becomes the bigger problem. Here, a low tire pressure doesn't help, so it's best to keep it at about 3 to 4 bar (45 to 60 psi). This will reduce the tire's footprint, while increasing the contact pressure, which in turn will tend to give a slightly firmer grip. Use the same backward-leaning riding position recommended for riding in the snow.

Avoid sudden movements, because any abrupt deviation can send you careening one way or another. Use relatively high gears, which limits the chance of a sudden force on the driven wheel. Steer around obstacles in very wide, gentle curves, and slow down as gradually as possible.

RIDING AT NIGHT

One of the most dramatic improvements over the last 15 years has been in bicycle lighting, and mountain biking has been the main beneficiary. The subject of lighting equipment and its maintenance will be covered in some detail in Chapters 24 and 34 respectively.

Despite the improvement in bike lights, the best time for nighttime riding is when there's a full moon. Unfortunately, the rangers of some of the most popular mountain biking areas, where nighttime riding is almost universally prohibited, know that too. That's the reason it may sometimes be tempting on a bright moon-lit night to turn your lights off—you'll be less likely to be caught. We don't subscribe to the no-lights idea, for fear of running into someone else with the same idea.

The dangerous spots are those areas where the previously open trail enters a wooded area. The difference between light and shade is so great that it seems like disappearing into a sudden void. Slow down significantly before you reach a dark area.

DEALING WITH THE HEAT

Although more emphasis is usually placed on dealing with cold weather, the other extreme can be just as important, especially if you are not used to being outside and doing hard physical work. It's also particularly important if you live in a temperate region and get out in a part of the world with much more sun and heat— such as coming from England to New Zealand, or even from Washington to Colorado.

Highland terrain and most of the southern hemisphere expose you to more ultraviolet rays than most of us are used to—and more than anyone should allow without protection. To minimize the damage, cover up as much of your skin as you can and use heavy-duty sunscreen for the rest (face, ears, neck, and so on). A protection factor of 45 is nothing excessive if you're out for several hours. Try out various kinds and make sure you get one that does not run off as you perspire.

Particularly in dry climates, you will not notice the loss of liquids adequately, as your perspiration will quickly evaporate. For any trip of more than an hour, drink plenty of water, starting even before you leave, and continue drinking at least every 15 minutes.

CHAPTER TEN

HEALTH AND SAFETY

R iding a bike—even off-road—is not an entirely riskless undertaking. Neither are many other pursuits. Accidents and other health hazards are very real risks everywhere. This chapter shows how you can minimize the risks.

In any discussion about bicycle safety, the main subject of interest seems to be the presumed danger of being involved in a collision with a motor vehicle. In off-road cycling that risk is less relevant, although it must be remembered that most mountain bikes are also ridden on ordinary roads with other traffic hazards most of the time.

Considering the various hazards, ranging from those to your own body and equipment to the harm or loss you may cause others, it may be smart to take out some kind of insurance. Personal liability insurance is perhaps the most important. In the United States and other countries without national health insurance, make sure you have adequate health insurance.

Learn how to deal with accidents, injuries, sickness, and other health-related emergencies that can occur while cycling. Do you really know what to do when you are bleeding, when you think you may have broken something, when one of your companions faints or is seriously hurt? Take a first aid course to be prepared for dealing with the unanticipated. That is a lot smarter than shutting your eyes, hoping nothing serious will happen. Even if you are spared yourself, you may be able to save someone else's life. If you can't take

Keeping out the dust. The rider in the foreground got himself a face mask to filter out the dust thrown up by his fellows in this early-days' California mountain biking event. *Gordon Bainbridge photograph*

a first aid course, at least read up on the subject—appropriate literature is included in the Bibliography.

OFF-ROAD DANGERS

What may astonish you at first is that the risk of being involved in an accident is actually greater on trails and paths than on roads with motor traffic. Keep this in mind when riding off-road. Many of the very characteristics that make cross-country cycling so enjoyable are also responsible for the increased risk.

Anticipate emerging wildlife, hikers, rangers, or cyclists, who may suddenly appear from around the next bend or from behind a bush or rocky outcrop. Practice

control of your bike, so you can react to the unexpected and control your bike even under difficult conditions. Braking, steering, and even falling gracefully can all be practiced and perfected.

PROTECTIVE GEAR

Protective clothing is necessary. Wear a helmet, gloves, and perhaps long-sleeved and long-legged garments, preferably double layers. A helmet serves to stop you from cracking your skull or damaging its contents when you fall off the bike, and you're likely to fall more than once when traveling in the outback.

If you fall on your head, the impact tends to smash the brain against the inside

Taking a spill at a NORBA double slalom event at Big Bear, California. *Bob Allen Photography*

of the skull, followed by the reverse action as it rebounds. Neither your skull nor the object with which you collide is likely to deform gradually enough to prevent injury. That's why energy-absorbing helmets with thick, crushable foam shells were developed. It's the crushing of about 3/4 inch of seemingly brittle foam that absorbs the shock. The minimum requirements for a safe helmet are those specified in the American standard ANSI Z-90.4; an even tougher standard is that of the Snell Foundation. The label inside the helmet will specify which standards it meets.

EVALUATING THE RISK

The likelihood of getting hurt—be it as a result of a traffic accident or a fall—increases dramatically after you get tired. This applies especially to cyclists carrying luggage and handling difficult terrain, and most dramatically to inexperienced riders.

More experienced cyclists have markedly fewer accidents and can go longer distances than beginners. This is one good argument for gaining experience and learning the necessary skills as quickly as possible.

FALLS AND COLLISIONS

Virtually every injury to the cyclist results from the impact when the cyclist falls off the bike. He either hits the surface, an object on or along his path, another person or vehicle, or his own bike. Four types of falls and collisions can be distinguished: stopping, diverting, skidding, and loss of control.

Stopping Accidents

In a stopping accident, the bicycle runs into an obstacle that halts its progress. Depending on the cyclist's speed, the impact can be very serious. As the bicycle itself is stopped, inertia keeps the rider going forward, throwing him against or over the handlebars. The kinetic energy of the moving mass will be dissipated very suddenly, often in an unfortunate location. Your genitals may hit the handlebar stem, or your skull may hit the ground or the object with which the bike collided.

The way to guard yourself against these accidents is to look and think ahead, so you don't run into any obstacles. If necessary, control your speed to allow handling the unexpected when a potential danger may be looming up around the next corner.

Diverting Accidents

A diverting accident occurs when the front wheel is pushed sideways by an external force while the rider is not leaning in the same direction to regain balance. Typical causes off-road are rocky ridges; on roads the same effects are caused by railway tracks, cracks in the road surface, the edge of the road, and by touching another rider's rear wheel with your front wheel. The result is that you fall sideways and hit the ground or some obstacle by the side of your path. Depending on how unexpectedly it happens, you may be able to break the fall by stretching out an arm, which seems to be an automatic reflex in this situation.

Characteristic injuries range from abrasions and lacerations of the hands and the sides of arms and legs to bruised hips and sprained or broken wrists. More serious cases, usually incurred at higher speeds, may involve broken collarbones and injuries to the face or the side of the skull. The impact of lesser injuries can be minimized by wearing padded gloves and double layers of clothing with long sleeves and pants. Wearing a helmet will minimize damage to the side of the head.

Diverting accidents can often be avoided if the cyclist is both careful and alert. Keep an eye out for the typical danger situations. Don't overlap wheels with other riders, and don't approach surface ridges at a shallow angle. When your front wheel touches the rear wheel of the rider in front of you, or if your handlebars are pushed over by an outside force, you may sometimes be able to save the day if you react by immediately leaning in the direction you were diverted, and then steer into the same direction to regain control.

Skidding Accidents

Skidding accidents often cause the cyclist to fall sideways, resulting in abrasions, lacerations, or, more rarely, fractures. Avoid skidding by checking the surface ahead and avoiding sudden steering or braking maneuvers and excessive leaning in curves. Cross slick patches—such as loose gravel and wet rocks off-road, railway tracks, sand, leaves, and even white road markings on regular roads—with the bicycle upright. Carry out the requisite steering and balancing actions *before* you reach such danger spots.

If you cannot avoid it, once you feel you are entering a skid, try to move your weight toward the back of the bike as much as possible, sliding back on the saddle and stretching your arms. Follow the bike, rather than trying to force it back.

Loss-of-Control Accidents

At higher speeds, especially in a steep descent, loss-of-control accidents sometimes occur. In this case, you can't steer the bike the way you intend to go. This happens when you find yourself having to steer in one direction when you are leaning the other way, or when braking for speed control initiates unexpected oscillations. This situation often develops into a fall or collision along the lines of one of the accident types described previously.

Prevention is only possible with experience. Don't go faster than the speed at which you feel in control. The more you ride under various conditions, the more you will develop a feel for what is a safe speed, when to brake, and how to steer to maintain control over the bike. Once the situation sets in, try to keep your cool. Don't panic. Follow the bike, rather than forcing it over. The worst thing you can do is to tense up and get off the saddle. Stay in touch with handlebars, seat, and pedals, steering in the direction of your lean. This way, you may get out of it without falling or colliding, though your nerves may have suffered.

TRAFFIC HAZARDS

Although mountain bikes are great for riding off-road, you'll often finish your ride on regular roads, exposing you to the dangers of traffic. Cycling in traffic does not have to be as dangerous as it seems. You can learn to handle it, as traffic is nothing but people moving. Because you are human yourself, and probably smart enough to understand the basic laws of physics and mechanics, you can learn to avoid the risks associated with such an environment on your bike as much as in your car.

The only defense against inconsiderate road users is not to provoke them. Give in, even if it seems highly unfair. These accidents are more likely on lightly traveled roads near small towns than in heavy traffic near a big city, and Sunday afternoons and holidays are particularly bad. Although this does not make the ideal cycling environment, try to avoid the quiet roads near small towns at high-risk times.

Anticipate not only the predictable but also the unexpected: the motorist looming behind the next corner or intersection, the dog appearing from a driveway, or the cyclist suddenly crossing your path in the dark without lights.

The latter subject deserves special attention. The only way to arm yourself is to make sure you do not cycle out after dark without lights, so at least *you* can be seen and your light will help you see the other rider. A bright light in the front and a big rear light or reflector facing back are essential; all the other reflective devices don't do a thing that the former wouldn't do more effectively.

Most accidents occur in daylight, even though the relative risk is greater at night. Whether by day or night, cycle with all your senses alert. In general, ride your bike as you would drive your car, always verifying whether the road ahead of you is clear, and taking particular care to select your path wisely at junctions and intersections. As a relatively slow vehicle, you must look behind you, to ascertain that nobody is following closely, before you move over into another traffic lane or away from your previous path.

On the road, don't hug the curb—claim your place on the road. Your place is somewhere to the right of the centerline of the path normally taken by cars on a wide road (assuming right-hand traffic). Keep at least 90 centimeters (3 feet) away from the inside edge, even if the road is too narrow to stay clear to the right of the normal path of motor vehicles. Don't dart

This is a forward dismount softened by powder snow. It is one emergency maneuver you can practice on your own. However, the rider should spread his or her legs to clear the bars to land feet first. *Bob Allen Photography*

Falling practice on a comfortable grassy surface—how else are you going to save yourself in case of a real emergency? *Gene Anthony photograph*

out and audibly identify obstacles or hazards in the road. Wait until your maneuver does not interfere with others following closely behind.

The most feared type of bicycle accident is the one that involves being hit from behind. These accidents are surprisingly rare but almost invariably very serious. Although there is hardly any possible defense to ward them off, it is worth considering that they are characterized by a number of common factors. They invariably occur on otherwise deserted roads, where the attention of motorist and cyclist alike are at a low, because both feel perfectly secure.

Inconspicuous clothing, a low sun blinding one or both participants, and a lack of the cyclist's awareness due to tiredness at the end of a long day are also common features. It may be smart to increase your conspicuity. Wearing light and bright colors, such as white, yellow, pink, or orange, may well help others spot you in time to avoid this type of accident.

TREATING INJURIES

The most common type of injuries are abrasions, referred to in cycling circles as *road rash*, even when incurred off-road. They usually heal relatively quickly, although they can be quite painful. Wash out the wound with soap and water, and remove any particles of road dirt to prevent infection. There may be a risk of tetanus if the wound draws blood. Even if you have previously been immunized against tetanus, get a tetanus shot within 24 hours of the abrasion if the last vaccination was over two years ago.

If you have never been immunized before, get a full immunization, consisting of two (different) shots within 24 hours, followed by two more after two weeks and six months, respectively. Apply a dressing only if the location is covered by clothing, since the wound will heal faster when exposed to air. Avoid the formation of a scab by treating the wound with an antibacterial salve. See a doctor if any signs of infection occur, such as swelling, itching, or fever.

in and out around parked vehicles and other obstructions along the side of the road. When making a turn, choose your lane early but only after checking behind you to make sure that it is safe to move over. Thus, to go straight at an intersection, make sure you will not be overtaken by vehicles turning right. To turn right, get close to the right-hand edge. To turn left, choose a path near the center of the road or the middle of a traffic lane marked for that direction well before the actual intersection, after having established that you will not be cutting across the path of vehicles following closely behind.

Signal your intention before you do such things as diverting, turning off, or slowing down. That applies particularly when cycling with others in a group, where the first person should also point

Sprained Limbs

In case of a fall, your tendency to stick out an arm to break the impact may result in a sprained or even a fractured wrist. In other accident situations this can also happen to the knee or the ankle. Spraining is damage to the ligaments that surround and hold the various parts of a joint together. Typical symptoms are a local sensation of heat, itching, and swelling.

Whenever possible, keep the area cold with an ice bag. Get professional medical advice if you feel a stinging pain or if fever develops, because it may actually be a fracture that was at first incorrectly diagnosed as a sprain. This may be the case when the fracture takes the form of a simple "clean" crack without superficially visible deformation of the bone.

Fractures

Typical cycling fractures are those of the wrist and the collarbone, both caused when falling: the one when extending the arm to break the fall, the other when you don't have time to do that. You or medical personnel may not at first notice a "clean" fracture as described above: there may not be any outward sign.

If there is a stinging pain when the part is moved or touched, you should get an X-ray, even if a fracture is not immediately obvious. You'll need medical help to set and bandage the fracture, and you must give up cycling until it is healed, which will take about five weeks.

Saddle Sores

The quality of your saddle and your riding position affect the development of crotch problems. If early symptoms appear in the form of redness or soreness, consider getting a softer saddle, sitting further to the back of your saddle, or lowering the handlebars a little to reduce the pressure on the seat.

During the hours you spend in the saddle, the combined effect of perspiration, pressure, and chafing may cause cracks in the skin, where dirt and bacteria can enter. The result can be anything from a mild inflammation to the most painful boils.

There is little chance of healing as long as you continue riding vigorously. Prevention and early relief are the methods to combat saddle sores. The clue to both is hygiene. Wash and dry both your crotch and your cycling shorts after every day's ride. Many cyclists also treat the affected areas with rubbing alcohol, which both disinfects and increases the skin's resistance to chafing, or with talcum powder, which prevents further damage.

You'll need at least two pairs of cycling shorts if you ride at all regularly, so you can always rely on a clean, dry pair when you start out. Wash them out, taking particular care to get the chamois clean, and hang them out to dry turned inside-out. Treat the chamois with either talcum powder or a special treatment for that purpose—preferably a water-soluble cream, which is relatively easy to wash out.

Knee Problems

Knee problems are prevalent among bikers. They are concentrated mainly with beginners and very strong, muscular riders. In both cases, the cause seems to be pushing too high a gear. This strains the knee joint, resulting in damage to the membranes that separate the moving portions of the joint and the ligaments holding the bits and pieces of the joint together. The problems get aggravated in cold weather, so it will be wise to wear long pants whenever the temperature is below 15 degrees Celsius (60 degrees Fahrenheit), especially if fast descents are involved.

Prevent excessive forces on the knee joint by gearing so low that you can spin lightly under all conditions. Avoid climbing in the saddle with pedaling speeds below 60 rpm. Choose a lower gear to reduce the force on the knees.

Tendinitis

Tendinitis is an infection of the Achilles tendon, which attaches the big muscle of the lower leg, the gastrocnemius, to the heel bone. It is an important tendon in cycling, because it transmits the pedaling force to the foot. It sometimes gets damaged or torn from cycling with too much force in too high a gear. The problem is aggravated by low temperatures, which explains why it generally develops in the early season.

To avoid tendinitis, wear long woolen socks whenever the temperature is below 15 degrees Celsius (60 degrees Fahrenheit). It may also help to wear shoes that come up quite high, maximizing the support they provide. Get used to riding with a supple movement in a low gear, which is the clue to preventing many cycling complaints. Healing requires rest, followed by a return to cycling with minimum pedal force in a low gear.

Numbness

Beginning cyclists, not used to riding long distances, sometimes develop a loss of feeling in certain areas of contact with the bike. The most typical location is the hands, but it also occurs in the feet and the crotch. The numb feeling is caused by excessive and unvaried prolonged pressure on the nerves and blood vessels. You can usually relieve the effects with rest, although they may at times persist for several days.

Once the problem develops, get relief by changing your position frequently, moving the hands from one part of the handlebars to another or moving from one area of the seat to the other if the crotch is affected. To prevent numbness in the various locations, use well-padded gloves, foam hand grips, a soft saddle in a slightly higher position, or thick-soled shoes with cushioned inner soles.

Backache

Many riders complain of aches in the back, the lower neck, and the shoulders, especially early in the season. This problem is largely the result of unfamiliar isometric muscle work, keeping still in a forward-bent position. This condition is also aggravated by low temperatures, so it is wise to wear warm bicycle clothing in cool weather.

To avoid the early season reconditioning complaints, the best remedy is not to stop cycling in winter. Two rides a week at a moderate pace, or extended use of a home trainer with a proper low riding position, will do the trick. Alternately, you may start off in the new season with a slightly higher handlebar position and,

Drink water frequently on rides or races exceeding one hour, especially in hot weather and on trips involving lots of climbing. One water bottle on your bike is really the bare minimum; for a half-day's outing you need at least two. *Bob Allen Photography*

once more, low gearing. Sleeping on a firm mattress and keeping warm also help alleviate or prevent the problem.

Sinus and Bronchial Complaints

Especially at cold times of the year, many cyclists develop breathing problems, originating either in the sinuses or the bronchi. The same may happen if you are used to cycling at sea level and suddenly get to the mountains, where the cold air in a fast descent can be very unsettling. Wear a baklava to keep warm and breathe trough it to warm up the air you breathe in.

After a demanding climb in cold weather, do not strip off warm clothing, open your shirt, or drink excessive quantities of cold liquids, even if you sweat profusely. All these things may cause more rapid cooling than your body can handle. You will cool off gradually and without impairing your health if you allow the sweat to evaporate naturally through the fibers of your clothing. This works best if you wear clothing that contains a high percentage of wool.

Sunburn

On a clear day, especially in high-lying areas, the exposure to ultraviolet rays caused by a couple of hours of riding may well be more than is good for you. Clothing is the most effective shield, because—unlike any form of lotion—it does not get washed and wiped away by your own perspiration. A long-sleeved jersey, a helmet or cap with a visor, and long pants can help prevent painful and potentially dangerous exposure.

Dehydration

When cycling vigorously for a prolonged period, especially in hot weather, you can lose a lot of liquid through perspiration. Yet the body needs a certain minimum percentage of liquid to function properly. The effect of excessive liquid loss can be a sudden feeling of exhaustion, dizziness, and even fainting. Unfortunately, there is no advance warning, so you'll need to plan ahead.

Dehydration is most likely to occur when you're out for more than an hour, although it can happen even sooner if it is very hot and you're working hard. Start drinking water before you leave on an extended trip in hot weather, and keep drinking at regular intervals.

If you do develop symptoms of dehydration, as described above, drink water and take it easy for about 10 minutes to recover. Except in extreme cases, that's enough to get you back riding your bike. After several days of significant moisture loss, such as on an extended multiday tour, there is a risk of losing not only too much water but also minerals, mainly salt, as evidenced by headache and nausea.

The above brief descriptions are not meant to take the place of sound medical advice. It's just that you may not have a doctor and nurse at hand when problems occur out in the wilds. Once you get back to civilization, it's a good idea to consult a medical professional about the symptoms and how best to avoid or alleviate them in the future.

CHAPTER ELEVEN

MOUNTAIN BIKING FOR FITNESS

Cycling for aerobic fitness tends to lower your resting pulse by making your heart strong enough to pump the blood through the veins with fewer, but bigger, strokes per minute. This is presumed to have two positive effects. Your heart becomes better equipped to take on increased workloads when needed, and it doesn't "wear out" as fast as it does when you lead a sedentary life.

Whereas aerobic output can be maintained with the oxygen you breathe regularly, anaerobic output levels are those beyond that point and rely on energy stored in the body's blood and muscle tissues. Anaerobic work can be maintained for short periods only and is much more exhausting, leaving you quite depleted afterwards. If you want to enjoy your riding, keep out of this range as much as possible.

AEROBIC TRAINING

To increase or maintain aerobic fitness, all you need do is ride your bike for periods of at least 20 minutes, about half of which must be at an extended pace, putting in a real effort continuously for 10 minutes or more each day, or 20 minutes if you train only four days a week.

Each of these rides should be broken up into three periods. First, warm up at a modest output level for at least five minutes. Second, ride at your target level for at least 10 to 20 minutes, depending on the training frequency. Third, slow down and gradually cool off for at least five minutes.

On a mountain bike you can get quite a workout without going very fast while climbing hills. If you start your ride at the bottom of a hill, it'll be very difficult to warm up gently—you'll have to start pounding away grinding up that hill. Similarly, if you reserve the downhill stretch for the last part of your ride, you'll be cooling off all right—but far too suddenly. So the message is to choose your course so that you have at least five minutes worth of level riding at the beginning and the end of your trip.

Most riders underestimate the effort needed to achieve a training effect—it is hard work during the time in the target zone. To establish whether the pace you are riding is adequate, find out what your minimum training pulse should be and make sure you maintain that during the period of exercise. Check your pulse with a heart rate monitor. Your minimum required training, or target heart rate (THR) depends on your age and is most conveniently estimated as follows:

THR = 180 minus your age in years

To train effectively for aerobic fitness, follow the following steps:

1. Warm up by riding about five to ten minutes at relaxed but gradually increasing pace before the actual training session begins.
2. Increase your riding speed gradually over the next couple of minutes, checking your pulse every minute, until you reach the training heart rate.
3. Maintain that output level (but you may have to increase or decrease riding speed to do so, depending on the terrain) for the required period of 10 to 20 minutes, depending on the number of times per week you train.
4. At the conclusion of the training session, ride at a relaxed pace for five to ten minutes to cool off gradually until you are no longer perspiring, before getting off the bike.

Fit to Ride

One aspect of training for performance that is only too often overlooked is specificity. Simply put, to train for riding a bike, the best training is actually riding a bike. To improve performance in hill climbing, go climb hills. Even so, these basic specific exercises may well complement some of the other exercises described below.

CALISTHENICS AND STRETCHING

These two types of exercise comprise a complex of simple movements to loosen joints and increase the flexibility of muscles. Some of these exercises may also help develop muscles that are not adequately trained by riding the bike. In addition, light exercises of this kind are useful to warm up before hard rides and to recuperate more quickly afterwards.

The difference between calisthenics and stretching lies in the continuity of movement. Each type has its adherents, and it's probably safe to say that a combination of the two is best. When it is cold, stretching should be done inside. Strenuous stretching should always be preceded by some form of warming up, either cycling, jogging, or calisthenics. Neither calisthenics nor stretching exercises are a substitute for cycling. They merely complement it and improve your physical condition. Specifically, these exercises have the following effects:

1. Increase movement angles of the joints used in cycling.

2. Strengthen muscles that are used isometrically in cycling.

3. Condition the muscles to use a larger range of movement between maximum contraction and maximum extension.

4. Prevent aches or cramps resulting from tenseness while cycling.

In calisthenics, joints are loosened and muscles conditioned as the body is bent and subsequently stretched in a swinging motion over the greatest joint angle possible (this angle will usually increase significantly with repeated practice).

Of the muscle pairs at any joint, the single muscles that are stretched in calisthenics are strengthened. In stretching, joints and muscles are conditioned to extend fully by forcing them statically in an extremely extended or contracted position, which is reached gradually and then held for at least 30 seconds. The illustration depicts some cycling-specific stretching exercises.

The last word on the subject of stretching has not yet been said. Although most American sportsmen and their coaches are firm believers in it, there have been a number of studies by chiropractors in recent years that suggest these exercises do more harm than good.

BREATHING EXERCISES

Efficient breathing technique can have a significant impact on your general feeling of well-being and athletic performance. In addition to the effect on breathing depth, influencing the amount of oxygen that can be absorbed, there is also an effect on the nervous system: deep and regular breathing allows the brain to better control movements, reactions, thoughts, and emotions, both during exercise and when at rest. The latter effect may well allow the cyclist to divide his powers more effectively, to make more intelligent decisions, and to train more consciously.

Breathe in and out several times as deeply as possible. When exhaling, try to push the last puff of air out of the farthest corner of the lungs; when inhaling try to take in as much air as your lungs will allow. First do this standing up, bending forward when pushing the air out, raising the upper body fully when breathing in. Follow this by a set of these when lying on your back, keeping the body relatively still. Two sessions daily, comprising perhaps ten respiration cycles each, are adequate to maximize your effective lung capacity. A good time to do breathing work is in between sets of calisthenic exercises or after a moderate-power bout of work on the windload simulator.

WINDLOAD SIMULATOR TRAINING

The windload simulator, also referred to as the turbo-trainer, is perhaps the best stationary equipment for bicycle-specific training. It consists of a stand for the bike with a set of rollers that drive wind-turbine wheels (or nowadays often electric devices that give the same kind of variable drag that increases with speed). As the speed of the rear wheel increases, either due to faster pedaling in the same gear or to the selection of a higher gear at the same pedaling rate, the air resistance increases exponentially, resulting in the drastic increase in required power typical of cycling at higher speeds under real-world conditions.

It is a good idea to install an electronic speedometer with additional functions for pedaling speed and to use a heart rate monitor. This provides you with the ultimate in stationary training and monitoring equipment—an exercise physiology lab of your own.

WEIGHT TRAINING

Weight training is useful for developing your various leg muscles for greater pedaling force, as well as for developing some of the statically loaded muscles of the back, shoulders, and arms. These latter muscle groups don't get much strengthening during biking, although they are sorely needed to restrain your body while you pedal with all your might. Work on the muscles that ache after a longer ride—usually those of the arms, shoulders, back, lower arm, and stomach. Use dumbbells, stretch bands, or a special weight training machine.

MASSAGE

Although it may not appear to be a training practice, massage has long been recognized as a suitable way of improving both performance and training progress, as well as preventing cramps and injuries. It's nice to have a specialist massage you, but you can do it yourself quite effectively.

Massage improves the enzyme and blood circulation systems to the muscles. During hard, repeated muscle exercise, small fissures are formed, and wastes (mainly lactates) accumulate in these fissures within the muscle. Massage encourages the removal of these wastes and restores the flow of blood that assists recovery.

Procedure for Self-Massage

1. Take a brief shower or merely wash the legs in warm (but not hot) water, and dry them thoroughly. There is no real need to use massage oil.

2. Lie comfortably on your back, at such a distance from the wall that you can stretch your legs above you, as shown in the upper illustration.

3. Grab the middle of one of the thighs firmly with both hands, surrounding the muscle bundles; rub forcefully with long, even strokes down from that point toward the hip. Continue this for about one minute.

4. Now do the same for the section of the thigh from the knee down to the location just beyond where you started under the preceding point. Apply similar regular strokes, continuing for about one minute.

5. Repeat the work covered in the two preceding points for the other thigh.

6. Move back from the wall to take the position shown in the lower illustration, with the knees bent and the lower leg horizontal.

7. Carry out a similar massage of the lower legs, working toward the knees, as described above for the thighs.

8. Briefly massage the muscles of lower and upper legs over their entire length with about ten long strokes.

9. Afterwards, rest a few minutes, lying on your back with the legs raised, covered with a dry towel if it is cool.

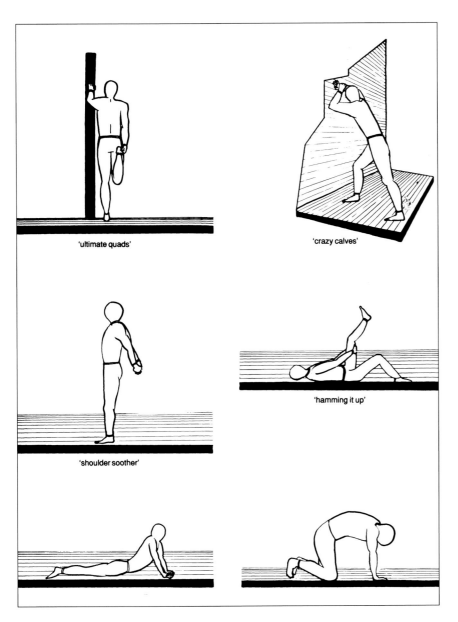

'ultimate quads'

'crazy calves'

'shoulder soother'

'hamming it up'

Stretching exercises. We don't claim to be experts on the subject of stretching, but these are the stretching routines commonly recommended for mountain bikers.

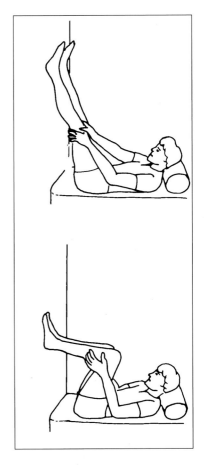

Massage for the masses: do-it-yourself. It only takes about ten minutes and significantly speeds up recovery after a hard ride.

MOUNTAIN BIKE TOURING AND ORIENTATION

The introduction of the mountain bike has led to a revival of bicycle touring. After all, a bike that is rugged enough to handle the off-road, geared low enough to handle steep hills, and that brakes well enough to stop you anywhere is what touring cyclists have always wanted.

CHOICE OF EQUIPMENT

Your mountain bike itself is probably suitable for touring the way it came from the shop. As long as it has bosses, or braze-ons, for water bottles and luggage racks, you are well on your way. Install racks both front and rear to distribute the load more evenly. Choose racks that are sturdy and that match the locations of the bosses and eyelets on your bike. For the front, "low-rider" racks are the most suitable, distributing the load as shown in the middle detail of the illustration.

If you will be touring at night and in wet regions, the addition of lights will be obligatory, and fenders may be appropriate.

As you won't have many opportunities to recharge batteries once underway, use disposable batteries rather than rechargeable ones. If you prefer generator, or dynamo, lighting, get the metal roller replaced by a 1-inch diameter rubber wheel, which makes much better contact. Adjust it to contact the side of the rim rather than the tire, which greatly reduces resistance.

When selecting and equipping a mountain bike for touring, keep in mind that you will usually be best served by simple equipment. We suggest not using suspension forks, because they may need maintenance when you are nowhere near a bike shop. Avoid the temptation to equip your bike with really cool lightweight components—you're much better off with simple components from the major manufacturers, stuff that can be repaired or replaced most easily.

Other items to avoid are anything that can't be made to work if something wears out or gets damaged. Take, for example, indexed gearing and twistgrip

shifters. They work great, as long as they do. But when a problem develops, you're stranded, unless you can fix things yourself. An old-fashioned top-mounted friction shifter, or at least a top-mounted index shifter with a selector that allows you to put it in friction mode, is much more suitable for touring. Similarly, brakes that require special levers to operate properly are less suitable than simpler models that will work equally well with a lever out of the recycled parts bin.

PACKING THE LOAD

There is a wide selection of bicycle bags available, and it should not be hard to find some that appeal to you. Don't just go for the optics but for practicality. The openings must be big and the closures designed to cover them up with a generous overlap. Drawstring designs are compact when half full as well as when completely stuffed.

Pack your bags with due consideration. Put things that belong together in the same bag, and put stuff that you need first or

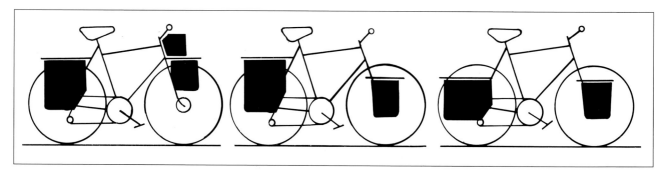

Three alternatives of load distribution for luggage on your mountain bike. The method shown in the middle detail has been found to have the least negative impact on your bike's handling characteristics.

Three ways of carrying a load on a mountain bike. The easiest way to carry a small to moderate load is to use a backpack, and that's quite suitable for a day trip, although you may find in hot weather and long climbs that perspiration makes the backpack quite uncomfortable (TOP). For longer tours, it's most common to load the bike itself up with panniers and other bags. It makes the bike harder to handle, especially if you ever have to carry it over obstacles, but is fine for most touring situations. Finally, you can use a trailer, and if you do, this BOB one-wheel trailer seems to be just the ticket: its single wheel rides in the same track as your bike, so you'll hardly notice it's there—until you need to dismount and carry the bike, when it's an even bigger headache than a bike that's heavily loaded with panniers. *Bob Allen Photography*

quickly close to the outside. Put raingear in an outside pocket so that the rest of your luggage does not get wet while you get it out. Make sure the bags you use in the front are evenly packed so that they are about equally heavy on both sides (this is much less critical in the rear). Keep the handlebar bag lightly packed and use it only for things you need regularly and those of value, as it is the only bag you can easily take with you when you leave the bike.

Attach the bags on the bike in such a way that the load is reasonably divided and the bags are firmly attached. The bags must all be tied down to the bike at the bottom as well as at the top. To attach bags other than those with integral attachments, don't use bungee cords but webbing straps or leather belts with buckles.

PLANNING YOUR TOUR

Start planning your tour well ahead of time. It not only makes the experience more predictable and less frustrating, it also extends the pleasure to include the time of preparation. Once you have decided on the general location, decide how to get there and buy detailed maps of the area, as well as a guidebook to find out what the points of interest are and what kind of conditions to anticipate. Study these with your particular purpose in mind. Get fully acquainted with the maps and their legend so you can interpret them quickly and accurately out in the field.

Once you have selected your general route, make sure it can be divided up into bite-size portions for each day, reaching a location suitable for an overnight stay. The distance you can cover in a day depends very much on the terrain. For touring on regular roads, 60 to 70 miles (90 to 110 kilometers) is generally a safe maximum, giving you about five hours of cycling and enough time for meals, snacks, breaks, and taking care of other needs along the way. Under off-road conditions, it is probably safe to halve these figures. A 35-mile off-road tour can be quite a challenge, even though the distance seems modest.

Decide whether you will be camping out each time or will have either frequent or occasional opportunities to seek shelter in hotels, hostels, or motels. Although the latter approach may not seem like the ultimate outdoor experience, it can be very convenient, and it is often possible by choosing your route just a little differently to return to the back country the next day.

Get a small notebook in which you write all your planning information, from the selected route and the details of your travel connections to your packing lists.

Before the actual tour, try out all your equipment. The best way to do so is by going on a weekend camping trip not too far from home, trying to replicate the actual conditions of your tour as much as possible. You'll be astonished how many things you'll decide to do differently, how many things you would have forgotten, and how many things you could have left home. Take notes of these and correct the pertinent lists in your notebook to make sure you don't waste time and effort on the actual tour.

Inform at least one acquaintance about your plans. Not just casually—leave this contact person a day-to-day itinerary (your TCP, or Time Control Plan) and make a firm commitment to keep him or her informed about your whereabouts during the trip. Put the contact person in charge of checking with you and informing safety patrols in the area where you

are touring when you do not report as planned. Your own responsibility will be to report to this person exactly as planned and keep him or her informed about any changes in your itinerary, either before or after your departure. This way, if anything should go wrong, all the pertinent information will be available to search for you and bring in help quickly and accurately.

EXECUTING THE TOUR

Consult your map frequently en route. Don't wait until you are lost before getting the map out, because that way you'll not even be able to establish where you might be, much less how to get back on the right track. If worse comes to worst, retrace your ride back to the point where you were last certain of your correct location and start again from there, paying better attention as you go this time.

Each time possible, make your call to the contact person and tell him or her not only that you have safely reached your planned destination for the day but also what kind of problems you have had, and any change of your plans for the next days. All this may sound exaggerated, but it takes a lot of worry off you and others in case anything unexpected happens. Again, usually nothing goes wrong, but it is a relief just to be able to confirm that your tour is proceeding according to plan.

When you get out into the backcountry, it is imperative that you can find your way around. And if you do get lost temporarily, you should know how to survive and get back home safely using a map and compass.

MAPS

There are several types of maps you are likely to encounter while planning for a mountain bike trip onto public land. The most common, the most reliable, and probably the most suitable is the topographic map, from *topo* meaning "place" in Greek, and *graphein* meaning "write" or "draw." When talking about topographic maps, we will be referring to the USGS maps. In other countries, similar maps are available.

Topographical maps give a three-dimensional representation of the land's

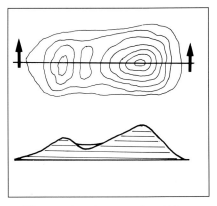

The meaning of contour lines. When there are none, the terrain is level; when there are many close together, the terrain is steep and mountainous; everything else falls in between.

physical features in a two-dimensional format. This is done with the aid of contour lines, with each line designating points of equal elevation. Every fifth contour line is colored a heavier brown than the others and is referred to as the index contour, with the exact elevation written somewhere along the line. The distance between the contour lines shows the steepness of the grade. The contour interval is designated at the bottom of the map (usually 20 or 40 feet). To find the slope percentage between contours, divide the contour interval (vertical distance in feet between contours) by their horizontal distance in feet and multiply by 100. What this number tells you is how many vertical feet you travel for every 100 feet traveled horizontally.

Latitude and longitude numbers are given in each corner of the map. Parallels, or lines of latitude, run east to west geographically. They intersect lines of longitude, or meridians, which run geographically north to south, at right angles. The first meridian, zero degree longitude, runs through Greenwich, England, and all other meridians run in degrees, minutes, and seconds east and west of this location. One hundred and eighty degrees away in either direction from Greenwich is the International Date Line, halfway around the world.

Parallels begin at the equator, which is zero degree latitude. North and south of this line, parallels run in degrees, minutes, and seconds toward the earth's poles, which are both located at 90 degrees. Crested Butte, Colorado, one of the mountain biking capitals of the world, is located at longitude 106.59 W, latitude 38.52 N. One degree corresponds to 60 minutes, one minute to 60 seconds.

Because topo maps are categorized according to the fraction of the earth's curvature they cover, they will be designated accordingly. Most topographic maps are one half of a degree (30 minutes), one quarter of a degree (15 minutes), or one eighth of a degree (7.5 minutes). The designation for this is in the upper right corner under the name of the map. You can verify this number by comparing the difference between the longitude or latitude numbers in the corners.

There will be a scale explaining what one unit on the map is in relation to one unit on the actual landscape. This scale can be found in the lower center of the map, and its ratio depends on what degree of map you're using. For instance, the scale for a 15-minute series map is 1:62,500—meaning that for every one unit of distance on the map, there are 62,500 units to cover the distance in the field. One inch on this quad represents approximately 5,208.3 feet (slightly less than a mile) in the field.

The smaller the denominator (the second figure) of the scale, the larger the relief features on the map will appear, and the more detail is available. The denominator 24,000 (the scale for a 7.5-minute map) is smaller than that of a 1:62,500 map, and so will yield more detail. The more detailed the map, the less land can be covered on that one sheet. A good map for off-road biking might be a 7.5-minute map.

There is a quadrangle location map showing where this particular quad is in relation to the state in the lower right-hand corner of each topo map. The names of adjoining quads are shown along each edge and in the corners of the quad proper.

Different colors and symbols are used on topographic maps to represent land features and objects, respectively.

Blue represents hydrographic features: lakes, streams, rivers, swamps, snow, and ice. Brown designates the hypsographic features, represented by contour lines and contour indexes.

Asking the way in Central Turkey. Touring on what are considered regular roads by local standards can be quite challenging in many parts of the world. But in many of these areas there are at least people around to help you out if you get lost. *Dieter Glokowski photograph*

Green represents vegetated areas dense enough to hide a platoon (27 people) from aerial observation in one acre.

White indicates areas of little or no vegetation, and includes boulder fields, meadows, and nontimbered areas above tree line.

Black indicates anything named, made, or designated by man: buildings, borders of public and civic lands, benchmarks, the names of ridges, lakes, and mountains.

Red is part of the United States Public Land Survey Grid, more commonly known as the township and range system, used mainly for surveying purposes. Important roads are also shown in red.

Purple is used to show revisions made since the last dated issue of the map, making it a very important color, and one that a lot of people don't pay as much attention to as they should. A quad's date of issue (in black) can be found on the right side of the bottom margin of the map, printed beneath the quadrangle name. In most cases that date is "dated," the map having been surveyed from the air and issued quite a while ago. In the years that have followed, many pertinent changes may have take place, and those have been recorded in purple. This means that field checks of aerial updates have not yet been done. Many times changes have occurred that have not even found their way into

purple ink yet, so look at that issue date and realize that it may not be as accurate as it once was, particularly as regards man-made features. Trails, roads, junctions, land ownership, all these things may not be the way they once were.

Learning to use a topographic map takes time and concerted effort. To the well-trained eye, these maps reveal an astonishing amount of information. The best advice is to take a topo map of a favorite and close-by biking haunt, go to it and read the landscape and relate it to the map. Find the relationship between the two. Learn to recognize what a ridge line or a valley looks like on paper. Do contour lines in drainages point up, toward higher elevation, or down? Look at a steep hill. What does it look like on the map? Feel the spatial relationship between a particular scale of map and the actual terrain.

The knowledge and experience you gain from intimacy with the map will help you find your way. Here are some additional points that will help you in the route-finding process.

Orient your map. It's hard to make sense of the map if you are trying to place terrain features with what you're seeing on the map when you're looking north while your map is facing west. Find True North, and then lay your map out so that north on the map is actually facing the day's

Hope you're going the right way. Here the only road leading east is obviously not too busily traveled. *Dieter Glokowski photograph*

Camping out in the wild adds a new dimension to mountain bike adventure. It can be done without formalities in many countries of the world—as long as you have access to water. *Bob Allen Photography*

north. Now the direction of features you are surrounded by corresponds with that of the same features on the map.

Use what is known in the orienteering world as "collecting features" as points of reference while traveling. Collecting features are simply those landmarks that pave the way to a specific destination. Streams, benchmarks, ridge lines, and open meadows can all be collecting features. Take note of them, mentally or otherwise, and be aware as you pass them by on the way to your final destination. Use them as points of reference.

As you're riding, look back every once in a while in the direction you're coming from. Pick out salient landmarks. Landscape features can look very different from the opposite direction. If you need to backtrack for any reason, this technique will assist you in confirming that you're on the right track.

Keep your map readily available so that you will use it. Like the water bottle, you are most likely to use it if it is within easy reach. Keep the map in a Ziploc bag to protect it, and fold it to show the area you're in.

USING A COMPASS

Knowing how to use a compass is a good skill to have. Although you will not often need to use one, it is nice to have the skill when the need arises. As a substitute you can use the angle of the sun. Being able to figure out the direction from the angle of the sun is not as difficult as it may seem. Paying attention to the sun consistently so that you become acquainted with its position at different times of the day is the hardest part.

We tend to enclose ourselves in four walls and a ceiling so often that we do not make a habit of gazing toward the sky. Once you do start to do so, however, you'll find that the sun is very consistent and faithful. It really does "rise" in the east and "set" in the west, keeping a southern orientation here in the northern hemisphere. When you're out riding, practice figuring out the direction and guessing the time of day by just looking at the sun. Verify your estimate with the aid of the compass and your watch. It doesn't take long to become fairly accurate.

An orienteering compass consists of three basic parts:

1. Magnetic-tipped needle—the red end always points toward the magnetic North Pole.
2. Compass housing marked with an orienteering arrow and orienting lines, with a graduated 360-degree dial marked around the compass housing. The bearing is read at the index pointer.
3. A baseplate marked with the direction-of-travel arrow and the index pointer.

There are two basic ways of using a magnetic compass: from map to terrain, or from terrain to map. It will help you visualize the map bearing process if you take out a map and compass while you learn.

In going from map to terrain, you are usually taking map bearings, or true bearings. To indicate direction in the field, two basic conditions must be met:

1. Set the dial to the desired degree reading. If the degree or direction is known, simply turn the dial so that the correct reading appears at the index pointer.

2. Without changing the dial setting, position the entire compass so that the orienting arrow is in line with the magnetic needle and the red end of the needle lies between the two orienting points.

Your line of travel will follow the sighting line on your compass. As long as you keep the magnetic needle "boxed" within the orienting arrow, you're set to travel in the direction of your sighting line. Some high-quality compasses have a mirror with a sighting line for extreme accuracy, with accompanying directions on how to use it.

To obtain your bearing from a map, lay your compass on the map with the baseplate parallel to the line on the map upon which you wish to travel. Next, hold the compass in position on the map, and turn the dial so the meridian lines on the compass are exactly parallel with any meridian line on the map, and the letter N on top of the dial corresponds to north on the map. This has now set the degree reading to your destination. Read at the index pointer. Now use the compass by the sighting line or by sight.

If you want to take a bearing from the terrain, simply hold the compass in front of you, with the sighting line pointing in front of you. Pivot yourself and the compass around together as one unit until the sighting line points toward the object on which you are taking the bearing. Turn the graduating dial until the orienting arrow and the magnetic needle are lined up, or "boxed," with the red end of the needle lying between the two orienting points. The degree reading at the index pointer is the bearing you want to take.

DECLINATION

You can't mention map and compass without talking at least a little bit about declination. It is generally known that Magnetic North is not the same as the True North Pole. Presently, Magnetic North is located near Bathurst Island in northern Canada, and it slowly moves around as the earth's magnetic lines of force change position.

Maps and directions are almost always based on True North, which is static. Magnetic declination is the angle between these two points. Where True North and Magnetic North are in the same direction, the declination is therefore zero. The line of zero declination in North America runs west of Hudson Bay down along Lake Michigan to the Gulf Coast in western Florida. At any point west of that line, a compass needle will point east of True North, or in an easterly declination. Westerly declination is any point which is east of the zero declination line. In North America, magnetic declination varies from 30 degrees east in Alaska to 30 degrees west in Labrador.

On topographic maps, declination is given in the bottom left corner. If you want to use a compass with your map, and need to take declination into account, there are two ways you can do so. The easiest way is to draw lines of magnetic declination on the map before entering the field. Just take a straightedge and extend the degree of declination line up through the center of the map. With this line as your guide, continue drawing Magnetic North lines one inch apart across the entire surface of the map. You now no longer need to compensate for declination because these lines correspond precisely to the compass needle.

GETTING LOST—
AND FOUND AGAIN

If you are lost, the first thing to do is to acknowledge the fact and save yourself a lot of angst and energy. Once a state of "lostness" has been acknowledged, you can move on to much more pressing and important needs, such as taking care of yourself and those with you.

If you feel fairly confident that you can retrace your movements and find your way again, you might opt to do so, being careful not to get so far away from your original position that you figure "they'll never think of looking for me over here." Pay attention to the sun's position, listen for traffic, and look for signs of cultivation. With the right preparation, being lost isn't such a horrible thing. Do not expect it, but anticipate that it could happen and be prepared for it.

CAMPING OUT

At the end of the day, it is time to start the tea brewing, the pasta water boiling, and to call some place home for the evening. Finding an aesthetic and proper place to bed down is a relatively simple and pleasant task, though finding a good minimum-impact site sometimes takes time. Making the right choice is an important way to make sure your impact on the area is as low as possible. Expend the energy necessary to do it right. Here are a few considerations when looking for a suitable spot:

1. Know the regulations. In regard to camping, there is a wide variance of protocol, even within the same land agency. Policies are dependent on land-use priorities, location, and type of ecosystem. They are good guidelines to follow, and can help you when on private land as well.

2. When selecting a campsite, distinguish between high- and low-impact sites, and choose the latter.

3. In some high-use areas, it may be prudent to camp on an already highly impacted area; with the right behavior, you and your party will do no further damage. When selecting a site like this, avoid enlarging the site by confining your tent and kitchen areas to already compacted areas. Stay on established traffic routes and away from areas that are obviously undergoing rapid soil erosion.

4. Avoid lightly impacted sites. These are areas that have obviously been used but still maintain some vegetative integrity. If left alone, they will rejuvenate quickly. With continued use, however, they rapidly deteriorate beyond the point of recovery.

5. Consider your relationship with the water. Streams and lakes can eas-

Taking a splash. On excursions and tours into the outback, you may have to count on conditions you can't predict—such as having to cross a stream in the desert. *Bob Allen Photographyy*

camps should be a good distance away from such trails.

7. For purely aesthetic reasons, camps should also be located away from designated biking or hiking trails, preferably out of sight altogether. Surely you would not be thrilled yourself when mountain biking in the wilderness to round a corner, exhilarated by the beauty of the scenery—only to be confronted with a tent right on the path.

8. Think about the durability of the substrate you are on, and avoid the fragile ones. Grasses seem to be more tolerant than woody-stemmed plants and tree seedlings, but plants in general don't like to be camped on for very long. Forest duff (the layer of decomposing detritus that overlies the mineral soil) is a good choice, as is rock and snow.

9. When looking for the perfect place for your tent, think flat (a slight concavity will collect rainwater), think high (for water runoff), and think safety. Be aware of potential hazards: standing dead trees, rockfall, flash flooding, wind, and wind-carried debris. If you move rocks to stake down the tent, or move branches, pinecones, or other debris to accommodate comfort, put them back where they were found before you leave. Wipe out all traces of your presence.

10. Spread your bikes and packs away from the tent, and away from each other's; this will prevent a lot of disturbance in a concentrated area, and will avoid creating a path that zeroes in on your sleeping quarters. Distributing your gear between your tent, your bike, and your panniers will also prevent you from having to run to the tent every time you need something.

11. If you are going to stay in an area for an extended period of time, you may want to move your campsite every couple of days. Moving just 100 yards away can make a lot of difference in terms of the environmental impact you have on an area.

12. Keep your kitchen clean and a fair distance (50 to 100 feet) away from your bedding. This also minimizes your impact, and keeps night creatures away from you while you're in the snooze mode. Make sure your food is inaccessible to the local animal populations.

13. Leave all sites as you found them—or better, if others have done damage before you. Don't dig trenches for tents, cut standing trees or their branches, or pull up plants or embedded rocks. This is a quiet form of eco-defense, and is wise care.

MAKING FIRES

Before deciding on a fire, make sure that regulations allow it, that you've obtained any permit necessary, and that you are familiar with any restrictions. Double-check the area, making sure it can supply an adequate source of fuel. There should be enough deadfall around that you can pick up what you need from the ground. If there is little deadfall available, or if you would need to take dead twigs from the surrounding trees, then you are not in an area suitable for fire building.

Always be aware of potential fire hazards, keeping the fire away from tents, ground vegetation, trees, and their root and branch systems. Two methods of fire building will be described below: the *mound fire* and the *pit fire*.

The Mound Fire

1. Once you have decided that it is OK to build a fire, find a good source of inorganic, or mineral, soil. River beds are excellent sources. Any soil that does not have a lot of dirt or organic material in it is satisfactory. You can transport this material by shoveling it into a stuff sack turned inside out.

2. Lay a thick layer of this soil out on a square of fireproof material, which you can get at a good hardware store or outdoor shop. Usually this material comes in blanket sizes, which you can cut up. Layer the soil

ily be contaminated by people moving, cooking, and sleeping in close proximity to them. This can happen when you drop things into the water, or through runoff later on. Use biodegradable products. People's close presence also inhibits wildlife from using their accustomed water sources. Camping a minimum of 200 feet away from water sources is required in many government-controlled areas, and it is a good practice to follow wherever you are.

6. Don't camp on game trails. Sometimes they are obvious, other times obscure. Trails made by deer and other animals can be an acceptable route to follow while traveling (if they're going in your direction), but because many animals are nocturnal,

thick enough so that, in combination with the fireproof material, it insulates the ground underneath from getting scorched. The best places to put your fire would be on mineral soil, a flat rock, a thin layer of duff, or any other area where there is not much vegetation.

3. Collect small twigs no longer than your hand and no thicker than your middle finger—and a good many that are even thinner.

4. Stack the tinder very loosely in a random pattern narrowing toward the top, with the thinnest twigs near the bottom, then light the fire at the bottom and progressively add thicker pieces as it burns.

5. When you are ready to dismantle the fire, burn all the wood down to white ash, which can be spread out around the ground or dispersed on a nearby river or creek once it has cooled. Return the inorganic soil to its proper place. This is much better than leaving the old campfire ring of blackened stones and half-charred wood.

The Pit Fire

This is another type of minimum-impact fire, though in many circles this method is not as favored as the mound fire.

1. Dig a pit several inches deep in mineral soil, keeping the sides vertical and the pit shallow enough to allow for air circulation. Make sure there is no vegetation or duff surrounding the pit that could inadvertently catch on fire. You may want to place mineral soil around the perimeter and keep it moist.

2. When you start digging, remove any vegetation and its roots as gently and in as much of a single unit (soil, roots, and plants) as possible, trying to keep the root system intact. Lay this aside several feet from the fire pit itself, keeping it moist with a cover of damp soil. Cover all of the roots.

3. Collect tinder and build the fire as described above for the mound fire.

4. Afterwards, clean up the same way

Going down a rocky trail, carrying the bike and all its luggage, in Eastern Turkey. *Dieter Glokowski photograph*

you would a mound fire. Fill in the pit and replace any vegetative block that you may have cut away. If there are any air pockets underneath or around the sod blocks, the soil will settle, leaving a depression, and roots will desiccate.

Because complete combustion is difficult, refrain from burning food scraps and nonwood material. This refuse is a pain to clean up, and heats the ground more than combustible wood.

HYGIENE IN THE OUTBACK

This is where we get into what is for some still a delicate topic, namely that of human waste disposal. As more people frequent the outdoors, and stay out for longer periods of time, the more essential it is to understand and abide by guidelines for proper feces disposal. Here are some basic concepts as you strive for the most ecological way to go about the business:

1. Minimize the chance of other people and animals running into your feces (referred to as *it* from now on).

2. Minimize the chance that it will find its way to a water source.

3. Maximize the rate of its decomposition.

The first goal is most easily met by burying it in individual "catholes," though this does not guarantee that animals will not dig it up. Dig a small pit in a flat surface about 6 inches deep, making sure it is within an organic soil horizon. This ensures as much biological decomposition as possible. Breakdown will be minimal where the soil is cold, wet, or sterile (inorganic). Be certain you are at least 200 feet away from the nearest water source, and that there is no surface moisture present where you are digging. Having kept the topsoil intact, replace it and camouflage the hole as necessary.

One of the main concerns in all of this is to stay clean yourself. Soap is not naturally found outdoors, and its use is discouraged. To wash your hands is to use water and friction. Rubbing your hands together vigorously and rinsing well should do the job. You can increase friction by using sand or rocks while rubbing your hands together. If you do need to use soap, choose a biodegradable type but still rinse it off well away from lakes and streams, so that it has time to break down and filter within the soil.

CHAPTER THIRTEEN

MOUNTAIN BIKE RACING AND BEYOND

Mountain biking has become a significant international sport, accepted since 1990 by the Union Cycliste Internationale (UCI), the world's governing body of cycling, and starting with the 1996 Atlanta games, it's now an official Olympic discipline. In the first part of this chapter, Charles Kelly presents his insider's view of mountain bike racing—as it started and as it is practiced today. The second part contains an overview that looks at all the aspects of mountain bike competition, together with some recommendations to help you get involved in the sport.

INSIDER'S VIEW OF MOUNTAIN BIKE RACING

The urge to compete is part of the human condition, and we can rest assured that the first time two cyclists approached a trail, one tried to get there before the other.

Even before the term *mountain bike* was coined, there were informal off-road races that bore no resemblance to the traditional European sport of cyclo-cross. The first I know about took place in 1969.

The world of mountain biking now features two main varieties of competition, cross-country and downhill, and the downhill is further divided between long-course races and "dual slalom," head-to-head races run on a short course marked with poles in the fashion of a ski race.

Downhill racing was the first to evolve, but I am surprised that it has joined the list of legitimate cycle sports.

Rocket science old and new. Today's most publicized form of mountain bike racing is the downhill, and that's how it all began, too. The contrasting equipment testifies perhaps more to commercialization of the sport than to real progress. The early mountain bikers who raced down Repack on Mt. Tamalpais on custom-built mountain bikes did so on rather simple looking equipment. (left). Eric Palmquist, shown here at the Mammoth Mountain Eliminator, is a more recent exponent of the game (above). His bike has front and rear suspension, and his outfit seems borrowed from a ski jumper. *Photographs by Wende Cragg (left) and Bob Allen (above)*

There is no equivalent among traditional cycling events, and considering the conservatism that has been a major part of international cycling, it is almost shocking that downhill would be given World Championship status complete with rainbow jersey.

The first downhill races are lost to history, and the one most commonly referred to as the origin of this form of racing is the Repack Downhill, a loose series of 24 events that took place in Fairfax, California, from 1976 to 1984.

The Repack race started on a morning in October 1976, when six Fairfax riders got together at the top of a steep hill to establish for all time who was the fastest descender. The results were not expected to be of any consequence to anyone who was not present, and the participants expected that they would do this once and then find other forms of amusement.

The Repack race was a major impetus to the development of the new breed of bikes, because it was a legitimate test of durability and because all participants were looking for the technological "edge" that has become a hallmark of modern cycling.

The Repack era ended in 1984, because the last race, with nearly 100 riders, was an official NORBA event and took place with official "approval." This approval was rescinded when the nature of the event became clear to authorities. Repack was over, a victim of its own success.

Repack racers had always dreamed of putting on a similar race at a ski resort, with a lift to the top and miles of downhill on service roads. The thinking was that skiers were permitted to take major personal risks, and there must be a way that these areas would permit cyclists to assume the same risks.

In 1985 Don Douglass had the same thought, and he secured permission to use the service road at Mammoth Mountain ski resort for a race. This was a considerably more vertical descent than Repack, and there was a gondola to the top that could easily hold bikes and riders. Douglass called his event the *Kamikaze Downhill* after the suicidal pilots of World War II, and it has

There is something special about the start of a modern cross-country mountain bike race. This is the World Cross Country Championships held at Chateau D'oex, Switzerland. *Bob Allen Photography*

entered the history of mountain biking as the first of the "modern" downhill races.

Downhill racing is a good metaphor for the development of the off-road sport. The first events featured people on crude machinery, wearing workingman's garb of jeans, work shirts, and baseball caps, and racing for nothing more than pride. A modern event features unbelievably sophisticated and specialized machines that are virtually engineless motorcycles, riders wearing body armor and several square feet of sponsors' logos, and prizes in the multiple thousands of dollars. In 1976, speeds approached—but probably did not exceed—55 kilometers per hour (35 miles per hour). In a modern event, speeds of over 105 km/h (65 miles per hour) are not unusual. In downhill races conducted on snow, even higher speeds are possible.

Although not all mountain bike events include downhill races, it is one of the major features of races held at ski resorts, which are the natural beneficiaries of mountain bike racing. It was at ski resort races that the dual slalom mountain bike race format emerged. Like the downhill, it may be a misnomer to call this a "mountain bike" event, because the bikes are designed and set up strictly for this short, downhill, handling-intensive race. Dual slalom is not

an official UCI world championship event, but it may eventually be one. More than any other form of bicycle racing, downhill and dual slalom meet an important criterion for sports in America, namely that they are easily televised.

There is no comparison between cross-country and downhill races in their capacity to be captured by the TV camera. For the same reason that cross-country ski races are not popular television fare, cross-country mountain bike racing will never work for TV coverage. First, cross-country races tend to be devoid of drama, because lead changes are relatively infrequent. Second, because the course goes all over the map, it is hard to shoot, and a shot of one rider does not usually show his or her relationship to others. By comparison, bicycle road racing is easy to present because the action can be held where cameras can approach easily, and the riders tend to stay in groups. A cross-country mountain bike event can go on for several hours, and TV presentations have not yet been carried "live," because severe editing and voice-over are required to present it.

Downhill and dual slalom have everything visual that the cross-country race does not, and this is why they will continue

Fun at a double slalom event. Like many of the modern high-speed downhill races, these events are often held at ski resorts. *Bob Allen Photography*

cial" to anyone else. Finally, there is that feeling of an adrenaline rush so sought after today, and mountain bikers will take it where they can find it.

Downhill brings an automatic controversy with it. The image of riders shredding slopes at more than 50 miles per hour is not one that is popular with all outdoor user groups. The televised images that accompany the development of the downhill sport will also be used to demonstrate irresponsibility to those who are looking for it.

AN OVERVIEW OF THE SPORT

Mountain bike racing all started in the United States, and to this date there are probably more races held here than anywhere else in the world. The sport's origin can be traced back directly to the casually competitive sport of downhill racing. Even today, with the number of mountain bikes sold each year surpassing the sales of all other adult bicycles combined, sporting competition still plays an important role, both in the technical development of the mountain bike and in its actual use. Racing is both a popular amateur participation sport and one in which accomplished riders are making real money.

There has been cross-fertilization between conventional road and cyclo-cross racing on the one hand and mountain bike racing on the other. Indeed, some of the greatest names in road racing and cyclo-cross are now also competing in mountain biking events, and vice versa. The World Championships, alternately held in Europe and America, annually pit riders from all over the world against each other, and some of these events are now so popular that television coverage is a sought-after commodity.

As in road racing, competitors are assigned categories by their national sanctioning organization. Unless you've earned your laurels in road or cyclo-cross racing, you'll be assigned the lowest category for your age and gender group. From then on, only good results are going to move you up, until some day you may be assigned the Expert, or even the Professional, category. Just the same, many

as the staples of TV mountain bike coverage, with cross-country relegated to secondary status. Cross-country races are won on the climbs, at between 3 and 10 miles per hour, with little visible action. Downhill and dual slalom are won by speed and handling; crashes are frequent, the lead can change at any time, the action can be condensed, there is a standard for comparison, and goals are clearly defined. Strategy and tactics are at a minimum. Anyone can understand downhill.

Television is not the only reason that downhill is here to stay. It is clearly the

most popular event among the riders also. At a big mountain bike race, one that has many events spread over several days, the downhill will see the most entries. Fitness is not seen as an issue, and weekend riders who feel they have the handling skills can compete with anyone. This may or may not be true, but it works as enough of a rationale that people who wouldn't dream of riding five miles uphill will attempt to race that distance downhill. The standard of a time for the course is attractive, as friends can compare among themselves and compete in contests that aren't "offi-

Missy Giove is one of the best in the business of downhill racing. Her custom Cannondale illustrates cutting-edge downhill racing technolgy with its high-tech triple clamp forks, hydraulic brakes, and complex crank system. *Bob Allen Photography*

The closest thing to what was once billed as a "Tour" but is actually a thinly disguised race. This is the RADS Hike-A-Bike up Telonix at Laguna Beach, California. *Bob Allen Photography*

events don't have quite so many participants that all categories are run separately. Often, several categories are run together.

A day at the races in mountain biking usually includes several different events for the different categories of riders. The types of events included are described below, and in many cases there will be separate races for women and tandem riders, as well.

MOUNTAIN BIKE VERSUS CYCLO-CROSS

Cyclo-cross is a form of bicycle racing through rough terrain that has been a popular winter-season sport for many years, especially in Europe. In cyclo-cross, light drop-handlebar bicycles are used. Like the mountain bike, they have wide-range derailleur gearing and cantilever brakes. But that's where the similarity

ends. Unlike mountain bikes, cyclo-cross bikes are lighter and more fragile drop-handlebar machines that run on skinny (though also knobby) tires.

The way the cyclo-cross bikes stand up to the abuse of off-road cycling is by means of timely replacement. In fact, this equipment replacement procedure is now driven to the point of absurdity. In many races, competitors not only change bikes after every lap of the short course, to give the mechanics a chance to get them back in working order, they may even show up with different bikes for different sections of the course.

Mountain biking can be seen as a healthy reaction to this obsession with equipment replacement. It makes it possible to complete a race with just one bike, a true test of both man and machine. The same

bike that is used uphill will also go down and ride through mud and sand and over rocks. Instead of being carried over lengthy sections of the course, as is customary in cyclo-cross, it will carry the rider most of the way.

The first ones on record to use fat-tire bikes a cyclo-cross race were Russ Mahon and Carter Cox, who brought their "ballooners" to the 1974 cyclo-cross race in Mill Valley, California—without much notice. It was probably Gary Fisher who first served notice that the mountain bike was for real. At the 1980 California Cyclo-Cross Championships, he showed up with his fat-tire bike and ran away with the Senior championship title. This proved that the mountain bike can not only do things no other bike can do but can also do things for which more specialized equipment is intended.

Trials competition resides on the opposite end of the offroad spectrum from downhill racing. Riders utilize specialized and ultra-trick bikes. A rider's balance and bike handling skills are essential for success. *Bob Allen Photography*

MOUNTAIN BIKE RACING ORGANIZATIONS

Initially, the U.S. national bicycle racing organization, the United States Cycling Federation (USCF), was slow to recognize the potential of mountain bike racing. Almost since its inception, mountain bike racing has largely been sponsored by the National Off-Road Bicycle Association (NORBA). Although NORBA was founded in 1983 as a member-run organization, the elected directors saw fit to actually sell the organization to Glenn Odell, one of its founding members—disenfranchising the membership in the process.

Although the new owner was a benevolent and honorable man, the principle of selling out to private ownership (unbeknown to most of the members) set an ugly precedent. The various conflicts with the USCF might have been resolved more elegantly and permanently if there had been at least a pretense of membership control. Odell put a lot of time and effort into lobbying for access (a concern now handled by IMBA, the International Mountain Bike Association) and gaining insurance for the membership, while his industry-backed entourage was more interested in competition and commerce.

The combined tasks of organizing races, controlling the membership, dealing with a board of advisers, and fighting political battles were more than any man could carry out alone. Three years later the organization was sold to another individual, and nasty squabbles soon started. By then, NORBA had become nothing more (or less) than a race sanctioning body. Though essential for competition, this left the critical issues of access, safety, and membership participation ignored.

Finally, the organization was sold once more, this time to the USCF, which thus became the governing body of road, track, cyclo-cross, and mountain bike racing. This way, at least mountain bike rac-

Today, a good trials bike doesn't look a bit like your regular mountain bike: it has small wheels, a high bottom bracket, very fat tires, and a ridiculously low saddle. *Bob Allen Photography*

ing is in competent and powerful hands, and the conflicts between road racing and off-road racing organizers are cleared out of the way for good.

OFF-ROAD EVENTS

All competitive off-road events offer the novice the unique opportunity of participating on equal terms with the best. Even though some form of differentiation, similar to the categorization that is established in USCF-sponsored racing, is creeping into the sport, many races are still open to all comers with the appropriate credentials, which may be no more than a liability waiver and a twenty-dollar bill.

Real national celebrities in the world of off-road racing may be within touching distance, at least at the beginning of a race. They move ahead fast, while the novices are fidgeting to get into the right gear. Because most of these events are not based on the principle of numerous laps around a compact course, typical for cyclo-cross racing, the slow riders don't get in the way of faster ones. Although quite a few organizers are beginning to distinguish between the real gonzos and those of us who are out for the fun of it, this is not an athletic class society. Consequently, it is possible for a talented and determined newcomer to rise to stardom within a much shorter time than is customary or possible in regular bike racing.

Downhill

The oldest form of the mountain bike race, this is a scramble down a steep open hillside or trail. The terrain may be marked to show where you are supposed to ride and where you're not. Generally it's run as a time trial, with competitors starting at two-minute intervals. This type of event is now more akin to downhill skiing than to any other form of cycling.

Because it is spectacular and easy to watch, television coverage of downhill racing has been more extensive than of other forms, bringing with it more money from sponsors, more advertising, and more equipment development. Nowadays, some of the racers are indeed the same people doing the same thing on skis during the winter, and looking at the way they are dressed, they might as well be on skis. They generally use full-suspension bikes; most of the successful racers ride machines specifically developed for this discipline only.

Double Slalom

This is one of the recently introduced events made popular by television coverage. It's carried out on a very short and steep downhill course and very similar to ski-slalom. Two riders start together and the winner moves on to the next round.

Cross-Country

Most conventional mountain bike races fall into this category of mixed-terrain riding—some uphill, some downhill, and any number of laps around a course. Originally, these races were more typically held over a longer distance, but now more compact circuits are used and traversed several times. This makes it easier for organizers and spectators to have an overview of the entire race. It's the most true-to-life form of mountain bike racing, as it's more like riding under naturally prevailing conditions and requires elements of all off-road techniques.

Uphill-Downhill

In this kind of event you first work up a sweat before you get to break your bones on the way down. Separate times are generally recorded for the two sections and then totaled. Consequently, there may be three winners in any one race: the fastest rider uphill, downhill, and overall. Some of these races are hardly longer in distance than the downhill; others may take you over many miles.

Challenges and Enduros

These are other types of events out of the old book that the modern sanctioning organizations dropped by the wayside. A challenge can be a long uphill-downhill race or one with varied terrain. Though the route will be marked in some critical areas, you may be offered some flexibility of choice, with some daredevil always finding a new and shorter route, which may subsequently be named after him or her. Sometimes, the newly discovered shortcut becomes the established route, which may result in the same race becoming more of a challenge from year to year.

An enduro is more like the typical cyclo-cross race: many laps on a relatively compact course of perhaps one or two miles. The course includes varied terrain. The placings at the end of each lap are recorded, with a certain number of points awarded to the first six riders after each lap. The point ratings are accumulated, and the rider with the highest number of total points is declared the winner.

Trials

This is the kind of event that is highly competitive but has nothing to do with speed. It probably started as observed trials, which was developed mainly in the New England states and traces its heritage back to motorcycling practices in those same parts of the country. The idea is to ride what seems like an impossible course without putting a foot on the ground. Bikes with very high bottom brackets, direct steering, small wheels, very soft tires, and extremely low gears are used, and the riders stand up more than they sit in the saddle.

Observed trials competition is the ultimate test of skill and requires an entirely different temperament than the speed-and-

thrills stuff practiced mainly in the West. Originally, putting on an event like this was a bit of an organizational miracle, because you had to mark off the terrain accurately and you needed about as many observers as you had participants. Because not too many spectators and participants could be accommodated, this kind of game originally did not get as much coverage as it deserved as long as competition was held in natural surroundings.

These days, trials seems to have degenerated into stunt riding events held at specially constructed obstacle structures. Although competition isn't dead yet, many of these events are mere demonstrations, used to attract attention to other kind of cycling events, ranging from bike swaps and fund-raisers for youth programs to bike shop openings. As opposed to the original observed trials held out in the natural environment, they can be easily adjudicated by the officials and watched by the public.

GETTING READY TO RACE

To train effectively and to understand the development of the various skills involved, you are referred to the book *Mountain Bike Racing* by Tim Gould and Simon Burney. Join a club and your national sanctioning organization to get a license.

For your first races, you will be assigned the lowest category, although if it's a smaller event you can enter in the open class. Only after proving yourself with a series of good placings are you admitted to the next higher category, until some day, if you're diligent and very good at it, you may finish up in the Expert class, or even in the Professional category. Because your license is recognized internationally, you can participate in foreign countries as well as at home.

CHAPTER FOURTEEN
MOUNTAIN BIKING FOR WOMEN

Mountain biking is a great form of sport, recreation, and transportation for women, too. In this chapter, Jacquie Phelan, founder of WOMBATS (Women's Mountain Bike And Tea Society) explains some of the ways for women to succeed in the world of mountain biking. The first five sections give a general overview of solutions to problems that confront many women bikers; the final section is a first-hand account of women's racing.

DEALING WITH BIKE SHOPS

Take out a yardstick and stand against a door jamb, mark off your height and measure it. Remember this number of inches or centimeters. Then, with no intention of buying a bike, walk into the store, peruse the bikes, and hang out at the counter. You're simply testing the particular shop for its warmth, a great indicator of its ability to serve you. When someone asks if they can help you, say the usual "No, I'm just looking, thanks." This really throws them for a loop. They have to refer to the sales tips in the trade magazine, or fall back on their own communication

Jacquie Phelan, author of this chapter, riding a historic mountain bike: one of the first "Little People's" bikes designed and built by her husband Charlie Cunningham. Don't be fooled by the luggage rack or confused by the drop handlebars: Jacquie has long been at the top of women's mountain bike racing. *Gordon Bainbridge photograph*

One of the best women's cross-country racers ever—Juli Furtado. Now retired, Furtado is seen here riding in the Cactus Cup circuit race in Scottsdale, Arizona. *Bob Allen Photography*

skills. If, miraculously, the person is a woman, she probably will have no trouble seeming approachable. In this case, you're in luck, because only a small number of bike shops employ women.

For years, the bike shop has operated as a sort of boys' clubhouse, just like hardware and auto parts stores. I don't think it's because boys in bike shops hate women, it's just that we baffle them, and not enough women frequent shops to make the employees feel comfortable around the average female. The clubhouse atmosphere arises because men have an awful lot more time to hang out than we do, as most of us are working both for a salary and unpaid at home. If you want to experience a *women's* clubhouse, check out the thrift shop some time when on the prowl for alternative clothing.

OK, so now leave the shop, run back to your doorway, and measure your new height, after interacting with the shop. If the number is smaller than what you originally measured, find a new shop: those people rely on the brilliant tactic of humil-

iation to demonstrate their awesome bike knowledge. If the number is equal to or greater than your original height, it's a good shop. Head back there and buy a bike: they are happy to share their enthusiasm, even if you are just a fledgling and don't know what it's all about. (Hint: "it" is about metal. If you're not into teeny pieces of expensive metal, then you speak a different language than the average bike shop employee.) I don't believe that the brand of bike is as important as the attention given to fit and follow-up. Excellent service is what you really need from a shop.

Thanks to that wallet of yours, though, and this recession we've been in for a decade, there is a noticeable willingness on the part of the employees (and shop managers and owners) to learn our lingo.

Really Good Signs
1. A woman employee.
2. Bike gear for women—clothes, gloves, and shoes.
3. Small, well-built bicycles already assembled for a test ride.
4. Books on the shelf aimed at the new female rider.
5. A good magazine selection—a sign of the shop's commitment to the spread of information to anyone who comes through.

Extra Touches
A cooler with drinks to buy.
A coffee machine.
A tea thermos.
A chair.

Really Bad Signs
1. Employee asks you out on a date during the sale.
2. The minute you walk in, the employee averts his eyes and wanders off to do something else.
3. Three employees don't look up from their conversation when you enter.

BIKE CLOTHING: TRADITIONAL AND ALTERNATIVE

When you look at what people wear for riding, you'll find that there are distinct

categories. Here, the garb tends to be neon logo-infested Lycra tops and black shorts or tights. Luckily, there is no ban on originality in bike gear—the only considerations *you* have are practicality and comfort.

To the delight of most of the drivers overtaking me as I blazed cluelessly along back in the 1970s, I wore nylon running shorts and a skimpy cross-strap dance leotard that let my entire back turn brown, except a thin "X." Twenty-somethings love a tan; let 'em—fry now, cry later.

I never had a chafing problem. When I finally inherited a pair of Czech bike shorts made of wool with a genuine chamois, I discovered the quasi-infantile delight of the bikie diaper. That piece of tough but supple animal skin made me feel armored, and I mean that in a good way. Meanwhile, the wool always felt warm in winter and awesomely cool in summer. That was a mystery, but I didn't ask questions.

Then came my first wool jerseys, short- and long-sleeve, also inherited and therefore well worn. You could find them in bike shops (though less and less frequently until they came back in fashion with an $85 price tag), but the used ones are softer, pre-shrunk by the original owner (preferably a 180-pound guy who accidentally threw it in the dryer) and full of good karma and big chainring stories, even moth holes if you're lucky. Wool jerseys are pretty amazing garments, but a bit tricky to wash.

Then I discovered the joy of cashmere (I call it "crashmere") one day in the Purple Heart thrift shop down on San Francisco's Valencia Street. It's a very special goat hair that even wool-sensitive people seem to tolerate without breaking out in red dots. For three bucks max (any more and you won't want to do the Wombat surgery about to be described) you get an old sweater that can be turned into two useful garments: arm warmers and a vest. Simply hack off the sleeves at the armholes, and run a bit of elastic around the top (or be like me and just tuck in the baggy wide end—your jersey has elasticized sleeves, usually). It's modular clothing at its best. When you heat up, just shove them down around your wrists.

Descending fast in rough terain. Melissa Briley at Park City, Utah. *Bob Allen Photography*

I seldom wear the vest—it's just too warm for our temperate clime—but when I travel to Colorado or Minnesota, I pack the vest. You can layer it—it has to be next to your skin—and add a thin long-sleeve sweater or jersey and a windbreaker and beat the winter cold.

T-shirts are great under a few circumstances:

1. You are staying within five miles from home, and you never stop riding the whole time.

2. You are climbing a mountain and then staying up there in a heated house.

3. You are in denial about how freezing cold T-shirts are on every single little descent on a cool day's ride.

The fact is, cotton next to sweaty skin makes for refrigeration. "Cooled by evaporation" is the term, I believe, and cotton is really good at conserving your sweat and clinging to your shivering gooseflesh until you finally wise up, strip everything off and put the wool or polypropylene directly next to your skin. Oh, and if you don't have a special brassiere intended to wick moisture, you're doubly doomed. Try wearing your cotton bra over your Wombat "hack vest" for the descent, and then remedy the error with a quick call to Title IX Sports in Berkeley, California, 1-800-655-5999.

The most useful lightweight underlayers I have are made of polypropylene: a sleeveless white undershirt and a zippered turtleneck long-sleeve in dark blue. The dark colors soak up more warmth from the sun, perfect in winter. My favorite pants are the furry stretch pile tights (mine are from Patagonia); second best are corduroy Levi's, I kid you not. Cords are nice and stretchy and much warmer than jeans, which feel like cold cardboard on my legs, never mind the seamy intersection in the crotch of ten layers of denim . . . Jeans also seem to make my knee track wrong—they literally derail the patella, unless they're super-baggy.

If they're mid-calf or longer, socks can turn any pants into cycle pants. You know about the chainring tattoo, don't you? It's really tough to get out of fabric. Try Simple Green de-greasing soap. On a bare calf, this imprint can be wiped off with a dab of anything greasy daubed on a napkin: mayonnaise, butter, Pennzoil, makeup remover. Soap's OK, but the grease trick is much swifter and impresses the heck out of your companions. Works for your hands, too, after you've wrestled with a chain or fixed a flat.

Skirts, I've found, are great riding wear, preferably knee length or shorter. You just have to forget about keeping them clean. Too long and billowy and they'll jam in the rear brakes, too tight and you can barely pedal. I wear a tartan kilt on the trails and a Mr. Rogers button-front cardigan to confound the sartorially prejudiced hikers in Marin. In a kilt, they're not sure I'm really a biker, just a wheeled vision in kick-pleated plaid.

When riding in "sensitive" areas, remember that a full-pro outfit has the opposite of a calming effect on the frazzled nerves of that hiker doing a walking meditation in nature's cathedral. In the dirt, I always refrain from wearing clothing with lettering. But I like taking things to their logical extreme. On pavement, on the other hand, it's crucial to stick out as much as possible, and this means neon, especially a chartreuse windbreaker, and maybe even a helmet add-on toy, to stick out above the cars.

WHAT TO CARRY

Let's take a peek in the fanny pack, backpack, messenger bag, or pannier. Off-road, you'll probably want one of the first two, because they don't restrict your body English.

What goes in? In order of importance: windbreaker, sunscreen, food, eyewear, money, tiny chain tool, and map.

The pump must live on the bike. If you have more than one bike, you must have a pump for each one, lashed tightly on with Bat butyl, because the Velcro bands that come with the pump tend to let you down after a few months.

A water bottle is crucial—please consider a bomber cage by Blackburn—every convenience store carries the ideal one-and-a-half-liter bottle, already full of healthy water, for less money than the traditional puny bike bottles. These big, clear Evian-type bottles don't leach plasticizers into the water the way the bike bottles do (just smell the insides of each and make up your own mind). The CamelBak, a kind of backpack filled with water, is another option, but it also imparts plasticizers into your water supply. On the other hand, it is a terrific crash pad to bounce off of.

RIDING TOGETHER

A degree in sociology wouldn't hurt, to help you translate the gestures, posturings, and cryptic utterances that precede a group ride, but allow me to translate the most common:

1. By far the most popular pre-ride ritual is the *laying on of the excuses*. Why does anyone need to tell you about their lingering cough, their backache, or the fact that they haven't been on a bike in three months? To protect themselves against your unspoken derision at their pathetic 18-miles-per-hour average pace (mind you, the typical Wombat cruises the woods at about five miles per hour).

2. The second most popular pre-ride ritual is running back and forth between toilet and water faucet, letting off and taking on water while everyone else either does the same thing or waits impatiently. This is to gauge one's popularity. If you're really popular, your ride pals will put up with your lack of ride-readiness. If not, they leave.

3. Last but not least is the likelihood of your friends (I use this term loosely) taking you on a death march on your first real foray into the dirt. It's almost safer to go out alone a few times, just to noodle around for an hour, so you don't return home ragged, swearing off bikes forever. But no, your friends want to show you a good time. The problem is, it's *their* idea of a good time; they have long forgotten what constituted "fun" when *they* were beginners. In fact, they purposely deleted it from their memory, a forced amnesia brought on by the extremely low status beginners have among the cognoscenti.

Beginners are like colts, puppies, and baby rats: pure enthusiasm in the saddle.

Estella Villasenor riding in the scenic splendor of Hidden Valley at Moab, Utah. *Bob Allen Photography*

That's why it's important to treasure your beginner status—it passes soon enough—and exchange some of that enthusiasm for your know-it-all buddies trail expertise. Fun equals a ride for no more than two hours (saddle time), punctuated with a picnic made of genuine sandwiches and cookies, not space food, in any sort of weather.

How to tell you're getting tired: the thought crosses your mind, "I wonder how much farther..." If you catch yourself thinking this, or hear a companion uttering it, *stop*! Pull out a map, drink something, eat something, build up your reserves. Eat and drink immediately when you feel you need it. We don't have gas gauges, but that thought and similar ones ("When is the hill going to top out?" "I wonder what's for dinner?") are your stomach and brain crying out for respite and replenishment. Try it—your friends will think you're a mind-reader.

Don't hesitate to say, after an hour and a half, "I think I have just enough oomph to get home, can we turn around now?" If I'm with people who I know will not want to do this, I secretly lay down trail marks at every junction. Without even dismounting,

I drag a toe in the dirt through the curve and give it a wiggle so it looks like a sine wave, not a skid mark, and this way I can Gretel my way home without inconveniencing any of the hammerheads that want to forge ahead. It's better to return with energy left than to ride bedraggled. A pooped cyclist crashes more frequently.

TRAIL ETIQUETTE

1. Cough and slow down to alert others of your presence. "On your left" went out of style last year when the Olympics dumped a few million more cyclists on the trails. Give hikers a choice, fer gawd's sake!

2. Keep voices down—no yodeling—let the birds and the jets be the noisemakers. Besides, nobody on a bike can hear you anyway.

3. When you stop, pull over to the side, out of the path of others, rather than hogging the trail or the road. If others have to swerve to avoid you, you're in the way, and group riders are most guilty of this. Pack riding should be *verboten* in the dirt except in races. Herds of hikers are a hassle, too, but at

least they don't scream by at speed. Groups should never be bigger than four. Break up, if your group is five or more. True, it will string out as you go, but why make a nasty impression in the first mile of trail where all the other users are? By the time your pack is strung out, there's usually no one to appreciate the single-strand beauty of your low-impact group.

4. Within two miles of any car parking area, ride super-duper slow and respect the dogs, strollers, mothers, and slow walkers of all ages. You'll get away soon enough, so keep cool.

5. If you find yourself ragging on people the way I am ragging on you, don't be surprised to find an extremely unreceptive audience, no matter how right you think you are. Enough said. Find a bike you love and ride, baby, ride.

THE YOUNG HISTORY OF MOUNTAIN BIKING'S WILD WOMEN

The first women on bicycles, riding around unchaperoned in the late 1800s, are off-road's first heroines. Paved roads were invented long after the bicycle captured the hearts of thousands of women the world over. Every advance that women have made can be traced to the industrial revolution's greatest gift, the bicycle. Suddenly women could, with a machine that cost no more than a month's wages, navigate the roads without the need for a wagon, horses, or a chaperone in the form of a relative or spouse. Even women's clothing was revolutionized to accommodate the new freedom of movement, and naturally, the first women paid dearly for their bravery.

A hundred years later, to put it in perspective, there are millions of women pedaling their produce to market in the Andes, pedaling to work in Peking, and pushing their heavily laden bicycles over mountain passes to safety in war-torn Yugoslavia. And there are a few of us in the "overdeveloped" countries who are discovering our wild side astride two knobby wheels.

Alison Dunlap in the heat of cross-country competition. *Bob Allen Photography*

Wende Cragg is the first woman I can think of who regularly rode in the late 1970s with the Marin County gang of riders that included Charlie Kelly, Gary Fisher, and Fred Wolf. She was strong and determined not to be left behind. Joe Breeze easily lured her out on rides with the promise they would stop and identify spring wildflowers. She was one of the first to get one of Joe's original hand-built chromoly Breezers, and as she only weighed 120 pounds, she appreciated the lighter-weight machine. She entered and won the National Cyclo-Cross Championships in 1979.

At the time, the status of cycling in the United States was so informal that promoters (even of a National Championship event) were free to put on any kind of event they saw fit, and a certain Oregon promoter had looked forward to honoring both a man and a woman. The USCF had rules, however, and the Colorado official who flew in for the event told the two women entered they weren't permitted to finish if they were lapped by the men. Wende ignored him and finished anyway, to the promoter's delight, but the United States Cycling Federation official threatened to rip the stars-and-stripes jersey she'd earned right off her back if she ever wore it again at a cycling event. (The USCF disallowed women in cyclo-cross for years after this, only reinstating a women's championship in 1986.) Because Wende was a budding photographer, her pictures are the sport's very first images of itself, and they have appeared far and wide (including right here) as a valuable chronicle of our infant sport.

Soon after, Charlie Kelly met and fell in love with Denise Caramagno, a brash young New Yorker who'd moved to Marin and loved mountain biking's

Going down. One of the top downhill racers, Leigh Donovan, at speed during the 1997 World Downhill Championships held at Chateau D'oex, Switzerland. *Bob Allen Photography*

One way for men and women to stay together is on a mountain bike tandem. Of course, it's a great way for different strength riders to stay together, regardless of sex: there are quite a few men who couldn't keep up with some women riding singles.

maverick image as much as the bicycle itself. She rode and raced in 1980 and 1981. Her claim to fame is greater than just being an early racer: with Kelly, she founded the sport's first journal, the brilliant *Fat Tire Flyer*. For six years (1980 to 1986) the magazine irreverently promoted "the world's smallest sport," with editorials by Charles Kelly and cartoons like "Ricky Cha," the Rastafarian dope-smoking, Zen rider, and "Mud Pup," a bicycle that took its owner on rides. The rider in this case

was a beautiful teenage girl named Edie, based on Denise, who commissioned the cartoon, and the image of a free-flying bicycle with a woman on board would help to cement the sport's early acceptance of women as heroes.

In 1980 I met Gary Fisher, and by the following year he was my boyfriend, coach, and chauffeur to the races. We were road racers, but luckily there was a free weekend in June, and he found a fat-tire bike I could borrow, so we raced up in Whiskeytown at what became the race

against which all others were measured. I won it easily, beating all but six of the 75 men. Gary, of course, won overall, and our career as mountain bike racers was set.

The relationship didn't survive all those road miles to and from the races, but I met everyone I would need to know for the next few years: the Marin gang that founded NORBA; Charlie Cunningham, the man I would spend the rest of my life with; and a new character inside myself named Alice B. Toeclips, who lived to ride her bicycle.

CHAPTER FIFTEEN

ACCESS AND ADVOCACY

Mountain bikers are not always welcomed everywhere, and in many cases we must be on our guards to retain (or regain) access to terrain that is suitable for our sport. In this chapter, Phillip Keyes, who has been active in this arena for many years, summarizes the arguments on both sides of the issue and proposes a strategy for mountain bikers to follow.

Many of us bought our bikes and headed for the woods to seek a little peace and quiet and get a bit of exercise amidst the beauty of Mother Nature. It's disturbing to realize that mountain biking is not always welcomed with open arms by our fellow trail users. Sometimes we get the hairy eyeball from a passing hiker, and sometimes it gets worse: the author's favorite trail now features a picture of a bike with a big "X" through it.

Riding a mountain bike has become a political act. Whether we like it or not, there are people who would prefer that we not tread on public lands. Instead of being welcomed by other people in the woods, we're sometimes scowled at and made to feel as if riding our bikes was somehow criminal. Whether you call it "trail bicycling," "off-road cycling," or "mountain biking," riding a bicycle on public trails is political. We are all emissaries of our sport, diplomats of the mountain bike community. We must show that off-road riding is a "green" activity, on par with hiking, horseback riding, cross-country skiing, and trail running.

Mountain biking raises the environmental consciousness of many of us who

A group of New England Mountain Biking Association members acting as volunteer terrain maintenance workers in Wompatuck State Park, Hingham, Massachusetts. Forested areas like this one require frequent clearing of woodfall—a different kind of maintenance than what would be required for steep barren hillsides or lush mountain meadows. *Philip Keyes photograph*

have become passionate about this sport. It has brought a whole new generation and group of people into our parks and open spaces, and has taught them to care for the trails. Even those who begin by simply "using" the trails soon find out what a wonderfully beautiful place they are in, and it's not long before they want to protect and steward the trails. As mountain biking grows, it will soon become one of the primary user groups of public lands, and as this happens we will become one of the principal protectors as well.

THE PROBLEM WITH BIKES

Let's face it: in most areas, mountain bikers are the new kids on the block, and it's only natural for other traditional user groups, such as hikers and equestrians, to question our right to use "their" trails. Mountain bikers have only been on the trails in significant numbers since the late 1980s, and initially many land managers and traditional trail users thought of mountain biking as a temporary fad and a short-lived annoyance. When this "fad" showed no signs of waning, land managers and organizations representing traditional trail users needed to figure out what position to have about these "kids."

In many cases, it was easier for land managers to ban all bicycle use on trails rather than spend the time and energy developing strategies to regulate mountain biking. Only recently has the National Park Service expressed a willingness to open certain sections of their trails to mountain bikes. Some powerful trail groups, such as the Sierra Club, pigeon-holed mountain bikes as being in the same class as motorized vehicles, and therefore they felt that existing bans on the motorized set should be applied equally to mountain bikes. It took nearly a decade for the Sierra Club to recognize mountain biking as a legitimate trail activity.

It's ironic that many people who discover the pleasures of off-road cycling do so coming from a background of other environmentally "green" outdoor activities such as hiking, cross-country skiing, trail running, and the like. They are shocked to find themselves on the other side of the table, accused of being anti-environment by groups to whom they would otherwise be sympathetic. Mountain bikers have much common ground with groups involved with the conservation movement, and there is much to gain by toning down the hostility and giving us a chance to prove ourselves.

With few exceptions, most mountain bikers believe in the conservation of open spaces and in trail preservation. The biggest threat to trails around the globe certainly isn't biking: it's the outright destruction of trails by poorly planned development. Better to join together to save the trails and find solutions to the real problems facing our public lands and open spaces than it is to bicker and point fingers.

UNDRESSING THE ARGUMENTS

In this section we'll consider the arguments brought against allowing mountain bikes in the natural environment and see how well they hold up in a rational analysis.

"Bikes are bad for the trails."

One of the earliest but still most common anti-bike arguments made is that mountain biking is damaging to the trails.

Supposedly, mountain bikes simply cause inordinately high amounts of trail damage, resulting in erosion and trail degradation. Yet thus far there has not been any scientific study supporting this claim. On the contrary, Joseph Seney's 1990 study, "Erosional Impacts of Hikers, Horses, Motorcycles, and Mountain Bikes on Mountain Trails," substantiated the following results:

1. Trail damage by bicycles was not found to be significant.
2. The differences between bicycle and hiker impacts were difficult to distinguish based upon the measurements of water runoff, sediment runoff, or soil compaction.
3. Horses produced significantly more sediment runoff than the other groups because they dug up the trail. The differences between the other groups were not significant. Sediment runoff is bad for trails because sediment is the glue that holds the trail together.
4. Horses and motorcycles produced significantly less water runoff than hikers and bicyclists. The greater the water runoff, the healthier the trail.

All trail use has an impact, and the key to a healthy trail lies in its proper construction and maintenance. The amount of use a particular trail receives is significant. Parks and open spaces surrounding urban areas are under the greatest stresses due in large part to the increased numbers of visitors, not just to mountain bikes. Many times these trails simply cannot sustain this high level of use without trail maintenance. More and more, mountain bikers are becoming part of the solution instead of the problem by holding trail maintenance days and sponsoring work parties on public lands. It is key that all of us help in this effort.

"Bikes are dangers to others."

Another major argument against mountain biking is that mountain bikes are dangerous to other trail users. Safety is indeed an important issue, particularly when it comes to reckless riding. But this is a behavior that can be modified and isn't

intrinsic to the bicycle itself. However, all it takes is one gonzo mountain biker to zoom past an unsuspecting family or to spook a horse to create the image that all mountain bikers present a danger. Riders must yield trails to equestrians and hikers. That means stopping for horses and slowing way down for hikers. Remember that walkers generally go about three to four miles per hour and that bikes travel on average about seven to ten miles per hour. Thus what is slow for a walker is a lot slower than what is slow for a biker. Err on the side of slowness and use the opportunity to say "Hi" and spread some goodwill. Be a diplomat and not a terrorist.

"Bikes ruin the natural experience."

The last major anti-bike argument is that bikes simply don't belong on the trails because they take away from the natural experience other trail users are seeking. This argument mistakenly presumes that mountain bikers do not appreciate the sense of adventure and the natural tranquillity that our trails provide—this is not the case. It is also mistaken to presume that the presence of a cyclist automatically denigrates the peace and beauty the trail provides. Bicycles don't have engines or cause noise pollution. In fact, sometimes the problem is that we are too quiet and can't be heard when we approach another trail user. Our presence shouldn't be taken as any more of an affront than would the presence of any other person in the woods.

Underneath the idea that cyclists take away from the experience of other trail users is the notion that the experience of hikers or equestrians is somehow more "pure" and of higher value that the experiences sought after by cyclists. Where I live, near Walden Pond, Thoreau developed his philosophy on foot, not on bike, and many of the locals still believe that the only way to appreciate the forest is on foot or on hoof. If I had to guess, I think old Henry David would have enjoyed spinning a few gears had he had the opportunity. Transcendentalism and mountain biking go hand in hand. None of us should regard our own trail experience as inherently better than anyone else's.

Marilyn Price, of Mill Valley, California, started an outreach program called Trips for Kids to introduce inner-city youngsters to the fun of mountain biking. One of her projects is this bike maintenance workshop. *Neil van der Plas photograph*

MOUNTAIN BIKE ADVOCACY

Sparked by a rash of trail closures, mountain bike advocacy groups popped up across the United States in the late 1980s. By the mid-1990s, almost every major city in the country had an organized group. Some of the first organizations were the Concerned Off-Road Bicycle Association (CORBA) in Los Angeles, the Bicycle Trails Council in the San Francisco Bay area, the Dallas Off-Road Bicycle Association, the Southern Off-Road Bicycle Association in Georgia, the Mid-Atlantic Off-Road Enthusiasts in Washington D. C., and the New England Mountain Bike Association in Boston. These groups quickly became embroiled in trail politics and set the stage for a national advocacy movement.

In 1988 a small advocacy group was started in southern California with a grandiose name, the International Mountain Bike Association. With no paid staff and little money, the all-volunteer group positioned itself to give voice to all mountain bikers and represent their interests to public agencies and the media. Central to IMBA's goal was to dispel the unfounded criticisms used to support bicycle trail bans and to gather information proving

that mountain biking is "an environmentally sustainable and socially responsible use of public trails." Understaffed and underfunded, IMBA operated out of the home offices of its few dedicated founders and was kept afloat by the generosity of its benefactor, Al Farrell.

One of IMBA's first major successes was to convince the national leadership of the Sierra Club in 1994 that "mountain biking is a legitimate form of recreation and transportation on trails, including single-track, when and where it is practiced in an environmentally sound and socially responsible manner." This was a major breakthrough for IMBA and a huge philosophical change for the Sierra Club, which opened the door for the two organizations to work together on more pressing problems of concern to everyone, such as the selling off of the nation's open spaces.

By June 1994, IMBA was able to bring their cause to the next higher level by hiring its first paid executive director, Tim Blumenthal, and setting up a staffed office in Boulder, Colorado. Since that time, IMBA has become a professional advocacy and lobbying organization that has been successful in bringing together more that 350 local advocacy groups to present a

unified coalition of trail users, representing more than 62,000 mountain bikers. This movement crystallized in January 1996 when IMBA organized the first-ever national mountain bike advocacy summit held at Biosphere II deep in the Arizona desert. Attended by more than 160 mountain bike advocates, and members of the bike industry and the press, the summit showed that IMBA had successfully created a national movement and was ready to lead the cause to the nation's capitol.

And that they did. Later that same year, IMBA began discussions in Washington, D.C., with the National Park Service to open up some trails to bicycles. The Park Service was one of the early and largest land managers to close its trails to bicycles, citing that preservation and not recreation was its key mission.

In Marin County, the National Park Service's ban on bicycles in the Golden Gate National Recreation Area was upheld in court, renewing the tensions between the Park Service and the mountain biking community. However, IMBA studied hundreds of potential areas and trails, and created a target list of 25 areas on National Park Service lands that would be suitable for mountain biking, such as the North Rim Trail of the Grand Canyon National Park. As of this writing, there is hope that many of the proposed trails will be opened to cyclists.

As a testimony to the effectiveness of local advocacy, IMBA maintains a tally of the number of miles of trail IMBA-affiliated groups are able to open to bicycles. In 1996 alone, the number of miles was over 700, indicating that advocacy is not only successful at preventing closures but is increasing the riding opportunities for all of us.

THE INTERNATIONAL SCENE

In Canada, the Canadian Mountain Bike Association (CMBA) formed in 1996 and is still in its infancy. As an independent affiliate of IMBA, the CMBA hopes to promote and protect mountain biking along the same lines as IMBA. Its early goals are to set up a dedicated office with a part-time staff and create representatives in each province in order to forge a national organization. On the local Canadian front, however, each province boasts many off-road advocacy groups that have been protecting the sport. CMBA hopes to act as the liaison and clearinghouse for all the groups on the front lines, and has received funding from the Bicycle Trade Association of Canada.

In Europe, mountain bike advocacy has a long way to go, and it is curious that an area with such a rich history and passion for bicycle racing has not been on the vanguard of mountain bike advocacy. Yet by the mid-1990s, the Europeans became the dominant force in the off-road racing circuit, so with a bit of effort, they may catch up to the United States in the race to save the trails. In 1996, IMBA met with the UCI, the international governing body of bicycle racing, during the mountain bike World Championships in Cairn, Australia, to propose that the UCI appoint an IMBA contact for each of its 190 cycling federations around the world. This global network would help bridge the gap between mountain bike racing—the UCI's main focus—and mountain bike advocacy, and help ensure that race courses are environmentally sound.

GIVING BACK TO THE TRAILS

One of the primary goals of many advocacy groups is to work with land managers and help keep the trails in good shape. This is especially important in high-impact areas near major urban centers, where the trail systems weren't designed to accommodate large numbers of users, especially with the scanty budgets available for the management of public lands. By getting involved with their local riding areas, mountain bike groups can help design new single-track trails that better meet the needs of mountain bikers.

Bicycle patrols have become another method of giving back something to the parks. They can be used to educate mountain bikers about the do's and don'ts of the particular area and they can provide assistance and a level of comfort and security to all trail users. Some patrols are certified in CPR and Search and Rescue techniques.

Singletrack riding, as practiced here by Charlie Stocker in Montana, is considered the hardest practice to defend. Although it may be true that encounters with other users are more likely to turn into confrontations, there is no evidence to suggest that mountain bikers do disproportionately more damage there. *Bob Allen Photography*

THE CHANGING IMAGES OF MOUNTAIN BIKING

Many of the problems that mountain biking has faced have been a result of the marketing images of mountain bikers as irresponsible, juvenile, gonzo eco-terrorists. These images in large part are the creation of marketing specialists who use the "extreme" aspect of mountain biking to sell their products. The gonzo images are reinforced by the occasional rider who blisters down some narrow trail and nearly broadsides a family taking a stroll. All it takes is one incident for the whole sport of mountain biking to be painted with the same negative brush. That's why it's critical that each of us ride as diplomats to our sport. This isn't to say that we should never enjoy a thrilling descent or push ourselves and our bikes to the limit. But we should know when and where to let it all hang out, and when to back off, be cautious, and tone it down.

What was once the domain of the young and the restless is now an activity common to those with mortgages, kids, and college funds. Mountain biking is no

Former Trials World Champion Robbie Powell (far right) with a group of cyclists at the opening of a trail in the formerly closed-off Diepwalle Forest outside Knysna, South Africa, where a small herd of elephants still roams. Cyclists in South Africa have more serious access problems than in most Western countries, due to a long history of restricted access to lands administered by government agencies like the Forest Service.

longer a fringe sport—it is now firmly a part of the mainstream. Although many of us may bemoan this fact, it also has a positive side: mountain biking must be taken seriously as a socially accepted activity. Mountain biking is here to stay. It is a sport that must be governed, not banned.

RACING AND LAND ACCESS

Mountain bike racing still fuels the public image of the sport, pushes mountain bike technology, and provides the marketing backdrop that sells bikes. Racing has done much both to help and hurt the sport. Yet, more and more, national-level racers are using their influence to support mountain bike advocacy. Top-level racers are the heros that many look up to and seek to emulate both on and off the trail. As such, they are uniquely able to use their positions to educate the next generation of bikers to ride responsibly and join their local advocacy group.

Penny Davidson, the United States national downhill champion, has used her influence at many of the national races by setting up an IMBA Awareness Expedition, a program of recreational rides, kids'

rodeos, and social events designed to spread the IMBA Rules of the Trail. Pro riders such as Ned Overend, John Tomac, Susan DeMattai, Dave Weins, Travis Brown, and Juli Furtado, just to name a few, have all begun to play an active role to help IMBA and promote advocacy.

Getting local racers involved with land access has been difficult, but one program in New Jersey called Pay Dirt has been able to bridge the gap successfully. The Pay Dirt program rewards racers of the New Jersey State MTB Cross-Country Championships with a chance to get first-place points for volunteering ten hours of trail maintenance. Considering the series contains only nine races, volunteering to do trail maintenance can play a significant role in the overall point series. There are also prizes given to racers with the most volunteer hours.

GETTING TO THE NEXT GENERATION

Kids and bikes have always been a natural, and in 1987 Marilyn Price began a program called Trips for Kids, which brought inner-city kids out on mountain bike excursions in the San Francisco Bay

area. Now with a volunteer base of more than 150 and much support from the bike industry, the Bicycle Trail Council of Marin, and IMBA, Trips for Kids has chapters in San Francisco, Los Angeles, and Denver. The program combines social activism with mountain biking and teaches kids the skills needed both to ride responsibly and to repair their bikes.

IMBA'S RULES OF THE TRAIL

The most important thing any mountain biker can do to protect our privilege to use the trails is to follow IMBA's Rules of the Trail. Our riding behavior has a huge influence on how we are perceived as a user group, and this perception is key if we are to continue to ride off-road.

Ride on open trails only. When cyclists ride illegally, it sends a message that we don't care about the trails or trail policies. Scofflaws undermine our ability to work with land managers and clearly make us part of the problem, not the solution.

Control your bicycle. Of all the arguments against allowing bicycles on trials, the one that land managers must listen to the most is that of public safety. If you ride recklessly out of control, you're a danger to yourself and everyone in your path. Although there has been no reported case of a pedestrian being killed by an off-road bicycle, it is a worst-case scenario that must never happen.

Always yield trail. Bikes must slow way down for hikers and must stop completely for equestrians. Use the time to be friendly to your fellow trail user, and ask the horse-back rider how the horse is with bikes.

Never spook animals. Mountain bikes are great for discovering wildlife because they are quiet and swift. But we must remember that although we enjoy using the land, it is the animals' habitat, and we should respect them and not scare them away.

Leave no trace. This principle goes way beyond mountain biking and is the principal code of conduct for any outdoor experience. Don't discard punctured tubes or energy bar wrappers—leave only the waffle prints of your knobby tires. Leaving litter reinforces the mistaken image that mountain bikers don't care about the trail.

Although a few tourist regions are beginning to object to mountain biking in exotic destinations, most unpaved roads and trails are still open to mountain bikers on public and private land. *Bob Allen Photography*

THINGS YOU CAN DO

Here's a list of the actions you can take to help minimize the likelihood of cyclists being banned from the great outdoors.

Ride Responsibly

It can't be said it enough: each of us must be a diplomat for our sport.

Join Your Local Mountain Bike Club

Paying your annual dues to your local club will be some of the best money you've ever spent. In addition to sponsoring trail work and all the other advocacy efforts your club performs, you frequently get a newsletter and an opportunity to meet and ride with a bunch of other mountain bikers. It is a great way to keep up-to-date with what's happening locally and learn about new places to ride. Even better, offer to get involved.

Join IMBA

This organization is unparalleled in its ability to work for you at both the national and local levels. Quite simply, they are doing big things on a small budget, and they need every dime they can get.

Get Involved With Your Local Park or Conservation Area

These places are starving for volunteers, and a little goodwill goes a long way. Whether you volunteer as part of a group or individually, it lets the local land managers know that mountain bikers are willing to give back to the trails.

COUNTERPOINT: A NOTE FROM ROB VAN DER PLAS

This chapter, written by Philip Keyes, nicely summarizes the issues, at least as it concerns the American situation. One issue I would like to clarify, though, is that the American insight into events in foreign countries tends to be limited. To give an example, when I suggested writing an article about access problems for a Dutch cycling magazine, I was told not to bother. Why? Not because they're way behind but because they're way ahead. The question of access simply is not an issue in most European countries because there has always been access for cyclists to lands that in the United States might have been restricted. It may be a problem in some localities (I know of Swiss ski resorts that ban cyclists from the trails maintained by the tourist board), but by and large, access is not as big a problem in most of Europe.

PART III

UNDER-STANDING YOUR MOUNTAIN BIKE

CHAPTER SIXTEEN

THE MOUNTAIN BIKE AND ITS FRAME

In the chapters of this third part of the book, we'll take a close look at the technology that makes mountain biking possible. In each of these chapters, you'll find both a general description of a major functional group of the bike and appropriate selection criteria to help you choose your equipment.

Before getting any further into this material, you may want to refer to the illustration on page 17 in Chapter 3, which names all the parts of the bike.

THE FRAME

The frame is the mountain bike's backbone—the structure that holds it all together. The frame on a mountain bike differs from that of a road bike to accommodate the particular kind of use and abuse for which it is intended.

The illustration shows the components that constitute the frame. The main frame comprises four large-diameter tubes: top tube, seat tube, downtube, and head tube. The rear triangle consists of two seatstays and two chainstays. The smaller members are the bottom bracket, seat lug, upper and lower head lugs (assuming it is a lugged frame), and bridge pieces connecting the pairs of seatstays and chainstays. Finally, there are dropouts and braze-ons, minor items attached to the tubes, such as brake pivot bosses, cable anchors, stops, guides, and bosses.

Today, most mountain bike frames are welded. Conventionally, quality frames have been made by brazing the tubes together with lugs. It is also possible

to braze the tubes together directly, referred to as fillet-brazing. Some frames are made with tubes that are bonded together with internal lugs or are built entirely of carbon-fiber-reinforced resin.

The welding process commonly used for mountain bike frame construction is TIG-welding. In this process, the heated zone is protected against corrosion by a stream of an inert gas. The lugless joints of a TIG-welded frame are markedly more abrupt than they are on a fillet-brazed frame. TIG-welding is cheaper than fillet brazing but works very satisfactorily on tubes with slightly thicker ends.

Cheaper welded frames may be MIG-welded. This is an automated process resulting in a rather big, crude-looking weld bead at the joints. Because MIG-welding requires greater tube wall thicknesses, such frames are likely to be heavier.

FRAME QUALITY

To size up the quality of a frame, first check the diameters of the various tubes. At least the downtube should be of a larger diameter than the one used on a road bicycle of the same material. This is necessary to accommodate the higher stresses resulting from the rougher treatment and the more generous lengths, slopes, and clearances of the mountain bike. (Aluminum frames require tubes that are bigger in diameter than their steel equivalents of the same strength and rigidity.)

Also observe the other details. If the joints are smooth and without gaps, the bike is probably of a higher quality than if they

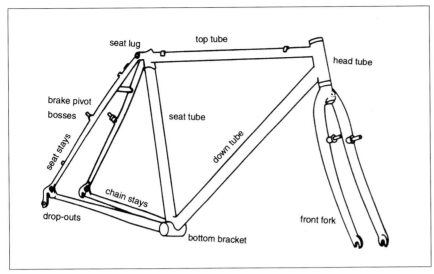

The parts of the frame. This illustration shows the common names of all the components used on a conventional mountain bike frame without rear suspension. Some special frames, especially those made of carbon- or Kevlar- reinforced resin, are not constructed in this way.

are rough and show gaps. Finally, check the finish: a smooth, even coat of paint generally indicates a more carefully built machine.

FRAME GEOMETRY

There are a few differences between the typical geometry of a mountain bike and that of a road bike for the same size rider:

1. The mountain bike has a higher bottom bracket.
2. The mountain bike's top tube is lower. This, in addition to the higher bottom bracket, results in a considerably shorter seat tube.

3. Although the seat-tube angle should be roughly the same, the mountain bike has a shallower head-tube angle.
4. The mountain bike's top tube is slightly longer.
5. The mountain bike has longer chainstays.
6. The mountain bike has a longer wheelbase (the distance between the wheel axles).
7. The clearances for the wheels are more generous on the mountain bike.

Many manufacturers nowadays include drawings showing the geometries of their

various models in their catalogs, so you can shop around. Just the same, don't buy a bike without having tried it out, even if the geometry seems perfect on paper.

The bottom bracket is typically 30 centimeters (12 inches) or more off the ground. This height is required to provide adequate ground clearance in rough terrain and to prevent damage to the biggest chainring. Even higher bottom brackets make a bike more suitable for extremely rough terrain.

The top tube is lower to allow a low enough saddle position that makes it possible to reach the ground while seated and to let you straddle the bike more easily when you are standing still. In general, it should be about 2 inches lower than on a road bike for the same size rider. The combined effect of the higher bottom bracket with that of the lower top tube should result in a seat-tube length, or nominal frame size, that is about 7.5 centimeters (3 inches) less than it would be for a comparable road bike. You should be able to straddle the frame of a bike (with wheels installed) with both feet flat on the ground and lift the front wheel off the ground by 12 to 15 centimetrs (5 to 6 inches).

Table 1 in the Appendix shows recommended seat-tube lengths, measured one of two ways, as well as straddle heights. In terms of straddle size, the frame should be about 2 to 3 inches less than your inseam leg length.

The seat-tube angle determines how the seat will be centered relative to the drivetrain. For most sizes, 72 degrees is just

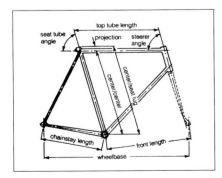

Frame geometry designations. This illustration shows the names for the various measures of sizes and angles on the mountain bike frame.

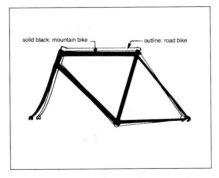

Comparison of typical mountain bike frame geometry with that of a conventional road bike.

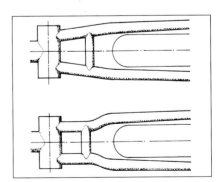

Two ways of chainstay design to give the mountain bike's rear wheel enough clearance. The method illustrated in the lower detail, with the distinctly curved stays, is more effective for really fat tires.

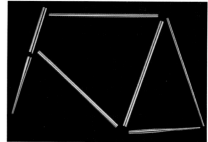

A mountain bike from Marin with a conventional frame and a respectable component group, consisting mainly of Shimano Deore XT components.

RIGHT (BOTTOM): Despite the bad rap bike manufacturers often get, many of them base their designs on the results of some real testing using sophisticated analytical equipment, such as this Megalog system, first developed to fine-tune racing motorcycles. *Photograph courtesy Mobil-Tech*

ABOVE (TOP): A frame is nothing but a bunch of tubes connected to form a rigid structure. Here's one tubing manufacturer's view of what goes into a frame. *Photograph courtesy Mannesmann*

about right. Very small bikes typically need a steeper seat-tube angle to achieve the proper position for a short-legged rider.

The head-tube angle influences the steering characteristics, the overall wheelbase, and the comfort or springiness of the front end. Any angle between 68 and 72 degrees may be right, depending on the size and the bike's intended use. It may be as shallow as 68 degrees for a sluggish but comfortable bike that goes downhill without risk. It should be more like 72 degrees for a bike that gives a nimbler, though rougher, ride—one that demands more skill on a steep descent.

The longer top tube results in a low, stretched-out position, it helps protect your knees from hitting the handlebars when standing up on a steep climb, and it provides a long wheelbase. For beginners, bikes with a slightly shorter top tube for any given frame size tend to be more comfortable. About 3 to 4 inches more than the seat-tube length (measured center-to-center) is about right for most riders, but more is OK for experienced riders.

Longer chainstays provide greater clearances and contribute to the longer wheelbase. Short chainstays and the resulting shorter wheelbase provide better climbing and sprinting characteristics. Chainstays that are less than 43 centimeters (17 inches), provide a nimble ride, whereas higher figures result in more comfortable descents.

You need at least 5 mm (3/16 inch) lateral clearance on either side of the rear tire. Bikes with small clearances don't take the really fat tires. Measure the distance between the pairs of chainstays and seatstays at a point 33 centimeters (13 inches) from the drop-out centers; then deduct 10 mm (3/8 inch) to determine what is the fattest tire that will fit with adequate clearance.

DIFFERENT FRAME DESIGNS

Over the years, various frame designs have been introduced that look quite different from those used on the conventional bike. Some of these are mere fads, others may be here to stay.

On smaller frame sizes, it has become customary to use a sloping top tube—higher in the front than near the seat. This allows the use of a reasonably long head tube (the most critical factor for adequate rigidity and predictable steering).

A briefly popular design was characterized by raised chainstays. This allows the use of a very short wheelbase and prevents the chain from getting caught between the tire and the right-hand chainstay (referred to as "chain-suck").

Another eye-catching frame design is the one used by GT, on which the seatstays cross the seat tube about 3 inches below the seat lug and continue on to the top tube. It's based on a French touring design by specialty frame builder Jo Routens. Although there's nothing wrong with it, it has no discernible advantage on mountain bikes.

Then there are the various frames with suspension. Even if the bike has a front suspension only, the frame should really be designed with that in mind, as the distance by which the fork gives must be accommodated. Today, many frames are

Shimano's mountain bike component groups have gone through many incarnations. This was the Deore XT version before the introduction of the V-brake. Although for many years Shimano would not break up component groups, you will now often see bikes with most of the components from such a group, complemented with parts such as SRAM's Grip Shift twistgrip shifters. And the pedals found on even quite nicely equipped bikes may be of a much lower-quality component group, due to the fact that most potential buyers intend to replace them with clipless pedals— most of which are not CPSC-approved because they don't come with reflectors.

actually designed with the suspension fork in mind, but adding a suspension fork to an older frame may detract from the bike's handling characteristics. Frames with rear suspension are an even more complicated matter, requiring very special frames designed around the particular type of sus-

pension used, and there are now many different designs on the market.

FRAME MATERIALS

Quality frames may be made of alloy steel, titanium, stress-relieved aluminum, or fiber-reinforced resin. Whenever steel

is used, the tubes should be butted, meaning the wall thickness is thinner in the center section than at the ends where the tubes are joined.

The first mountain bikes were made of steel tubing without lugs, as at that time none was available to fit the large diameter tubes needed. There are now lugs available to fit the large-diameter mountain bike tubes, and some excellent mountain bikes are still constructed this way, although the majority of frames are now TIG-welded.

TIG-welded frames built with high-strength alloy steel tubes should have a tube wall thickness of 1.2 mm in the butted sections and no more than 0.8 mm in the center section. Anything thicker and heavier seems to result in a harsh and less nimble ride, even though the difference in weight is only on the order of one or two pounds in all.

Any tubing referred to as Hi-Ten (high tensile), or some similar term, is merely carbon steel. Such frames are both heavier and weaker on account of the material's inferior strength as compared to steel alloys.

The type of tubing used is generally acknowledged by a sticker attached to the seat tube.

Aluminum tubing varies greatly from one make and design to another. It should be made of even greater diameters and wall thicknesses than steel tubes to be adequately rigid and strong, respectively, due to the material's inherent characteristics.

Titanium falls somewhere in between, being about as strong as steel but lighter and more flexible; titanium tubes should be slightly larger in diameter than steel tubes.

FRAME DETAILS

Several other points affect the quality of your frame. The drop-outs (the flat parts in which the rear wheel is installed) on a steel frame, should be thick and rounded, indicating that they are made of either forged or investment-cast steel. These are superior in strength and rigidity to the type made of flat, stamped steel plate. On aluminum frames, the drop-outs should have removable stainless steel fixtures bolted on. Otherwise, they had

Frame detail: oversized head tube on a TIG-welded steel frame, showing meticulous welding detail.

Cable routing detail under the bottom bracket: one cable runs up to the front derailleur, the other back to the rear derailleur.

Another way of doing it: seat lug cluster on a Ritchey custom-built frame without quick-release seatpost clamp. Also note the cable routing for the rear brake. That's the kind of workmanship and attention to detail you can get only on hand-built frames like this one.

better be really thick, to the point of being ugly, because thin aluminum ones will bend or break too easily.

The slot for the rear wheel in the drop-outs may be either vertical or horizontal. Vertical drop-outs allow closer clearances between the wheel and the chainstay bridge, resulting in a more rigid rear end. Because the wheel cannot be adjusted by pushing it forward more on one side than on the other, this kind of drop-out requires precision when building the frame. Check from behind, looking along both wheels, to make sure the wheels track, meaning they are perfectly aligned, when the axle is at the top of the slot on both sides. If they don't, only a frame builder or an experienced bike shop mechanic can correct that problem.

There is a derailleur eye on the right-hand drop-out. It should be at least as thick as the rest of the drop-out, to make sure it does not get bent, which would result in derailleur misalignment and consequently in unpredictable gear shifting.

The bridge pieces between the chainstays and the seatstays should be attached with perfectly smooth and unin-terrupted welds or brazed joints. The same goes for the various other braze-ons, which should include the following:

1. Pivot bosses for the rear brake on the seatstays. Although there is a certain degree of standardization, check when replacing brakes that they match the bosses on the frame by inquiring about interchangeability at a bike shop.

2. A rigid cable stop for the end of the outer brake cable if cantilever brakes are used. (V-brakes do not need cable stops.)

3. Guides or tunnels for the brake and gear cables, including stops at those points where outer cable sections are interrupted.

4. Threaded eyelets for the installation of a luggage rack and fenders, as well as a hole in the bridge between the seatstays to mount fenders. Even if you don't plan to install such accessories, it doesn't hurt to know you can accommodate them.

5. Threaded bosses for the installation of water bottle cages. Three locations are suitable: the front of the seat tube, the top of the down-tube, and below the downtube.

6. One or more pegs or anchors for

the pump. A nice place is along the rear side of the seat tube, if the chainstays are long enough to provide adequate clearance there, leaving the front of the seat tube free.

FRAME FINISH

Steel frames get painted, and the better the paint, the harder it is. Many titanium frames and some aluminum ones are left bare, or merely covered with a transparent lacquer. Generally, paint does not adhere to aluminum and titanium as well, and because these materials build up a thin layer of dense oxidation that actually protects the underlying material, they can do without paint (although aluminum corrodes rapidly in a salty atmosphere, such as near the ocean or in areas where the roads are often treated with salt to remove snow).

Paint is about the only feature that most manufacturers have to distinguish their wares from those of the competition, and for that reason you will see some wild color schemes at times. Simple paint jobs have the advantage of being easier to touch up, keeping your bike looking like new much longer.

SEVENTEEN

THE WHEELS

Mountain bike wheels are like those of any other bicycle—they just have fatter and knobbier tires. They are spoked wheels with wired-on tires, also referred as clincher tires. Wired-on tires consist of a separate inner tube and a tire casing that is held on in a deep-bedded metal rim by means of wire-reinforced beads. The other components of the wheel are the hub and the spokes that connect the hub with the rim.

THE HUB

The hub forms the heart of the wheel. It is attached to fork or frame by means of a quick-release mechanism or by means of axle nuts. Although theoretically the solid axle used for wheels that are held with axle nuts is slightly stronger, modern quick-release hubs are adequate for mountain bike use, although high-quality nutted axles are still available for tandem wheels. Cheap mountain bikes may also have (crude) nutted axles.

The hub consists of a hollow shell with flanges, to which the spokes are attached. It rotates around the axle on a set of bearings in the hub shell. Bearings may be either adjustable cup-and-cone bearings or non-adjustable cartridge bearings. Either way, they should be equipped with good dust seals. The hub must have the same number of spoke holes as the rim, usually 32 on a modern mountain bike.

Special front hubs with larger-diameter axles are available for use with suspension forks. These help keep the fork blades aligned, which increases the steering predictability and the fork's life expectancy.

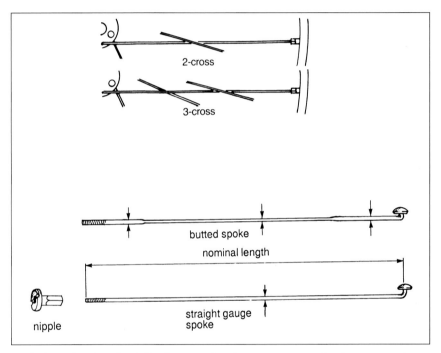

Spoke and spoking details. Top: how to tell spoking patterns apart. Simply count out the number of spokes on the same side of the wheel that any one spoke crosses to determine whether your wheel is one-, two-, or three-cross spoking. Bottom: How to tell butted and straight-gauge spokes apart. It also shows how spokes are measured.

The width of the hub is measured as the over-locknut dimension, which should correspond to the internal width between fork-ends or the drop-outs. For the front hub it's typically the same as for road bikes, that is 100 mm. For the rear hub this dimension may be as much as 135 mm, compared to 125 mm for most modern road hubs. The greater width gives the wheel more lateral stability.

The quick-release is not opened or closed by unscrewing or tightening the thumb nut, nor by using the lever as a wing nut, but by twisting the lever in the appropriate direction to tighten or loosen the internal cam mechanism. Only if the wheel does not come out with the lever set in the *open* position should you loosen the thumb nut one or two turns, not forgetting to tighten it again when installing the wheel, *before* tightening the lever.

THE SPOKES

Each spoke is held to the hub flange by its head, and to the rim by means of a

Different tires for different purposes. These tires from Specialized show a general-purpose pattern (left) and a dirt-grabbing (right) profile, respectively, the latter tire also being considerably wider.

screwed-on nipple. The nipple should be kept tightened to maintain the spoke under tension, preventing a lot of spoke breakages. The spokes run from the hub to the rim in one of several distinct patterns. The illustration shows one-, two-, and three-cross spoking patterns. Generally the three-cross pattern is most suitable for the rear wheel of a bike with 32 spokes; it really does not matter on a front wheel, unless it has a drum brake or disk brake (sometimes used on downhill bikes), for which two-cross spoking is recommended.

The rim with the tire must be centered over the ends of the locknuts. On the rear wheel, this normally creates an offset relative to the hub flanges, due to the presence of the freewheel on the right-hand side. The offset results in much higher forces on the spokes leading to the right-hand flange than in those on the other side. This leads to broken spokes on the right-hand side and makes it hard to keep the wheel trued. On modern bikes this is less of a problem than it once was thanks to the use of cassette hubs, which are not as uneven as hubs with separate freewheels. The more gears (resulting in more cogs on the right-hand side of the hub), the more likely this is to be a problem.

The spoke length is measured from the threaded end to the inside of the bend. Before replacing a broken spoke, or when buying spares to take along on a longer tour, check which sizes are needed for your wheels. They may be different for front and rear, and in the rear even from one side to the other.

Spoke strength is a function of their thickness and flexibility. They should be at least 2.0 mm (14 gauge or less—a smaller gauge number corresponds to a bigger diameter), at least at the ends.

Typical mountain bike wheel: 26-inch knobby tires mounted on an aluminum rim, laced to a quick-release hub by means of 2-mm thick stainless steel spokes.

Butted spokes have a thinner section in the middle and are as strong as plain gauge spokes that are as thick as their thickest section. These are less likely to break, due to their greater flexibility.

THE RIM

Mountain bike rims typically have the cross-section shown in the illustration, which also shows how the tire fits on, as well as the tire sizing convention. All mountain bike rims have a diameter of 559 mm at the point where the tire seats. The rims should be made of aluminum. In addition to being light, aluminum ensures much

better braking when wet than the chrome plating used on steel rims found only on cheap mass-market bikes. Stronger models are a little heavier, but on really rough terrain they are well worth the extra weight.

The rim should match the tire size. The trend in recent years has been toward narrower rims, like 20 mm measured inside. Narrow rims have an advantage in terms of rolling resistance and even puncture protection of the tire. The narrower seat forces a greater portion of the tire to bulge out, making the tire more cushioned and flexible.

The spoke holes in the rim should be reinforced by means of ferrules. To protect the tube, a strip of rim tape should cover the part of the rim bed where the spoke nipples would otherwise touch the inner tube.

THE TIRES

The size of the tire defines the nominal size of the wheel. Adult mountain bikes have 26-inch wheels with tires that may be anywhere from 1.6 to 2.2 inches wide. Hybrids generally have 700 mm tires of narrower width. These nominal sizes don't necessarily coincide exactly with their actual dimensions.

It all depends on the tire cross section, or width. The rim for a mountain bike tire has a rim bed diameter of 559 mm. Add to that twice the actual tire cross section, and you have the tire's outside diameter. Even though this system has been adapted as a (worldwide) ISO standard, it continues to be ignored by most manufacturers from the United States and their Asian suppliers.

The recommended tire width depends on the terrain. The minimum width suitable for any kind of off-road cycling is probably 47 mm (1.75 inches), whereas 59 mm (2.2 inches) is the cat's whiskers for very soft and

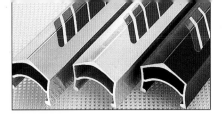

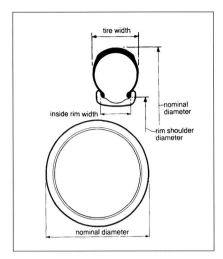

Rim and tire details. The top detail shows a cross-section through a rim with the tire mounted on it. Although most mountain bike rims have the shape shown here, they may vary in width and depth. This drawing also illustrates the meaning of the dimensions quoted for tire sizing.

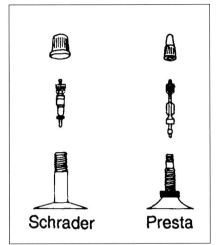

Presta and Schrader valves compared. The Presta valve offers less resistance to inflate, but the Schrader valve can be inflated with a gas-station air hose. They require different pump heads and the hole in the rim should be bigger for a Schrader valve than it should be for a Presta valve.

Campagnolo mountain bike rims—one of the few items still remaining of the prestigious Italian component manufacturer's offerings for mountain bikers. They're among the best available.

Most mountain bike wheels are held in places with a quick-release. Before removing and installing a wheel, first open up the brakes so that they clear the tire. See the text for instructions regarding the correct use of the quick-release.

very rocky ground. The 1.6-inch-wide tires found on cheaper imports are only suitable if you ride on well-surfaced trails.

The rolling resistance of a tire is a function of the extent to which the tire or the road deforms at their contact area. On a smooth, hard road surface, the only way to fly is with a tire that is inflated really hard. On soft ground, on the other hand, that tire had better be a little softer.

Soft ground calls for pressures of no more than 1.7 bar (25 psi) at low speeds, a little higher at higher speeds. On smooth asphalt or other smooth hard surfaces, you may go all the way to 5 bar (75 psi) for high-speed cycling. All other combinations lie somewhere in between. Experiment with tire pressures for different kinds of riding, frequently checking with a tire pressure gauge, until you have developed a feel for the pressure that is best for certain conditions.

There are numerous different tread patterns. What will be best for you depends on where and how you ride. The very knobby tires that are characteristic of early mountain bikes are still ideal for off-road cycling, especially on soft ground or snow. Knobs that are offset relative to one another, forming distinct interruptions between the rows of

knobs, provide good traction on soft and loose surfaces. Patterns on which the knobs are offset in a continuous pattern provide less rolling resistance but also less traction. Tires with a so-called negative tread pattern, with large projections and small recesses are the most durable.

Smooth tires, called slicks, work fine on regular roads and hard rocky surfaces, even when it is wet. They work best when inflated to a high pressure (about 4 bar, or 60 psi), as the pressure between tire and road is proportional to the inflation pressure, and the higher this pressure, the better the chance that water is pushed out from under the tire, which is essential for good contact.

Recently, tires have been introduced that are smooth on top and knobby on the sides; these offer low rolling resistance on smooth surfaces and good grip when cornering. To optimize their traction on rough surfaces, run them at about 1.7 bar (25 psi).

For icy conditions, there are studded tires. The Finnish Nokia Oy company has made them for many years, but only recently introduced them in a size to fit the mountain bike's 559 mm rim. IRC also introduced a studded tire, called Blizzard, which is more readily available in the

United States. Another interesting solution is a type of snow chain that can be installed around a standard tire—deflate the tire, put on the chain, and then reinflate the tire to tighten the chain.

TUBE AND VALVE

The tube is inflated by means of a valve, available in two versions. The Presta valve requires less force to inflate. Unscrew the round nut at the tip before inflating, and tighten it again afterwards. To inflate a Presta valve with a gas station air hose, you'll need an adapter nipple. Even if you have one, chances are the thing leaks air. This is the reason most manufacturers still install tubes with Schrader valves, as used on car tires.

Ideally, the tube should closely match the size of the tire, although most tubes stretch enough to go either from 1.5 to 1.9 inches or from 1.75 to 2.2 inches cross section. The lowest rolling resistance is offered by the lightest and most flexible tubes.

CHAPTER EIGHTEEN

THE DRIVETRAIN

The mountain bike's drivetrain comprises the components that transmit your effort to the rear wheel: pedals, crankset (comprising bottom bracket, cranks, and chainrings), chain, and freewheel with cogs. The derailleur system will be treated separately in the next chapter.

THE CRANKSET

The crankset (chain-set to our British readers) is the heart of the drivetrain. It comprises several different components, which will each be described in the following sections—the bottom bracket, cranks, and chainrings. Generally, all these components are supplied as a group of matching parts by the same manufacturer, but you can also select parts from various manufacturers or different models to make up the system.

THE BOTTOM BRACKET

Sometimes referred to as crank hanger in Britain, the bottom bracket is the set of bearings in the frame's bottom bracket shell, together with the spindle, or axle, to which the cranks are attached. Two types are in common use: the conventional adjustable BSA bearing and the system with machine bearings contained in a preassembled cartridge, often referred to as sealed bearings. On both types, the spindle has tapered square ends for the installation of cotterless cranks.

On high-quality bottom brackets, the spindle is hollow and the cranks are held with bolts; cheaper models use solid axles with threaded protrusions to which the cranks are held with nuts.

Either type of bottom bracket can be provided with some kind of seals to keep dirt out and lubricant in. But neither type can be perfectly sealed, so some kind of cleaning and lubrication will be required from time to time, even on things referred to as sealed bearings. This is actually easier on the adjustable model than it is on the cartridge type, which may have to be replaced in its entirety.

Although the cartridge bearing is often thought to be superior, the size of the bearings relative to the total unit is actually smaller than they are on the adjustable model, which makes them weaker, all else being equal. Consequently, as long as parts of adequate quality are used and they are adjusted and lubricated regularly, a conventional BSA bottom bracket can give excellent service. It is certainly not inherently inferior to the cartridge bearing variety, as is sometimes implied.

THE CRANKS

Virtually all mountain bikes have aluminum cranks that are attached to the ends of the bottom bracket spindle by means of a cotterless device. The crank has a square

The mountain bike's drivetrain. This is a high-end machine from Specialized, showing a crankset with triple chainrings, clipless pedals, and a Shimano HyperGlide cassette freewheel with matching chain. We'll look at the derailleurs separately in Chapter 19.

tapered hole that matches the square tapered end of the spindle. A bolt—or sometimes a nut, if the bottom bracket spindle is not hollow but has threaded projections—clamps the crank over the spindle, and a dustcap covers the recess from the outside. The type with bolts is preferable, because once the type with nuts has been disassembled, it'll hardly ever get back together firmly enough, resulting in creaking noises when you pedal.

The right-hand crank has an attachment spider for the chainrings. The pattern of the holes in the spider may vary from make to make and even from model to model. It must correspond to the particular chainrings installed. When replacing either cranks or chainrings, the interchangeability restrictions must be considered: count the number of attachment bolts (usually five, sometimes four on newer high-end models) and measure the distance between them.

The square taper is not standardized either. Consequently, you may find when replacing either the cranks or the bottom bracket that a crank either hits the chainstay or does not seat fully on the spindle. Consult a bike shop to find out what fits and what doesn't. A comprehensive source of interchangeability information in general is *Sutherland's Handbook for Bicycle Mechanics*, which the bike shop may have available for reference.

Cranks are made in several different lengths. Some mountain bike riders swear by longer cranks, rather than the standard length of 170 or 175 mm. This dimension is measured from the center of the bottom bracket spindle hole to the center of the pedal hole. If your legs are longer than average, 180 mm or even 185 mm cranks may be justified, whereas a shorter rider may be happier with 165 mm long cranks.

Usually, the crank attachment bolt or nut is covered by a dustcap, which protects the screw thread in the recess. This screw thread is used to pull the crank off the spindle for maintenance or replacement by means of a crank extractor tool. The right-hand crank has an attachment spider or ring, to which the chainrings are bolted. On many recent models, the bolt takes the form of an Allen bolt and a

The bottom bracket unit, shown here, is the heart of the drivetrain. This high-end unit with cartridge bearings is Ritchey's ProLite Ti—yes, that stands for titanium, and that's what the spindle is made of (a very expensive way to reduce the weight by about 30 grams).

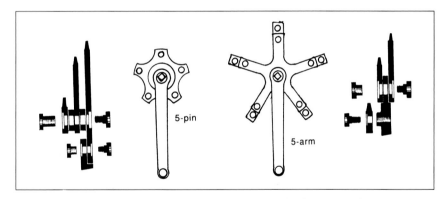

Connection detail for the chainrings on the mountain bike's triple crankset—which does not mean that it comes with three cranks but with three chainrings.

neoprene ring is placed around it, eliminating the need for a dustcap.

During the first few weeks, the crank's aluminum deforms so much that the connection between spindle and crank comes loose frequently until you have covered about 150 to 300 km (100 to 200 miles). For this reason you should carry the wrench part of the crank tool in your repair kit. Chapter 28 explains how to go about this work.

THE CHAINRINGS

Mountain bike-specific chainrings are available in sets of three, usually with 10-tooth differences, for example, 24, 34, and 44 teeth. (Smaller sizes, intended for use with smaller sets of cogs in the back to give the same gearing, are referred to as compact drive chainrings.) Because the numbers of teeth are a matter of gearing, we'll cover that subject in Chapter 19. Here we shall look only at the mechanical aspects of the chainrings.

The chainrings are attached to the right-hand crank with four or five bolts, by one of the methods shown in the illustration. The method shown in the right-hand detail is generally the more satisfactory. It results in greater strength and

If you thought chainring and sprocket teeth were just teeth, think again. The improvement in shifting ease and reliability of the last 10 years is as much due to careful orthodontic work on the chainrings as to the more publicized advances in derailleur and shifter design. The teeth on the smaller chainrings are designed specifically to aid the chain in shifting to the next smaller or bigger one at specific points.

rigidity, leading to fewer cases of bent and buckled chainrings. It also depends on the hardness of the materials used, which accounts for a lot of the price difference between superficially similar components. On cheaper bikes, the chainrings are made of thin stamped steel, whereas more sophisticated models are thicker and made of a hard aluminum alloy, machined to more exacting standards of accuracy. Even so, the steel ones work just fine when new, and their advantage is that the teeth can be bent (by the manufacturer) into some fancy pattern to improve shifting.

During the late 1980s and early 1990s, most mountain bikes were equipped with chainrings that were not truly round. The Shimano Biopace design was the most popular of these. The idea was based on some physiological fallacies dressed up with very scientific-looking graphs and formulas touted by Shimano and faithfully copied by editors of bicycle magazines.

Accomplished riders almost invariably preferred round chainrings even at the time. The only justification for the off-round designs may exist at inefficient low pedaling speeds that some novice riders may indeed use. This results in an irregular force distribution over the pedal cycle. True, the odd-shaped chainrings were one

way to solve that problem. But only temporarily. The preferable solution would all along have been to teach them to cycle at a higher pedaling rate, changing down to the appropriate gear to do so.

THE PEDALS

Mountain bikes are often equipped with clipless pedals, for which matching shoes are required. In the shop, though, even most of the expensive bikes may be displayed with cheap

Pedals old and new. Conventional pedals are used with toeclips and have the advantage that they can be ridden with regular shoes. Clipless pedals are more elegant, often lighter, and remarkably effective, keeping your feet in place, yet allowing you to exit them quickly in an emergency by merely twisting your feet slightly. You will need special shoes with matching plates installed,

pedals to keep the price down, knowing that you'll probably pay the extra to get clipless ones anyway.

Early mountain bike pedals were designed for more grip on regular shoes than those installed on road bikes. More recently, riders and manufacturers have found out there is no real advantage to such vicious, jagged-looking implements as the "bear trap" pedals borrowed from BMX bikes, so now quite elegant pedals are *en vogue*, even if they're not clipless.

Some pedals are made of resin-embedded graphite fiber, which are not very durable. When they get hard to turn, replace them with something better, preferably either clipless models or light metal pedals that have angled sides, front and rear, because these are the easiest to get on and off, whether with or without toeclips.

At least as important as the pedal's exterior shape are its guts. Two satisfactory designs exist: adjustable ball bearings and cartridge types on which bearings and spindle come as one replaceable unit (the latter invariably used on clipless models). Whether adjustable or not, the most important difference relative to any old pedal should be the need for a dust seal on the crank-side bearing.

When selecting clipless pedals, avoid models that have to be a certain way around to work, because it will be hard to coerce them into the right direction when trying to get your feet in. Shimano's SPD pedals, which are reversible, have become the unofficial standard, so most other manufacturers make sure their shoes and pedals match the same pattern.

THE CHAIN

Mountain bikes are equipped with the same 1/2 x 3/32 inch chains that are used on other derailleur bikes. These dimensions refer to the length between two consecutive pins and the internal width between the inner link plates, respectively. The chain should be long enough to wrap around the largest chainring, the largest cog, and the derailleur pulleys, while still leaving a little spring travel in the derailleur mechanism. (Avoid this combination of gears when riding; but your equipment should be able to handle it.)

You will need a narrow chain, such as the Shimano HyperGlide, if your bike has a freewheel block with eight cogs. The narrow chain has the same nominal dimensions and the same internal size, but the pins do not protrude as far. The disadvantage of the now popular kind of chains with "bulging" link plates is that they wear and literally stretch, requiring frequent replacement. They are now extremely popular on account of their greater lateral flexibility, which eases shifting.

The chain line is the path the chain follows from chainring to cog. It should preferably be parallel to the centerline of the bike. That's achieved when the intermediate chainring lines up perfectly with the middle cog on a freewheel block with seven cogs, with the point between the third and the fourth if it has six, and between the fourth and the fifth if it has eight cogs. Unfortunately, this situation is very hard to achieve, due to the constraints of the bike's geometry. Corrections to the chain line can be made by any combination of the following:

1. Adjusting the bottom bracket.
2. Inserting spacers.
3. Straightening the frame if it is bent.

Any of these jobs are best left to an experienced bike shop mechanic, although the basics are covered in Chapter 28.

THE FREEWHEEL

Today's mountain bikes are generally equipped with what is called a cassette freewheel hub. That's a rear-wheel hub to which the freewheel mechanism is attached in the form of a splined extension on the right-hand side, and the cogs are installed on it.

In the early days of mountain biking, most manufacturers used a screwed-on freewheel block with five, six, or seven cogs that was screwed onto the right-hand end of a (threaded) rear hub. Since then, the cassette hub has become almost universal.

The cassette freewheel mechanism is attached to the hub with a hollow

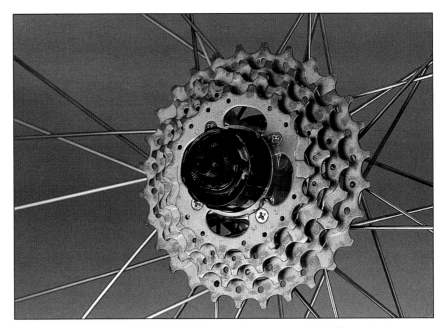

The big part of a freewheel cluster on a modern mountain bike. These four bigger cogs are installed as a unit, while the four smaller ones are slipped on separately on this Shimano XTR cassette freewheel.

Allen bolt and carries the wheel's right-hand bearing; the cogs are installed on it on splines and locked in place by means of a threaded ring or a threaded smallest cog. Most of the high-end cassette units now take eight cogs, and with nine-cog clusters now used on road bikes, they're beginning to show up on mountain bikes.

The advantages of the cassette system are easy cog replacement and a less pronounced difference between the left-hand and right-hand side of the rear wheel. The latter difference reduces the difference in spoke tension between left- and right-side spokes, which can be quite significant on a wheel with a screwed-on freewheel, leading to more frequent spoke breakage and other wheel problems.

DRIVETRAIN DEVELOPMENTS

Around 1992, SunTour, which was at the time still a force in mountain bike componentry, introduced the MicroDrive system, based on smaller chainrings and cogs, and Shimano soon followed with what it calls Compact Drive, now used on most bikes.

With these systems, you can still achieve the same gearing, but with fewer teeth both on the chainring and the cogs. Not only does this save some weight, it also increases the clearance between the ground and the chainrings. Finally, they also make it possible to keep the cranks a little closer together, a feature some manufacturers refer to as a "small Q-factor" (as though "narrow cranks" would be too descriptive).

Other ways to reduce weight and bulk include the use of an intermediate spider to mount the larger cogs on top-of-the-line rear hubs and, from small specialist manufacturers, a proliferation of expensive hollow parts.

Another interesting drivetrain development is the concept of two-wheel drive. This method can provide spectacularly improved traction and handling, advantages that are most noticeable on loose and slippery surfaces, such as wet slickrock, loose sand, snow, and ice. Different varieties are introduced at the annual trade shows with some regularity, but as of this writing none has reached the level of successful series production.

CHAPTER NINETEEN

THE GEARING SYSTEM

The gearing system comprises a front derailleur and a rear derailleur (sometimes called changer and "mech," short for mechanism, respectively, in Britain). The two derailleurs are operated by means of shifters mounted on the handlebars and connected to the derailleurs via flexible control cables. The rear derailleur moves the chain sideways from one cog to another on a freewheel block or cassette mounted on the rear wheel; the front derailleur moves the chain sideways from one chainring to another.

Since the various cogs and chainrings have different numbers of teeth, varying the combination achieves a lower or higher gear. As explained in Chapter 6, you get the lowest gear by selecting the small chainring in the front and the biggest cog in the rear. The highest gear results when you combine the large chainring with the smallest cog. All other combinations fall somewhere in between.

Nowadays, all mountain bikes come equipped with indexed gearing. That means that there are distinct stops on the shift levers for each of the gears, eliminating the need for fidgety adjustments when shifting. Older bikes had what is now referred to as friction shifters, and selecting the right gear was a bit more fidgety.

Although some component manufacturers claim universal compatibility of their equipment with most other makes and models of other components, this is in some cases true only for perfectly adjusted and unworn components. In practice, it may still

An overview of the mountain bike's gearing: front derailleur and rear derailleur, with which the chain can be moved from any of three chainrings in the front to any of six, seven, or eight cogs in the back.

be better to have a shifter from the same manufacturer as the derailleur, which in turn will work best on a matching freewheel. But since Shimano has become the de facto standard, most other manufacturers now make sure their items are fully compatible with Shimano drivetrain components.

The derailleurs used on mountain bikes differ from road bike models in that they accommodate the wide-range gearing typically used, and the shifters are designed to be installed on flat handlebars.

THE REAR DERAILLEUR

The rear derailleur comprises a spring-tensioned hinged parallelogram mechanism that pivots over a certain arc around the mounting bolt. A spring-tensioned cage with two little wheels, or pulleys, is attached at the end of the parallelogram. The chain runs through this cage, over the pulleys.

When the cable is pulled or released via the shifter, the mechanism moves over to the next position to the left or the right, corresponding to a different gear. As your pedaling motion pulls the chain forward, it is guided by the two pulleys in the cage to the next cog position, engaging the appropriate higher or lower gear.

The shifter has a ratchet mechanism that is stepped to correspond to the rear derailleur positions for the various gears. These specific positions are not pre-set in the derailleur but in the shifter. Consequently, in case of cable stretch or damage to any component, the system is likely to go out of adjustment. These problems are typically corrected by adjusting the cable at the shifter or the derailleur—see Chapter 29. For the rest, just keep the mechanism clean and lightly oiled.

The wide gearing range of mountain bike derailleurs is usually achieved with a relatively long cage, with the two pulleys lying quite far apart. In many cases, it is quite possible to get by with a short-cage derailleur, which is much less sensitive to damage than the long-cage variety. Because specifications change, ask someone in the bike shop to check whether the gearing combination you have in mind works with a short-cage model.

THE FRONT DERAILLEUR

The mountain bike's front derailleur, or changer, is a much simpler mechanism than the one in the rear. It is attached to the seat tube just above the chainrings and consists of a cage through which the chain is guided, attached to a simple hinge or parallelogram mechanism to move it sideways, carrying the chain over to the next chainring. Since there are only three possible positions (two of which—the smallest and the biggest—correspond to end points of the shifter's range of travel anyway), there's really not as much need for indexing. However, certainly since the increase in popularity of the twistgrip shifter, these too are now indexed. (Again it's the shifter, not the derailleur itself that's indexed.)

As far as maintenance is concerned, there is little to do here. It is usually enough to keep the mechanism clean and the pivots lightly lubricated. Make sure it is attached at the right height and with the cage parallel to the plane of the chainrings. If shifting is not accurate, an adjustment of the derailleur cable tension usually is all that is needed. When you can't reach the extreme gear or conversely overshift, dumping the chain, you should adjust the range of travel of the cage—see Chapter 29.

A close look at the rear derailleur and the way it guides the chain over the rear cogs.

SHIFTER MECHANISMS

Shifting has changed more than anything else since the start of mountain biking. During a two-year period, Grip Shift (or more generically twistgrip) seemed to be the name of the game but under-the-bar shifters (such as Shimano's Rapid Fire Plus) have come back. Up to about 1988 all mountain bikes were shifted with single-lever shifters that were mounted on top of the handlebars. Since then, double-lever shifters mounted under the handlebars were introduced, soon followed by the twistgrip. For use with drop handlebars, there are still bar-end models available, which are not indexed. Whatever type it is, the shifter controlling the rear derailleur is mounted on the right, and the one for the front on the left.

Twistgrip shifters are mounted on the handlebars where regular handgrips would otherwise go. On early models, the entire handle was twisted to change gear. That was a potentially dangerous configuration, since you could accidentally change gear when, for instance, you hit a pothole in your path. That's why Sachs first brought out its twistring model, on which the handgrip itself stayed steady, whereas the twisting mechanism was in the form of a ring at the forward end of the handgrip. Later Grip Shift followed suit and now all current models are divided into a part that acts as a handgrip and stays steady and a part that is turned to shift gear.

Top-mounted shifters usually have an auxiliary lever with which the indexing mode can be overridden in case there are alignment problems, leaving you at least the opportunity to shift in the so-called friction mode, just like older derailleur systems. This feature is a

The front derailleur is mounted just above the chainrings with its cage parallel to them.

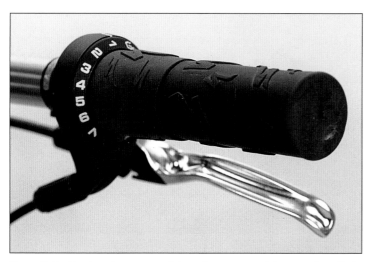

First off the block with twistgrip shifters for mountain bikes was Grip Shift.

There are other ways to skin a cat. First came top-mounted shifters (bottom), then came under-the-bar shifters, shown here with something Shimano rather redundantly calls "optical viewing" (top).

big advantage in case you go on longer tours farther away from "civilization," allowing you to use your gears even if the shifting is no longer indexed.

To ensure the most reliable and predictable shifting possible, make sure shifters and derailleurs are compatible with each other. Again, Shimano being the main supplier, it's easier to get stuff that is compatible with theirs. However, even with the same make, there are differences: low-end components are not fully interchangeable with high-end Shimano components—specifically the XTR models.

DERAILLEUR CABLES

The shifters are connected to the derailleurs by means of flexible control cables. The cable for the indexed derailleurs should be relatively stiff and thick, also requiring a larger-diameter outer cable. They are usually sold in complete sets of fixed length. One end of the cable has a soldered-on nipple, which is inserted at the shifter end; the other end of the inner cable is clamped at the derailleur in an eye bolt or under a notched plate with a pinch bolt.

Between the shifter and the derailleur, the cable is routed over and through guides mounted on the frame. If you use drop handlebars with bar-end shifters, the top end of the cable is routed along the handlebars, under the handlebar tape.

GEARING NOVELTIES

Two interesting alternatives to conventional derailleur systems come from Europe. Sachs makes a system called 3 x 7. It combines a seven-speed rear derailleur with a three-speed hub. Used without a front derailleur, it still gives 21-speed gearing, and 63 speeds if it's used in conjunction with a front derailleur.

The other system is the Mountain Drive from Switzerland, which replaces the front derailleur with a planetary gear system inserted between the chainrings and the cranks. It can be operated either from a handlebar shifter or simply by kicking against the center of the crank.

TWENTY

THE BRAKES

raking can have two purposes: to regulate speed gently or to come to a sudden stop. Whether you're braking to slow down or to come to a halt, you have to decelerate the bike. There's a lot of kinetic energy stored in the moving mass of bike and rider. The brakes are used to dissipate some or all of that energy. If you did not dissipate the energy by braking, you'd eventually do it by hitting the obstacle—with disastrous results.

TYPES OF RIM BRAKES

For the mountain bike, there are now really only two types of brakes in general use: cantilever brakes and V-brakes (also called direct-pull brakes). Older bikes may have U-brakes or roller-cam brakes, and a few use either hydraulically operated rim brakes or disk brakes.

Even the humble cantilever brake has gone through a slow evolution, becoming narrower, though not necessarily any better, as time went on. Newer versions of the cantilever, referred to as *low-profile* (more correctly *narrow-profile*) brakes are designed in such a way that they don't project sideways as much. Even the V-brake is really nothing but the next step in the evolution of the cantilever brake, on which the upward-pulling straddle cable has been replaced by a sideways contraction between the inner and outer cables, each attached to a brake arm.

On all rim brakes, a pair of brake pads is pushed against the sides of the rim when the brake is applied. On the cantilever and U-brake, this is done via a cantilever system pulled together with a connecting cable. On the roller-cam brake, the brake arms are spread apart at the opposite end by means of a wedge-shaped plate guided between rollers on the brake arms. On all of these, the brake arms are installed on pivot bosses that are attached directly to the fork for the front brake, to the seatstays or chainstays for the one in the rear.

The paramount criterion for a good brake is that it must be rigid, while still opening up far enough to clear the fat tires. All of these designs allow this, although you must ascertain whether the pivot bosses are installed in a position that allows the use of the particular brake selected. When comparing different versions of the same basic system, look for a type that provides maximum rigidity and smooth operation.

The most expensive V-brakes have a parallelogram linkage to keep the brake pads aligned with the rim. It works when new but adds complexity and is likely to lead to premature wear. Simpler models will probably last longer.

If your brakes don't work properly, first check to make sure the wheel rims are clean and dry. If that's not the problem, refer to Chapter 30 for adjustment and maintenance instructions.

BRAKE CONTROLS

The brake's control system consists of the brake levers and the cables. The brake lever should be rigid. It must work smoothly and be easy to reach, while allowing full application of the brake, leaving about 2-centimeters (3/4-inch) clearance between

The mountain bike's traditional brake is the cantilever. Although it has gone through an evolution of its own before it became the low-profile (a misnomer for narrow-profile) type shown here, they all work the same. The narrower the profile, the blunter the angle of the straddle cable should be to pull the brake arms forcefully together. That's why the oldest versions actually often work best.

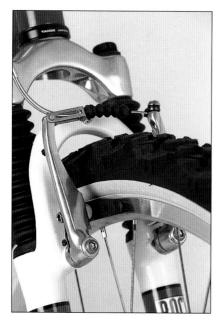
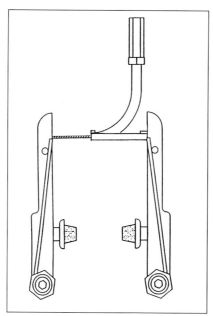
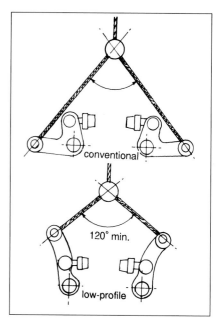

Today's fashion brake is the V-brake, first introduced by Marinovative (above right) as the "Cheap Trick" (belying its price tag and the use of titanium), and copied by Shimano and others as mass-produced versions (above left). Unlike other mountain bike brakes, it's self-contained, with the restraint for the outer cable as part of the brake unit itself. Looks like it's going to be the brake of choice for a long time to come, taking over in the same way the (also self-contained) sidepull brake has on road bikes.

On cantilever brakes, the angle at the top of the straddle cable should be a function of the brake's projection. On the more modern low-profile brakes (bottom detail) the angle has to be quite wide for the brake to work properly.

the handlebars and the lever. The type of levers designed for mountain bikes are quite suitable for any bike with flat handlebars, providing the attachment clamp matches the bar diameter. If you use drop handlebars, you will need road bike brake levers.

The cable has a soldered-on nipple that is hooked into a recess in the lever mechanism. The cable is partly contained in flexible outer cable and restrained at anchor points on the frame or, in the case of the V-brake, on one of the brake arms. Most friction is caused by the sections that run through outer cable, so keep those sections to a minimum.

All rim brake controls have an adjustment mechanism that allows you to take up any slack in the cable. In addition to the adjuster integrated in the lever, there may be an additional one at a cable anchor point. If you use a drop bar with road bike levers, this will be your only adjuster.

While the first mountain bikes had very big brake levers, the trend in recent years has been toward ever smaller ones. Gone are the motorcycle brake lever replicas, and elegant little two-finger brake levers are in. Because it is easier to design a lever

strong enough when it is shorter, this is a logical development. These levers allow you to hold the handgrip with the free part of the hand while braking with two fingers.

V-brakes give best performance only if special levers are used, as the amount of cable travel on the sideways pull of this type is less than the vertical pull on the straddle cable of a cantilever (or for that matter a roller-cam or U-brake). These levers have two different positions for the cable nipple, marked "V" and "C" respectively: the first one for use with a V-brake, the other position for use with a conventional cantilever brake—or for any other type.

To allow easy wheel removal and installation without affecting adjustment of the brake, the V-brake has a quick-release fitting on the brake arm to which the outer cable is connected. On cantilever brakes, the straddle cable can be unhooked. To do so, push the brake pads against the rim and at the same time remove the nipple that's held in a slotted brake arm. Something similar can be done with the cam plate on the roller-cam brake, twisting it out from between the rollers.

Although brake cables must be flexible, they should not feel "spongy," when compressed, to allow the application of adequate force. Relatively thick inner cables and non-compressing outer cables, preferably with a low-friction liner made of PTFE (more commonly know by the trade name Teflon) should be used. The cables should be routed as short as possible, providing they are not forced into excessively tight bends in any position of the handlebars.

The straddle, or connecting, cable on cantilever brakes should make a rather wide angle of 120 to 130 degrees at the apex to be effective. The most frequent cause of inadequate braking is too narrow an angle, which you can usually increase by moving the second clamping point inward to shorten the straddle cable, and making the necessary length adjustment of the main cable where it is clamped to the anchor plate.

Most modern cantilever brakes don't use a conventional straddle cable but attach the end of the inner cable directly to one brake arm, while there's a short cable that's connected with the other arm. There's no discernible difference in brake efficiency, but it is more difficult to achieve the right angle.

BRAKE PADS

The brake pads should be of a composition material that provides adequate friction even in the rain, which is not the case with plain rubber brake pads. Longer brake pads are not necessarily better. Although they may last longer, whenever it is wet they actually provide poorer braking than shorter ones. This is due to the fact that the pressure, and thus the ability to remove water between the brake pad and the rim, is greater for a smaller brake pad than for a long one.

Most brake pads can be adjusted in all three planes. For this purpose, they are attached to the brake arm with a bolt and a system of spherical and dished washers that allow angular movement in various directions—See Chapter 30.

BRAKE CHECK

Check the brake's effectiveness from time to time to make sure it won't let you down. First pull each lever with the bike standing still, making sure each brake firmly engages when about 2 centimeters (3/4 inch) of space remains between the brake lever and the handlebars.

Next, riding at walking speed, apply the rear brake fully. It should be possible to block the rear wheel, resulting in skidding. Then do the same with the front brake. In this case, the braking effect should be strong enough to make the bike tip forward if your weight is distributed naturally over handlebars and seat. Release the brake lever if it does.

If either of these criteria is not satisfied, adjust the brake according to the specific instructions for the type of brake in question described in Chapter 30. But before you do, check whether the brake pads touch the rim over their full width when the lever is applied and adjust the position of the brake pads—also described in Chapter 30.

Adjust the brake pads close enough to the rim to ensure they contact the rim fully when applied. Especially on older cantilever brakes, brake pad wear, if left unchecked, eventually causes the brake pad to slip off the rim and hit the spokes, whereas on U-brakes and roller-cam

Other mountain bike brakes that have fallen from grace. In the 1980s, the U-brake (above) and the roller-cam brake (below) enjoyed some popularity, at least in the rear. Both were usually mounted under the chainstays, which made for easier cable routing—and attracting more dirt that would interfere with proper operation. The Shimano sticker on the bike with the roller-cam brake is confusing because that brake was made under license from Wilderness Trail Bicycles by Shimano's then still-active competitor SunTour.

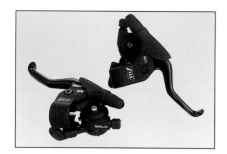

The Shimano levers shown are combined with under-the-bar shifters, but with the increased popularity of twistgrip shifters, separate brake levers are now once more available.

brakes the brake pads would eventually rub on the tire sidewall, which—though not as dangerous—may cause tire wear instead of good braking performance.

OTHER BRAKES

Ever since the introduction of the mountain bike, different brakes have been introduced. Although none have been able to edge out the cantilever and its close cousin the V-brake, some of these are quite interesting.

The various hydraulic brakes work equally well, with the difference that the one made by Magura is almost affordable, whereas most of the others are rather steeply priced. The advantage of hydraulic operation has long been established in motorized vehicles: virtually no losses due to resistance in transmission of brake force from the lever to the brake unit itself, resulting in very direct, while at the same time accurately controllable, brake operation.

Disc brakes, used in the front of some downhill bikes, are an issue apart. They are expensive and heavy, and the front fork and the front wheel really have to be designed around the brake.

How Gustav M works

1. The brake lever pushes a master piston, which presses hydraulic oil through the tubing into the slave cylinders. The master piston, when released, opens a small hole to the reservoir. The heated oil from braking can expand through this hole. This avoids overheating and locking of the disc brake. A membrane in the reservoir prevents air getting into the system when laying down the bike or turning it upside down. The membrane can expand about one cubic centimeter. When the brake pads wear, oil flows automatically back into the system by a second drilling in the reservoir, passing a seal when releasing the master piston. The pressure point of your brake remains always unchanged despite the wear and tear of the brake pads.

2. The two slave pistons, which are placed in the caliper press the outer brake pad against the disc. The caliper is moved horizontally on two guides (floating design); that is why the caliper moves outwards pressing the inner brake pad also against the disc. The specially designed seals in the caliper pull the pistons back. When the brake pads wear, the pistons slide a bit in the seals towards the disc and simultaneously a bit of oil is sucked back from the reservoir into the system.

3. Because of the dual piston design only on one side of the caliper, the spoke flanges on the caliper side can be positioned in a flatter, almost symmetrical angle. This allows to build a super strong, almost symmetrically spoked wheel. Such a wheel is absolutely critical for a disc brake because all of the brake forces have to be transmitted through the spokes.

4. Two slave pistons compared to a single slave piston with the same surface can realize a greater brake power because of the bigger friction diameter. The braking surface of the disc is narrower, resulting in a lighter disc. The caliper can also be built lighter and stiffer because the disc doesn't emerge as far into the caliper as a single piston.

1.

2.

3.

4.

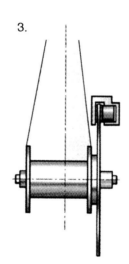

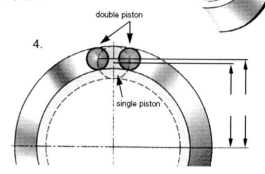

double piston

single piston

Illustration aus **bike** /Stacheter Design)

Disc brakes like those from Magura are necessary for the speeds attained in downhill racing. With each passing year, better materials and technology provides improved brake performance.

CHAPTER TWENTY-ONE

THE STEERING SYSTEM

The steering system comprises the front fork, the headset bearings, the stem, and the handlebars.

STEERING GEOMETRY

What keeps the bike following its own course at some speed is known as trail, the most significant element of steering geometry. Steering geometry is the entire interrelationship of angles and dimensions of the steering system. Trail is depicted in the illustration: it is the horizontal distance between the point where the front wheel contacts the ground and the point where an imaginary line drawn through the steering axis touches the ground.

Two front ends showing steering system components: with rigid front fork (above) and with suspension fork (left)

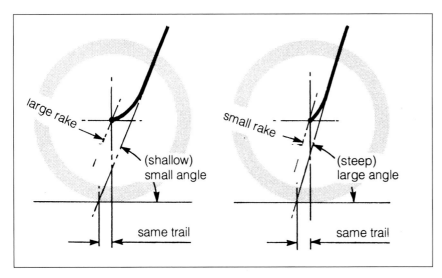

Steering geometry. This illustration defines the relationship between steerer angle and fork rake as they affect trail.

Projected and effective trail compared. At shallower steerer tubes the effective trail varies more with changes in fork rake than the conventionally referenced measure we call projected trail. The effect on the bike's handling is better predicted by the effective trail.

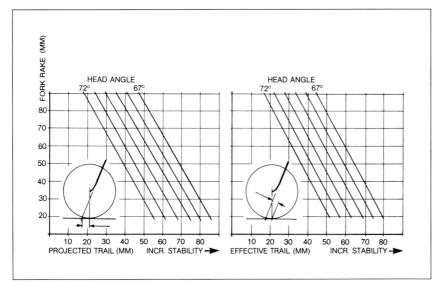

All bicycles have positive trail, meaning that the line through the steering axis intersects the ground at some point *in front* of the contact point between the tire and the ground. The bike's steering and handling would be very volatile if it were the other way round, referred to as negative trail. The amount of trail determines the stability and self-steering characteristics of the bike. Too much trail would make the bike sluggish to handle, so it becomes a matter of fine-tuning.

The bike's steering characteristics also depend on the steerer angle, that is, the angle between the steering axis and the horizontal plane. For any steerer angle, a particular amount of trail results in a certain stability. With a given steerer angle, the trail can be varied by selecting the fork design appropriately. This is achieved by selecting one with more or less fork rake. The rake is the distance by which the fork blades are bent forward. You'll probably never have to worry

about fork rake on a new bike: the manufacturer has taken care of that. But when replacing a fork, you have to get one with the right trail.

To obtain the kind of handling that agrees with off-road cycling, the mountain bike should have more trail than a road bike. This increases the bicycle's tendency to go straight, requiring less force to keep it on course when the front wheel is diverted by irregularities in the surface. The granddaddy of today's mountain bike, the Schwinn Excelsior, had a 68-degree steerer angle and a fork rake of 50 mm (2 inches), resulting in a trail of 60 mm (2 1/4 inches). There probably isn't a better configuration for downhill riding.

However, today's mountain bikes are used for lots of other things. Consequently, different designs are showing up more and more. The range of steerer angles varies from 67 to 72 degrees, with rakes that differ enough to make one bike a sure descender, the second a nimble climber, and another a stable low-speed trials machine.

The illustration summarizes the effect of various combinations of steering angle and fork rake, showing two different definitions of trail. The first is what could be referred to as simple or *projected* trail, the other one is what could be called *effective* trail, also referred to as *stability index*. The latter measure, derived in the right-hand graph, is the more accurate one, taking into account the effect of the angle at which trail and rake are measured relative to each other as a function of the steerer angle.

Although the difference between projected and effective trail is minor, it increases as steerer angles diverge more, accounting for the dramatic difference in handling characteristics between two bikes with identical trail but different head-tube or steerer angles.

THE HEADSET

The headset is the double set of ball bearings with which the steering system is pivoted in the frame. Headsets come in two distinct types: threaded and threadless. The conventional threaded type has a bearing race that is threaded onto the fork's steerer tube, whereas the threadless type (best known from its first manufacturer, Dia Compe, as the Aheadset) fits on a smooth steerer tube (and thus requires a special fork). The advantages of the threadless type are simpler adjustment, a slight weight savings, and less likelihood of the steerer tube breaking.

On either type of headset, the bearing cups are installed in the ends of the head tube, the bottom race is pushed onto the fork crown. Yes, they require different forks, with a threaded and a smooth steerer tube, respectively.

Headsets are available in a variety of sizes corresponding to the various steerer tube diameters in use: 1 inch, 1 1/8 inch, and 1 1/4 inch; the two latter sizes are referred to as oversize, or OS. The idea of oversize headsets was first introduced by Gary Fisher, who specified the 1 1/4-inch headset on high-end bikes, but since then the 1 1/8-inch size has become the de facto standard for most mountain bikes. Threadless types are now also available in 1-inch, 1 1/8-inch, and 1 1/4-inch versions.

The bearing balls (or on a few models, rollers) lie in the bearing races on the head tube, and they should be packed with clean bearing grease at least once a season. The bearing balls may be loose but are more usually contained in a retainer ring to keep them together. The fork race is held on a shoulder at the bottom of the steerer tube.

THE FRONT FORK

The front fork holds the front wheel and adds a little suspension—even if it's not billed as a suspension fork. This shock absorption property is greatest when the head angle is small and the rake correspondingly long. On the other hand, this also results in a weaker front end, given the same materials and wall thicknesses, as well as making a rather sluggish bike.

The conventional fork, whatever its other details, has a threaded steerer tube for use with a conventional headset. A threadless headset requires a fork with a smooth steerer tube. Whether threaded or not, the steerer tube diameter must match

The two types of headsets used on the modern mountain bike. On the conventional headset, the upper bearing cup is screwed onto the fork's threaded steerer tube, and the handlebar stem is clamped inside the steerer tube (above). On the threadless headset, the bearing races are held in place on the smooth steerer tube by the stem clamp. It is held down by a moderate force from a bolt in the top of the stem, which is clamped around it.

that of the headset and the frame's head tube. Most non-suspension mountain bike forks are of the unicrown design, on which the fork blades are bent inward near the top and welded to the steerer tube. On older bikes you may find some interesting forks, such as the ones with replaceable fork blades (the theory being that you don't need to replace the whole fork if you bend just one fork blade).

Not all unicrown forks are created equal. Some manufacturers take shortcuts, and many cheaper bikes come with uni-

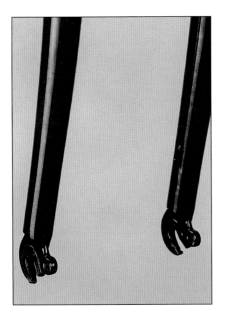

Fork ends, or front dropouts, are often equipped with little prongs at the end to stop the front wheel from falling out if the quick-release is not tightened. It defeats the object of a quick-release, but that's what the lawyers need to protect manufacturers against: claims from cyclists who sue them over accidents resulting from sudden front wheel disengagement. Perhaps a return to the old bolt-on front wheel hub would be a simpler solution, because even the most incompetent cyclist seems to know how to tighten an ordinary nut, whereas no amount of education seems to help the masses understand how to handle a quick-release.

crown forks that are not adequately reinforced. If the fork blades are made of butted tubing with significantly greater wall thickness near the top than elsewhere, the unicrown design works fine. If not, an additional reinforcing piece should have been brazed over the top of the curved section.

Pivot bosses must be installed on the fork blades to accept the brakes. Though a brake-bolt mounting hole, as required on a regular road bike with caliper brakes, is not strictly needed, either a normal hole or a threaded one comes in handy to mount a luggage rack or fenders, as well as the usual front reflector, which many riders quickly remove in favor of real lights.

Handlebar stem. Whereas early mountain bikes had one-piece units of bars with welded-on stems, today's mountain bikes have separate welded steel stems. This one is designed for use with a conventional headset.

(The little bracket does serve a secondary purpose of catching a cantilever brake's straddle cable if it should come loose, so you may want to keep it installed).

The fork ends should be just about as thick as the rear drop-outs, and investment-cast or forged models are much stronger than those made of stamped steel plate. If the bike is not intended primarily for racing, the fork ends should have threaded eyelets for rack and fender mounting. In addition, threaded bosses should be brazed on to the fork blades to install a rack. Bikes sold in Britain should probably have a threaded boss on the side to mount a lamp bracket for the type of light that is almost universally used there.

Nowadays, most fork ends have prongs sticking out at the ends. These irritating little things are sometimes referred to as lawyer's ridges because they were added by manufacturers in defense against a flurry of liability suits by customers who had failed to tighten the quick-releases, resulting in serious crashes because the front wheel suddenly came out of the fork with plain ends. Some riders who know how to handle a quick-release file those ridges off—but

don't hold the manufacturer responsible if your front wheel comes out.

In case of a fall or crash, the fork is the most likely component to get damaged. If there is no evidence of cracks or folds, it may be possible to have it straightened at a bike shop. If the problem is more serious, replace the fork.

If the steering gets sticky when turning the bars, even though it seems fine when going straight, it is due to a bent head tube, usually as a result of a collision. When replacing a fork that is bent, check the diameter and the length of the steerer tube, which must also be the same as the old one—assuming it was correct. To determine the required steerer tube length, deduct 2 mm (3/32 inch) from the sum of the stacking height of the headset (given by the manufacturer) and the length of the head tube.

HANDLEBARS AND STEM

Today, handlebars are not as wide as they were in the early days. A width of 55 centimeters (22 inches) is generally quite enough. If the bars are too wide, it may be possible to reduce the width equally on both sides following the instructions in

Bar-ends have become standard equipment on today's mountain bikes. The brand name of this one, Onza, has been sold a couple of times to different manufacturers after the original manufacturer went out of business. Manufacturers come and go in the mountain bike world, but some of the brand names stick around forever.

Chapter 31. Do that only if you have ascertained first that they can be held and the brake levers can be reached comfortably after this kind of surgery. This is very important if the bars curve in significantly, which was fashionable for some time, particularly on hybrids.

The materials can make a significant difference in terms of weight and price. Whereas cheap bikes have thick-walled steel or aluminum bars, high-quality handlebars are made of thin-walled, high-strength alloy steel tubing or even titanium. The latter material makes the bars a little springier and therefore more comfortable.

The stem connects the handlebars with the fork's steerer tube. Depending on the headset, the stem has to be of the right type. Stems for bikes with threaded headsets fit inside the steerer tube, whereas those for threadless headsets clamp around the steerer tube.

The collar that clamps around the handlebars should be at least 1 1/2 inches wide with two clamp bolts, and to prevent cracking of the handlebars at the location where they project from the stem collar, a reinforcing sleeve should be installed to spread the load.

Some stems have an integral guide and anchor for a front cantilever brake cable. On some models the guide takes the form of a roller, which ensures minimum cable friction. Whether it has a roller or not, it's a little inconvenient, as the brake has to be readjusted drastically whenever the handlebars have been adjusted, even if only slightly. The better solution is to have the cable stop clamped between the parts of the upper headset bearing.

The conventional stem for use with a threaded headset and fork is held inside the fork's steerer tube by means of a wedge-shaped item that is pulled up against the end of the stem by means of an expander bolt. The latter is accessible from the top of the stem—see Chapter 31.

On a bike with a threadless headset, the stem is clamped around the smooth steerer tube, preferably with two clamp bolts. The Allen bolt on top of the stem is not used to tighten the stem but to adjust the headset. Detailed instructions can be found in Chapter 31. The handlebar height on a bike with a threadless headset can be varied only by means of a different stem, one with more or less rise.

BAR-ENDS

Many mountain bike riders find that the straight handlebars do not provide adequate positioning flexibility. Consequently, manufacturers often mount extensions in the form of bar-ends that point up and forward from the ends of the bars.

Choose a model that clamps around the end of the handlebars (the ones that clamp inside, though elegant, may damage thin-walled handlebars). You may have to experiment a little before you find the optimum angle for the bar-ends, but once you have, you probably will not want to do without anymore. There are also one-piece solutions: handlebars with integral bar-ends; these are adjusted by rotating them in the stem collar.

Some cyclists prefer drop handlebars, and some manufacturers offer their bikes equipped with a special, spread-out version of drop bars. If you can't get custom-made drop bars for your bike, you can either buy a special model intended for use with a mountain bike, or you can use standard road bike handlebars. To get more leverage, which is desirable off-road, you may spread the ends of regular drop bars to about 50 centimeters (20 inches).

HANDGRIPS

The most comfortable handgrips are models made of a relatively firm type of foam. If you use drop handlebars, you can either install foam sleeves or conventional handlebar tape. Foam sleeves minimize the numbing effect on the hands caused by vibrations when riding over rough surfaces.

Since the introduction of twistgrip shifters, these now often take the place of stationary handgrips. They are held on with an Allen key clamp in the ring that holds the shift mechanism.

CHAPTER TWENTY-TWO

SADDLE AND SEATPOST

On the mountain bike, the saddle is almost invariably used in conjunction with a micro-adjustable seatpost and a quick-release binder bolt, with which it is clamped in the seat lug.

THE SADDLE

To be comfortable when a lot of weight rests on a saddle, as it does on the mountain bike more than on the road bike, while still allowing the legs to move freely when pedaling, the saddle should be relatively wide in the back and long and narrow in the front. Women, who tend to have a wider pelvis, should probably look for a model that is wider in the rear than the average mountain bike saddle. For most riders, the right saddle is one on which the rear portion is about 10 to 13 centimeters (4 to 5 inches) wider than the distance between the two protrusions on the pelvis that make contact with the saddle when you sit.

A couple of old pioneers and some other sophisticated riders prefer to use firm leather saddles, such as the Brooks models with coil springs in the back. These are hard to find and may require a special adapter to mount them to a modern seatpost.

THE SEATPOST

Virtually all mountain bikes now come with a forged aluminum micro-adjusting seatpost. The better ones are cold-forged, which makes them less susceptible to cracking. More important

Two seating groups: a conventional one (left) and one with a Hite-Rite installed (below). Common to both: saddle, micro-adjustable seatpost, and quick-release binder bolt.

than the adjusting detail are diameter and length. The inside diameter of the frame's seat tube can vary quite a bit, and the seatpost diameter has to match it. The length of the seatpost should be at least 30 centimeters (12 inches) to allow enough up-and-down adjustment while still clamped in securely.

There should be a marking on the seatpost indicating how far it may extend

Detail of a modern quick-release binder bolt. In view of the fact that most riders never seem to vary their seat height these days, it's probably a superfluous gadget, but it's become one of the hallmarks of the mountain bike.

outside the seat lug. If there is not, the minimum clamping length should be 65 mm (2 1/2 inches). If necessary, measure that point and mark it yourself using an indelible marking pen to make sure it is always clamped in safely.

Occasionally, interesting seatpost adaptations have been introduced. These include models with multiple adjustments to vary the position of the seat on the fly, and models with built-in springs. The latter can provide a respectable form of rear suspension, if they include an effective damping device.

QUICK-RELEASE BINDER BOLT

At times, you may want to lower or raise the saddle to optimize the bike's behavior in difficult terrain. Specifically, you will want to lower it when going down a steep descent. This is achieved easily by means of a quick-release binder bolt. It is loosened and fastened quickly and conveniently by flipping the lever. If it is too tight or too loose to fully release or hold the seat, first put the lever in the *open* position and then adjust the thumbnut on the other side. Don't forget to tighten the thumbnut to the point where the quick-release mechanism will work properly *before* finally twisting the lever to tighten it again.

SEAT SPRING ADJUSTERS

They're not as popular as they were in the early 1990s, but some of us still cherish our old Hite-Rites. Developed by mountain bike pioneer Joe Breeze, the Hite-Rite is essentially a spring that returns the seat to its original position, while allowing you to lower it under pressure.

The main advantage of the Hite-Rite is that the seat remains perfectly aligned when you quickly adjust the height. It also discourages saddle-and-seatpost theft.

MOUNTAIN BIKE SUSPENSION

Even though the mountain bike's fat pneumatic tires brought hitherto unknown comfort to off-road cycling, most riders find that a little more suspension would be nice. The real need for suspension is not so much for comfort but rather for traction and control: effective suspension helps keep the wheels on the ground and your hands on the bars.

The introduction of the RockShox telescoping forks around 1989 quickly took mountain bike suspension out of the category of curiosities, where it had been up to that time. Since then, RockShox have conquered a sizable segment of the market in every price range. Other manufacturers make similar products, and even rear suspension has become almost common, certainly in downhill biking.

In this chapter we will take a look at the various systems that are conceivable, their theoretical basis, and their practical applications.

Suspension components do add more complications to the bike. That may be acceptable if you either race or don't ride in very demanding terrain very often; but it can be a real nuisance. The problem lies in the often very short service intervals—often as low as 20 hours. To maximize their life expectancy, it's important to clean all suspension components after every use.

SUSPENSION TERMINOLOGY

Suspension devices consist of a number of parts that are common to most models. Most work on a telescop-ing principle, meaning that there are two cylinders, one sliding inside the other. Usually, the outside, larger-diameter cylinder is referred to as the slider tube. The smaller-diameter, inner tube is called the stanchion tube. Invisible from the outside are the spring elements—which may be coil springs, pneumatic cylinders, or elastomer elements. Finally, there are seals to prevent dirt from getting inside and flexible neoprene boots to cover the exposed portions.

On rear suspension units, there is generally an outer cylinder (comparable to the slider tube) with a piston (comparable to the stanchion tube) inside. Again the two main components are connected via a spring of some sort and there is a damping device as well as seals to keep dirt out.

The main measure of suspension is referred to as travel—the distance over which the wheel can go up and down. On front suspension systems the travel is measured from full extension to full compression of each system. On rear units, the amount of travel of the rear wheel can be significantly greater than the travel of the suspension unit itself by means of a cantilever design between the bike's rear triangle (seat and chainstays) and the suspension unit.

SUSPENSION THEORY

The theory of suspension recognizes that the unsprung mass should be minimized. That's another way of saying that the closer to the bumps, the more

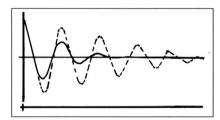

The effect of damping. An undamped suspension, represented by the dashed curve, makes the bike bounce up and down many times after an impact. With effective damping, represented by the continuous-line curve, the bike becomes stable quickly after the original impact.

effective the suspension. You can't get any closer to the bumps than the tires. And the tire's suspension effect can easily be fine-tuned by controlling the inflation pressure: let some air out in terrain that is particularly rough, especially if you go at some speed, and inflate them a little harder when the going is smooth.

Until the sudden advances in recent years, most other suspension systems had been mere compromises compared to the pneumatic tire. Not only did all of them leave a significant portion of the bike's mass unsprung (namely whatever is between the spring and the road), most of them also affected dimensions that should remain constant for effective cycling.

For the efficient transfer of power to the pedals, the distance between the rider's seat and the crank axle should remain constant while pedaling. Three other dimensions that should preferably

Two historic suspension bikes: the Slingshot seemed to do everything wrong by old suspension theory, yet it worked just fine, especially on climbs, where other suspension bikes are often sluggish (left). The first RockShox bike dates back to 1988, and this is the suspension fork that has taken the world by storm (above). *Bob Allen Photographys*

remain constant for maximum control are the wheelbase, the amount of trail, and the head-tube angle.

Finally, the suspension must be damped to be satisfactory. That means that after contracting, it should come to rest in the original position with a minimum number of oscillations. Two forms of damping are important: initial damping in response to a sudden load, and rebound damping on the way back. Hydraulically damped units are perhaps best at this, but it's not impossible to devise other methods of damping that are satisfactory.

In the front, a relatively upright steerer angle keeps the steering geometry most constant, so long as the right amount of trail is still provided.

In the rear, the best way is to design the mechanism to pivot around the bottom bracket, so there is no change in wheelbase and chain tension when the suspension is compressed relative to what it is under unloaded conditions. It also helps if the design is such that there is minimal lowering of the bottom bracket when the suspension is loaded.

These criteria are best served if the bike's frame is designed with the particular suspension system in mind. When looking for a suspension system, don't assume that what is best on a bike that is custom designed around a specific suspension should also work best when retrofitting an existing bike: retrofitting is a compromise that is most sensibly handled by something designed for that specific purpose.

Lastly on the subject of theory, an important concept is linearity versus progressiveness. A normal coil spring is a lin-

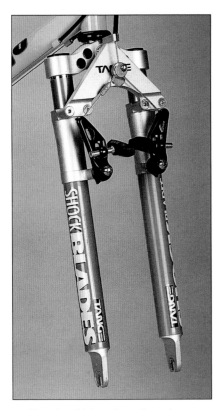

Tange's high-end polyurethane-sprung Shock-Blades, also showing some of the other relevant details such as the heavy-duty drop-outs and the reinforcing bridge to which the brake is mounted—the latter serves to keep the two slider tubes aligned.

"Suspenders" telescoping front fork. These are designed for "serious" downhill riding and are supplied as a complete package with the hydraulically operated disk brake shown. *Bob Allen Photography*

ear device: it deforms just about as far under the same force when it's almost fully compressed as when it's barely compressed. For a good bicycle suspension, you want something that's progressive: it should get harder to compress as you get closer to the end of the range. The advantage of progressive suspension is that it responds well to small unevennesses yet doesn't bottom out on big ones.

SUSPENSION REALITY

Much of the available body of knowledge, as outlined above, is based on experience with motorcycles, especially the concept that the unsprung mass must be minimized. As it turns out, this is much less critical on a bike than on a motorcycle.

This can largely be explained on the basis of the dramatic difference in weight between motorcycle components and those on the bicycle. An entire mountain bike may weigh less than does the front wheel and the unsprung portion of telescoping forks on a typical motorcycle.

Another example is the idea of a shock-absorbing seatpost, or the more sophisticated Softride Beam. Although conventional wisdom has it that you should keep the distance between seat and pedals constant, these devices work just fine. It seems to be quite enough to have something that is not so loosely sprung as to vary this difference up-and-down in response to tiny variations in load.

Clearly, you should not take any theoretician's word for it when it comes to the relative virtues of any suspension device. Instead, try several different models out for yourself or base your choice on reports from others who have experience with different types.

WHERE IT MATTERS

Many suspension bikes are great fun to ride, but only where there is a reason to use a suspension. That applies to downhill riding at speed, but not to riding on difficult narrow trails and in trials competition.

Once you decide to buy a bike with suspension, and you do have to use it where suspension isn't really suitable, lock it out altogether (if the model in question offers that option) or select the stiffest setting.

It seems particularly curious to see typical East Coast bikes, which have a geometry that clearly says "not built for speed but for technical trail riding" suddenly coming out with suspensions that may be perfectly good, but not for that kind of riding.

FORMS OF SUSPENSION

The various suspension systems can be divided into a few main categories, whether used in the front or the rear. They can be summarized as follows:

Pneumatic.
Elastomer in compression.
Elastomer in tension.
Torsion rod.
Leaf spring.
Coil spring in compression.
Coil spring in tension.

Each of these various systems has some advantages and disadvantages. All of them can be made to work very well or very poorly, last long or fall apart, depending more on their detail design and the quality of their construction than on their respective principle of operation. In the following section, we'll take a look at their operating principles.

Pneumatic

Probably still the preferred method, this system uses a chamber with compressed air as the spring. The air chamber can be enclosed in a flexible cushion so that the air does not leak out. Somewhere there may be a valve to let in more air to increase its pressure or let some out to decrease it as appropriate to the rider's weight. The advantage of pneumatic suspension is progressive compression: the more it gets compressed, the stiffer it gets, which is hard to achieve with any other suspension elements (most of which have a linear compression characteristic).

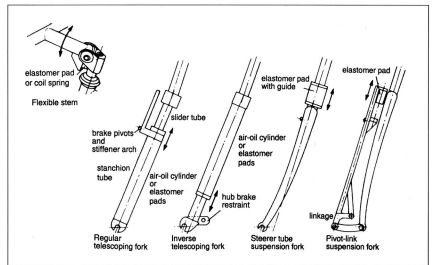

Overview of basic suspension methods. There are many ways to skin a cat, and although this drawing summarizes a good many of them, suspension engineers have come up with even more variants on these same themes.

Adjusting knob on a typical air/oil telescoping fork. The idea is to adjust the action for the weight of the rider and the type of terrain. Details are in the manufacturer's instruction manual.

An interesting variant of the pneumatic suspension principle is the Firestone pneumatic cushion. This is merely an air-filled rubber ball that can be installed between two points; it has been successfully used in the rear in combination with some form of friction damping.

Elastomer in Compression

A cushion of elastomers (a synthetic rubbery material) is compressed under the effect of the shock impact. Relatively cheap and simple to make, this method is used both in the front and the rear. In the front, it may be in the form of two parallel units in the fork blades; they look just like air-oil shocks but typically have less travel and less rebound damping, although with the improvements in materials, the difference between elastomers and air-oil systems is getting less. In fact,

some of the best forks available combine elastomers and air/oil devices.

Another design using the same material but a different approach is the one by Browning, used on Cannondale suspension bikes. It is a single element integrated between the headset and the fork crown. The advantage of this design is that the fork blades are solidly connected and thus can't move relative to each other the way they do on telescoping forks.

Typically, a combination of elastomer pads of different hardness is installed. Most of these units can be adjusted by selecting the appropriate combination of pads, which are often easily accessible for replacement. Today's elastomer pads can be quite sophisticated, and the stigma originally attached to elastomers compared to air cylinder systems is fast breaking down. The elastomers used by some of the best forks are called microcellular, meaning that they consist of many tiny air bubbles that are closed off to one another, embedded in the flexible elastomer material. These have very similar compression qualities to air cylinders, offering similar progressive compression characteristics.

Elastomer in Tension

Rarely used but potentially very simple and quite satisfactory if done

right, this is essentially an elastic strap, like a bungee cord, stretched between two points on a linkage mechanism. To work well, the linkage mechanism must be controlled to minimize lateral movement, and there must be an adjustable knob to control the tension for damping control. The first time we saw this principle applied on a bike was in the late 1960s on Captain Dan Henry's bike, which is described in some detail in Fred DeLong's excellent book *DeLong's Guide to Bicycles and Bicycling*.

Torsion Bar

Torsion bar suspension is based on the limited elasticity in twisting or bending of a more or less straight piece of a seemingly rigid material. It was used on a 1992 prototype titanium bike designed by Joe Murray—probably the lightest suspension bike ever devised.

Leaf Spring

In biking practice, the leaf spring will be a single fiber-reinforced member, rather than the conventional steel leaf spring as still used on many cars and trucks. The Softride Beam uses this principle to keep the saddle "afloat." Laterally, the thing must be rigid enough to resist sideways sway.

"Sweet Spot"-type rear suspension on Breeze Cycles' Twister full-suspension bike. The rear triangle stays rigid and pivots around a spot slightly forward of the seat tube, and vertically between the saddle and the bottom bracket.

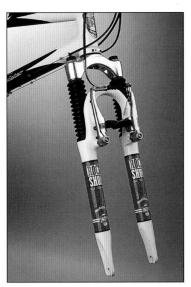

RIGHT: Sophisticated pivot-linkage front suspension fork for downhill racing from Interloc Racing Design.

RockShox Indy XC suspension fork. Available in versions with different travel range, this type of fork covers the "middle ground" between the low-price models and the most sophisticated downhill models.

Coil Spring in Compression

This simple method is often used in combination with some other elements, such as a hydraulic damper. Other models combine them with elastomer pads to limit the impact at final compression.

Many other types of these systems generally depend on a rather complex linkage system. By far the most cleverly designed of these are those by Mert Lawwill as used in the rear on the Gary Fisher full-suspension bike. Lawwill himself markets a front fork that uses the same principle, and promises to be a real winner.

These particular linkage systems keep the bike's geometry—its wheelbase, steerer angle, and trail—identical whether the suspension is compressed or not, resulting in excellent suspension and control over the bike.

Coil Spring in Tension

This system is only used on some custom-designs. It works essentially like the elastomer in tension. Again the design and construction of the linkage system is critical.

DAMPING

There are also different ways of damping, as follows:

Mechanical friction.

Hydraulic.

Hydraulic damping usually is in the form of a hydraulic chamber with a little orifice through which the hydraulic liquid passes slowly enough to form the right resistance. This system is used virtually only in telescoping forks (one in each blade) and rear-suspension cylinders. RockShox and Marzocchi are perhaps the best-known brands of air/oil pneumatic front forks, and Fox makes most of the rear-suspension cylinders of this type.

Other forms of adjustment include the fine-tuning of the damping system by means of selecting a different fluid for the hydraulic system. Generally, ATF 100 (a common automatic transmission fluid) is factory-installed, but more or less damping can be achieved by replacing it with a fluid with higher or lower viscosity, following the manufacturer's service instructions, which can be obtained via your bike shop or directly from the manufacturer.

STICTION

Stiction is an term made up of the words *stickiness* and *friction*. It refers to the directness of response to the impact of a force on the suspension system. Interestingly, it has been described both as a positive and as a negative feature. Experienced riders, used to the feel of control they get on an unsprung bike, consider some degree of stiction positive, because it limits the deflection to cases where the shock is so significant that suspension is really needed.

A little stiction may be a good feature—in fact it can be seen as initial damping—but too much stiction would make the ride too rough, and that's not why you get a bike with suspension. There is also a concern that where there is stiction there is deformation, leading to more wear and tear.

THE EFFECT OF SUSPENSION ON THE BIKE'S GEOMETRY

Except for the simple sprung stem, all suspension systems tend to change the bike's geometry. Somewhere, there must be room to accommodate the travel (the range of movement up and down), and as clearances on a modern mountain bike tend to be minimal, the only way to add suspension travel is by raising the frame.

In the front, a typical suspension fork requires about 2 inches more room, lifting the front end by that much. This in turns shifts the bike's head-tube angle to a shallower position—when uncompressed. As you hit an unevenness, and the fork is compressed, this angle changes to a steeper one again, and if the system is not well damped, the angle will change back and forth as the fork oscillates.

This can lead to somewhat unpredictable behavior, and it is one reason to keep the unit adjusted on the stiff side to maximize control.

Another measure of interest is the trail. As we've seen in Chapter 21, the fork rake and the steerer angle must be matched carefully, yet as the fork is pushed in, the steerer angle changes but the fork rake remains the same. Some manufacturers pride themselves in their advertisements on a presumably clever design that keeps the rake constant regardless of the angle. But curiously enough, this merely suggests that these manufacturers don't really understand the problem: in fact, the rake should vary to achieve the trail that is right for any particular steerer angle. By and large, systems with variable rake should be preferred to those with constant rake, and even those with constant trail.

In the rear, an important aspect is the response of the suspension to the force applied on the pedals. Preferably, the pivot points should be arranged in such a way that the tension in the chain, resulting from the application of force on the pedals, tends to push the rear wheel down, causing it to maximize traction. This is achieved by placing the pivot point high enough, preferably about in line with the point where the chain runs off the top of the chainring.

SUSPENSION FORK TRAVEL

To set up your suspension fork for your weight and riding habits, compare the deflection of the fork as you ride with the nominal amount of fork travel (that is, the distance over which the fork can be compressed), as quoted by the manufacturer. We recommend you set it up so that you take up 70 to 90 percent of the rated value. For example, if the rated travel is 65 mm (2 1/2 inches), you should compress the fork 45 to 60 mm (1 3/4 to 2 1/8 inches).

To check your fork's actual travel, tie a cable tie (a nylon fastener strap) around each of the stanchions, exactly at the point where they go into the slider tube when the bike is unloaded. Pull them snug enough so that they don't slide up or down except under force. As you ride the bike, the movement of the stanchions up and down in the slider tube will push the cable tie out of the way to rest at the maximum distance to which the two tubes have moved relative to each other.

Take the bike over the roughest terrain you expect to ride, going at the highest speed you normally handle. When you return, check the resulting position of the cable ties. If it's less than 70 percent of the nominal rating, you need a softer adjustment. If it's more than 90 percent, you need a stiffer setting. Just how that's done varies from model to model, and will be explained in the manufacturer's instructions that accompany the product.

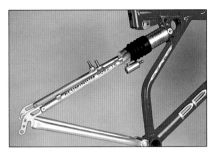

Rear suspension unit with on-the-fly infinitely variable damping that can be controlled from a lever on the handlebars on the ProDux Sidewinder, designed and built by the South African aluminum-frame pioneer Don Williamson. The proprietary shock unit is available only with the same manufacturer's aluminum frame shown.

SUSPENSION CARE

Suspension parts need more maintenance than the rest of the bike. To minimize wear and tear and to avoid as much maintenance work as possible, keep it clean and check it out. That is about the most important and most generally valid advice with respect to the maintenance of any suspension system. Keep the manufacturer's descriptive brochure with maintenance instructions that apply to your particular type and model.

After every ride, clean the telescoping or other moving parts very carefully. Use a dry cloth and wipe away from the mechanism, making sure you don't push any dirt particles inside. Then use a waxed cloth to go over it again to form a protective layer (don't use grease, as that would only attract dirt).

Adjust the tensioning or damping device (either a knob or a valve) to match your weight on the basis of the feel you get in the terrain. Don't adjust them too loose, thinking more cushioning must be better than less, because suspension is only meant to even out real bumps, not to make you seasick swaying up and down.

CHAPTER TWENTY-FOUR

ACCESSORIES

T his chapter will briefly describe the most useful accessories available for mountain bike use. Chapter 34 gives maintenance and installation instructions.

THE LOCK

We suggest you always carry a lock, even off-road, and lock the bike whenever you leave it unguarded. Toughest to crack are the large reptile-like chains with cylindrical shackles, followed by braced versions of the familiar U-shaped locks, such as the Badbones, although conventional U-shaped locks, like the Kryptonite, may be adequate. Another alternative is a heavy-duty plastic-coated cable with a separate lock, which should have a case-hardened shackle with a diameter of 7.5 mm (9/32 inch) to resist most common bike-theft equipment.

The U-lock is easily mounted on the frame by means of a bracket supplied by the lock manufacturer. Because mountain bike frame tubes generally have larger diameters than other bikes, and because these locks come in different versions, it will be best to take both bike and lock to the shop when selecting the bracket. Install the bracket so that it does not interfere with access to the water bottle.

An accessorized mountain bike. This older (1990) bike is outfitted with rear rack, front and rear lights, saddlebag, toeclips, and water bottle. There are many more gadgets you can install on your bike but we suggest you keep it to a minimum.

You can even get trailers for your mountain bike—a kind of baby-jogger conversion. Not suitable for a fast downhill run, but OK for level terrain and relatively smooth trails.

The cable lock is most easily carried in a bag hung from the saddle, though some models can be coiled up conveniently to hang behind the saddle. In that case, attach a strap on the back of the saddle to tie the cable down so it does not sway too much.

THE PUMP

At home, a big stand pump with hose connector and a built-in pressure gauge is most useful. You will need a smaller model to carry on the bike. There are special mountain bike pumps available that have a larger diameter than the models intended for other bikes, allowing you to pump more air, though at a slightly lower pressure.

These pumps are available with a plastic mounting strap to go alongside one of the frame tubes. A good place is behind the seat tube, if the frame's rear wheel clearance is adequate. Get a pump with the kind of pump head—the part that fits on the valve—to match the valves on your bike's tires (Schrader or Presta see Chapter 17).

Inflators with CO_2 cartridges have become popular. They are useful in a race, but for other purposes their time- and weight-saving features are not really worth the risk of "running out of air." Another popular pump is the telescoping pump, which is small enough to be tucked in the pocket of your cycling jersey, although it takes many strokes to properly inflate a tire.

WATER BOTTLE CAGE

On a trip that exceeds one hour, it is important to carry water, and you may need several on a longer trip in a hot climate. We recommend using only firm metal bottle cages. If there are several sets of bosses on the frame, choose the ones that allow the bottle cage to be mounted in such a way that you can conveniently reach the bottle while riding. The water bottle itself should be cleaned after every use, especially if you fill it with liquids other than water—energy drinks can grow dangerous molds after some time.

TOECLIPS

Nowadays, most high-end mountain bikes are equipped with clipless pedals. If your bike is not, you can mount toeclips to ensure your feet always have a firm hold on the pedals, while you can still use the bike with regular shoes.

LIGHTS AND REFLECTORS

Probably no single item has seen more improvement since the mountain bike first came out than lights have. Today, several manufacturers provide excellent high-intensity battery-powered lights that are so bright as to actually light up your way off-road, and so reliable that you can actually count on them.

Only battery lights are suitable for off-road use, because generators do not give enough light at the low speeds often achieved on the mountain bike. We suggest you look for the biggest and brightest you can find—the best have two separate lights: a high beam and a low beam. If it's a single light (and that also applies to the low beam of double light units), it should throw a relatively wide beam. To compare the quality of the beam pattern, shine several different lights straight ahead at a wall from the same distance. So many different varieties exist that precise instructions are elusive, but here are some hints.

The simplest acceptable lights are those that can be clipped to the handlebars. Usually these have a halogen bulb and are powered by two C-cells. You can get much brighter ones, but they require rechargeable batteries. A good solution would be a "modular" system—using the same light unit with upgradable features such as rechargeable battery pack and brighter bulbs.

The most spectacularly bright lights these days use metal halide bulbs—miniature versions of the system often used for street lighting, and it's not a bad idea, as these offer much more light output for the same wattage than other types. At a price, though: they're at least twice as expensive as the most sophisticated systems with halogen bulbs.

The Night Rider handlebar-mounted light set is a battery-powered light with high and low beam, neatly enclosed in a solid plastic housing and running off juice from batteries enclosed in a cannibalized water bottle.

Computers that are suitable for mountain bike use, such as this one by Avocet, tend to have large and simple displays with a minimal number of (preferably large) buttons. To keep operation simple, you don't want too many different functions.

On lighting systems with rechargeable batteries and wiring connections, occasionally check the connections. Recharge the NiCad batteries at least once a week, as these have a limited shelf life, which means they drain even when not in use. Lead-acid gel batteries have a much longer shelf life, but they too must be recharged regularly—before they are completely drained, as they should never be fully discharged.

A nice solution for the rechargeable battery is to have it contained in a water bottle for mounting in a water bottle cage on the frame, rather than have it a separate bag dangling from the frame—if you can spare a water bottle location for that purpose.

Most popular among rear lights these days is the flashing LED type, and they are indeed quite good. Instead of a battery-powered rear light, a really big reflector, mounted rather low, is equally visible to anyone who could endanger you from behind, assuming they have lighting themselves. Amber is more visible than red, so should be preferred wherever the law does not prohibit its use. (Many countries, and some states in the United States, require rear lights and reflectors to be red.)

Bicycle-specific reflectors are orientation-sensitive, because they reflect light only over a narrow angle back to the source. They must be installed in such a way that any markings are legible the right way around.

LUGGAGE RACKS

Special racks (carriers to our British readers) designed for the mountain bike's generous dimensions are readily available. The granddaddy of all modern racks is Jim Blackburn's welded aluminum model, and this is still the declared favorite of many riders.

In the front, the most popular is the so-called low-rider variety. These allow luggage to be carried where it least interferes with steering and bike handling—centered on the steering axis, just behind the front wheel axle. Unfortunately, they make it hard to transport the bike on most car roof racks. Front racks can't be used on bikes with suspension forks.

FENDERS

Fenders (called mudguards in Britain) are not suitable if you ride in thick mud because the stuff will build up inside and soon stop your wheel from going around. However, if you ride in rainy weather or merely on wet roads and trails, they can be useful. Several models are available, the widest and the longest ones being the most effective. Short clip-on guards don't do the trick.

CHAINRING PROTECTOR

This device, mainly sold under the name Rockring, protects the teeth of the large chainring from damage if you bottom out. It is installed in the same holes as the chainrings, so make sure you get the right version to match your equipment. It is of course also possible to install a strong metal guard directly on the bike, instead of on the chainrings, as a few international manufacturers do.

OTHER ACCESSORIES

In addition to the items described in some detail above, numerous other accessories are available, ranging from derailleur protectors and brake stiffeners to carrying straps and shoulder pads, all specially designed with the mountain bike in mind. And then there are the many more or less useful accessories for general bicycle use.

What among all these gadgets will be useful is up to you to decide. Our preference is to adorn our bikes as little as possible, while some others we know buy every new gizmo that hits the market. Only too often, these items are never installed—or, if they are, soon removed again.

Notwithstanding some honorable exceptions, the problem only too often is that many of these items have not been designed by experienced mountain bike riders, or if they are, they have not been adequately tested in practical use first. Don't hesitate to try things, but remove whatever doesn't live up to your expectations.

PART IV

MAINTENANCE AND REPAIRS OF YOUR MOUNTAIN BIKE

CHAPTER TWENTY-FIVE

THE BASICS OF MAINTENANCE

This chapter will be devoted to general maintenance themes, whereas the subsequent chapters are each devoted to the maintenance of a functional group.

SELECTING TOOLS

Probably 90 percent of all maintenance and repair work can be done with a very modest outfit. And of those tools, only a few are so essential that they should also be taken along on most bike trips on the road or trail. Tools can be categorized in regular, or universal, tools that can be bought at any hardware store, and specific bicycle tools that are available only from well-stocked bike shops or specialized mail-order outlets.

Quality counts when buying tools. You may find similar-looking tools at prices that vary by a factor of three. Don't choose the cheaper version, because the tool that costs one third as much doesn't last even a third as long. It never fits as accurately, leading to damage. After some unsatisfactory use, you'll probably decide to get the better tool anyway.

Below, you will find most of the common tools described. Don't be discouraged by the length of the list, as you don't really need every one of the items described here.

Refer to the section on *Tools to Take Along* for the really essential tools that should be bought right away. All the other tools can wait until you have a specific need.

Mountain bike components are built to metric threading standards, and thus metric tool sizes will be required. The size quoted in mm (millimeters) is the dimension across flats of the point where the tool fits.

UNIVERSAL TOOLS

These are the basic tools that can be purchased in any hardware shop.

Screwdrivers

The screwdriver's size is designated by the blade width at the end. You will need a small one with a 4-mm (3/16-inch) blade, a larger one with a 6- to 7-mm (1/4-inch to 5/32-inch) blade, and one or two Phillips-head types for the screws with cross-shaped recesses instead of the conventional saw cut.

Adjustable Wrenches

More commonly referred to by the Crescent trade name, the adjustable wrench is designated by its overall length. Get one that measures 150 mm (6 inches) and one that is at least 200 mm (8 inches), preferably even 250 mm (10 inches) long.

Box Wrenches

Known as ring spanners in Britain, these are the most accurate tools for tightening or loosening nuts and bolts with hexagonal heads. Like all other fixed wrenches, they are designated by the across-flats dimension of the bolt on which they fit. You will need sizes from 6 mm to 17 mm.

Open-Ended Wrenches

These are the most common wrenches available. They can be used when there is not enough access room for the box wrench. Get a set in sizes from 6 mm to 17 mm.

Combination Wrenches

This type has a box wrench on one end and an open-ended wrench of the same size on the other. Even better than a set each of the preceding items is to get two sets (yes, two: you'll often need to hold the head of a bolt while loosening or tightening the nut with the other) of these, again in sizes from 6 mm to 17 mm.

Allen Wrenches

Referred to as Allen keys in Britain, these hexagonal L-shaped bars are used on the screws with hexagonal recesses. Initially you will at least need 4, 5, and 6 mm, but eventually you may also run into the sizes 2, 2.5, 3, 4.5, 7, 8, and 9 mm. You can also get these as combination tools containing a whole series of sizes.

Pliers

Occasionally you may find a use for a needle-nose pliers, diagonal cutters, and something like a Vise-Grip. Don't use any one of them whenever another, better-fitting tool will do the job, as pliers often do more damage than necessary.

Hammers

These are classified by their weight. We suggest a 300-gram (10- or 12-ounce) metal-working model, which has a square head at one end and a wedge-shaped one on the other. In addition, you may need a mallet with a plastic head of about the same weight.

Files

These are designated by the length of their blade and their coarseness. Get a relatively fine 8-inch file to remove the occasional protruding spoke-end or a burr at the end of a part that is cut off or damaged.

SPECIAL BICYCLE TOOLS

The following list of tools made specifically for bicycle use includes almost all the tools you will be likely to need as a home mechanic. A much more modest selection—those listed under *Tools to Take Along*—will usually get you by when no really major operations have to be carried out.

A selection of tools, including both regular wrenches and pliers, as well as special tools for work on the hubs, the bottom bracket, the freewheel, and the headset.

Even more special tools will be mentioned as we get into the actual maintenance instructions. In many cases, you will have to consult a bike mechanic to make sure you get the size or model of any particular tool that matches the parts installed on your bike. For that reason, it is best to have the bike with you whenever buying tools.

Pump

Make sure you get a model that matches the particular valves used on your bike (Presta or Schrader, as described in Chapter 17).

Pressure Gauge

We suggest you invest in a pressure gauge to make sure you inflate the tires correctly, at least to use at home—again matching the valve used on your bicycle's tires.

Tire Levers

These are used to lift the tire off the rim in case of a flat (puncture) or when replacing tube or tire. Most mountain bike tires fit loosely enough on the rim to use only one or two, and some can actually be removed without. Select thin, flat ones that don't bend.

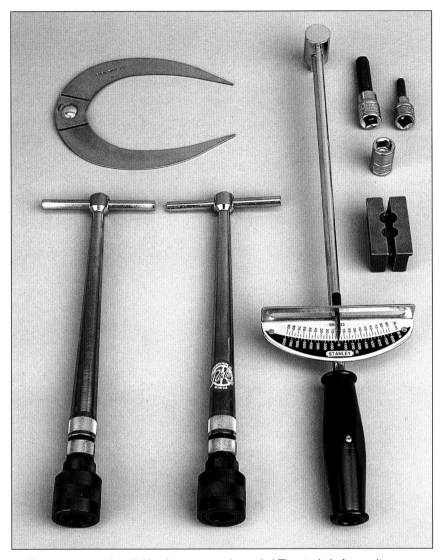

Even more special tools like these are rarely needed. They include frame alignment and correction tools and a torque wrench. Your bike shop will have such tools, and you'll be best advised to use its services for jobs requiring these tools.

Tire Patch Kit

This little box contains most of the other essentials for fixing a puncture: patches, rubber solution, and sandpaper. It is also handy for carrying other small spare parts. Replace the patches at least once a year, as they lose their adhesive quality with time. Also check to make sure the rubber solution is still reasonably full.

Spoke Wrench

Called a nipple spanner in Britain, it is used to tighten, remove, or install a spoke, either to replace it or in order to straighten a bent wheel. Get one that matches the spoke nipples used on your bike.

Crank Extractor

This tool is needed to tighten or loosen the cranks. Get a model that matches the cranks installed on your bike, as they vary from make to make, sometimes even from model to model.

Freewheel Extractor

Used to remove a screwed-on freewheel block or a sprocket on a cassette hub, which may be necessary to replace something as basic as a broken spoke. This tool must also be selected to match the particular freewheel used on your bike.

Chain Whip

This device may be needed to remove individual cogs from the freewheel. Depending on the kind of freewheel on the bike, you may either need two or one in conjunction with the manufacturer's special wrench, as outlined in Chapter 28.

Chain Rivet Tool

This tool is used to remove a pin that connects the links of the chain, so it can be separated for maintenance.

Cone Wrenches

These very flat open-ended wrenches are used to overhaul the bearings of a wheel hub. Available in several sizes—get two of each of the sizes needed for the hubs on your bike.

Bottom Bracket Tools

Needed for maintenance operations on the crankset or bottom bracket bearings. Many mountain bikes are equipped with bottom brackets that need quite specific tools for this work, so make sure to match the tools to the components on your bike.

Headset Tools

These are oversized, flat, open-ended wrenches, used to overhaul the steering system's headset bearings. Their size has to match the make and model of headset.

LUBRICANTS AND CLEANING AIDS

You will need some materials to help you clean the bike and its parts, as well as to lubricate for minimal friction and maximum durability. Use the following items:

Cloths

You'll need at least one clean and one greasy cloth. The latter is made that way by applying oil or bearing grease to a clean cloth.

Brushes

Get two sizes, about 20 mm (3/4 inch) and 40 mm (1 1/2 inches) wide.

Tools to take along—at least on a longer ride with limited access. On short rides, just a tire patch kit a pump, and a couple of Allen wrenches may be enough to see you through.

flat container to catch drippings or clean parts.

Penetrating Oil

Most convenient is a spraycan of thin, penetrating lubricant, such as WD-40. This is actually primarily formulated as a water dispersant, but it works fine for getting tight things loose. Wipe it off if you use it on aluminum, as it tends to mar the shiny aluminum finish if left on too long.

Chain Lubricant

Get either a spraycan or an applicator bottle of special chain lubricant.

Wax

Used to protect bare metal parts, any car wax will serve the purpose.

Cleaning Aids

Many cleaning jobs are done simply with a cloth and water, whereas some items may have to be cleaned with a mixture of solvent with about five-to-ten percent mineral oil.

TOOLS TO TAKE ALONG

The following is just our personal preference. In addition to this list, refer to the section on spare parts below for other items. Carry them in a bag tied to the bike. Alternately, you can make a pouch to fit your tools, carried either in a bike bag or tied directly to a frame tube or under the saddle. Here's what we suggest taking along:

pump (for mountain bike racing, use a CO_2 inflator instead)
4-mm screwdriver.
Two or three tire levers.
Tire patch kit.
6-inch adjustable wrench.
7- to 14-mm open-ended or box wrenches.
4-, 5-, 6-mm Allen wrenches.
Needle-nose pliers.
Spoke wrench.
Chain rivet tool.
Crank extractor.

Additional Items

In addition—depending on the length and the purpose of the trip—you may want

Solvent

Use a special biodegradable type available in bike shops.

Bearing Grease

Use any lithium-based bearing grease. Get it in a tube, rather than a can, so that it stays clean.

Oil

You can get a whole range of special bicycle lubricants, but in a pinch you can use SAE 40 motor oil or SAE 60 gear oil for most lubricating jobs.

Containers

Use an empty jar with a lid and a

to carry some of the spares listed in the next section. Equally important are a bottle of water installed on the bike, a tube of waterless hand cleaner, a cloth, and a first aid kit including a pair of scissors and a pocket knife.

Spare Parts

Here is a list of the spare parts you may find useful to carry on a longer trip. Just how many of these you should carry depends on the conditions of the trip. Be guided by the following list:

Brake cable (inner cable only, long enough for rear brake).
Derailleur cable (inner cable only, long enough for rear derailleur).
Spokes with matching nipples, making sure they are of the right length for both wheels.
Hooked emergency spokes as described in Chapter 27 for the right-hand side of the rear wheel.
Bolts, washers, and nuts in 4-, 5-, and 6-mm sizes.
Grommet (rubber seal washer) for pump.
Light bulbs and batteries for front and rear lights (if you will be riding in the dark).
Inner tube.

WORKSHOP AND BIKE SUPPORT

When doing maintenance or repair work at home, we recommend you provide at least a minimum of organized workshop space. It needn't be a separate room, nor must it be a permanently designated location. But while working on the bike, it should be adequately equipped for doing so.

The amount of space needed is quite modest: 2.10 meters by 1.8 meters (7 feet by 6 feet) is enough for any maintenance work ever done on the bike. Equip this area with the tools and the cleaning and lubrication aids listed above. In addition, you will need a workbench—although the kitchen counter or an old table will do. Ideally, you should install a sizable metal-working vise on the workbench.

The best way to support the bike is with a freestanding work stand. In an emergency, you can turn the bike upside-

The Blackburn Sportstand is an excellent way to support a bike that needs service.

down, after turning sensitive parts on the handlebars out of the way.

HANDLING COMMON PARTS

This section is devoted to the techniques for handling some basic mechanisms found in many places on your bike. This includes screw-threaded connections in general, cables and their adjustment, and ball bearings with their adjustment and lubrication.

THREADED CONNECTIONS

Essentially, all threaded connections are based on the same principle: a cylindrical (male) part is threaded into a corresponding hollow (female) part by means of matching helical grooves cut into each.

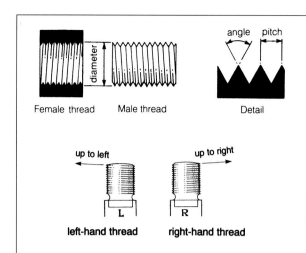

Female thread   Male thread   Detail

angle   pitch

up to left   up to right

L   R

left-hand thread   **right-hand thread**

Details of a threaded connection. The lower detail shows how to tell the left-hand and right-hand versions of a threaded stub apart; you'll need to know this to recognize which pedal goes on what side of the bike.

Close-up view of a threaded connection. As you see here, not just nuts and bolts but many other components, such as this headset, have threaded connections.

Modern control cables, as used for the mountain bike's gearing and brake controls, have a low-friction liner between the inner cable and the outer casing.

When the one part is threaded fully into the other, the reaction force pushes the sides of male and female threads against one another, creating so much friction that the parts are no longer free to turn, thus keeping the connection firm.

The illustration shows the details of a typical threaded connection, including an enlarged detail of a cross section through the thread. Screw threads are designated by their nominal size, generally measured in millimeters in the bicycle industry. In addition, the pitch, or number of threads per inch, and the thread angle may vary (either 55 or 60 degrees). Finally, some parts have left-hand (L.H.) threading, instead of the regular right-hand (R.H.) thread. L.H. thread is found on the left pedal, as well as on a few bearing parts.

Regular nuts and bolts are standardized—for a given nominal diameter, they will have the same pitch and the same thread angle, and they all have R.H. thread. Many other bicycle components are less standardized: there are at least three different industry standards for such parts as headsets, bottom brackets, and freewheels. Although mountain bikes are virtually all built to the BCI (British Cycle Institute) standard dimensions for most of their parts, non-standard dimensions may be used for some parts, such as oversize headsets. To avoid mismatching, always take the part to be replaced, as well as any matching component to which it is threaded, to the bike store when buying a replacement, so you can try it out there.

The way to loosen and tighten the connection is the same. One part has to be restrained while the other is turned relative to it—to the right to tighten, the left to loosen in the case of R.H. thread, the other way around for L.H. thread. The lower detail of the illustration shows how to tell them apart if they are not marked. Use exactly fitting tools to give the best possible hold and to minimize damage. Use tools that offer some leverage (a wrench with a long handle) on the part that is turned; the part that is merely restrained may be held with less leverage.

All threaded connections should be clean and lightly greased when they are installed. If you have difficulty loosening a connection, first squirt some penetrating oil, such as WD-40, at any accessible point where the male part disappears in the female part, and wait five minutes before proceeding. To allow a nut or the head of a bolt to be turned when it is hard down on the part it holds, a plain washer should be installed between the two. This allows you to tighten the joint more firmly.

To minimize the chances of coming loose, usually as a result of vibrations while riding, many threaded connections are secured one way or another. Several different methods are used to achieve this: locknut, spring washer, and locking insert nut. The locknut is a second nut that is tightened against the main nut, creating high friction forces in the threads working opposite ways. The spring washer expands to hold the connection when vibration would

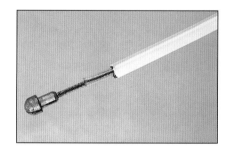

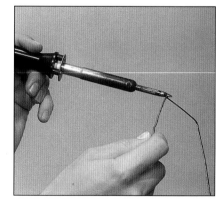

The cleanest way to finish the loose end of a cable is to solder the strands together, preferably before you cut it.

otherwise loosen it, and the locking insert nut has a nylon insert that is deformed by the threading, offering the required high resistance against loosening. If you have problems with parts coming loose, you may use any of these techniques to secure them.

A connection that comes loose frequently despite the use of such a locking device is probably worn to the point where replacement—usually of both parts—is in order.

CONTROL CABLES

Brakes and gears on the mountain bike are operated via flexible cables that connect the brake or shift lever with the main unit. The illustration shows details of a typical cable, including the pertinent adjusting mechanism. The inner cable takes up tension (pulling) forces, which are countered by the compression (pushing) forces taken up by the casing, or outer cable. To minimize the resistance of the inner cable running in the casing, the length of the outer casing is minimized by having part of the inner cable run free between stops that are mounted on the bike's frame.

A nipple is soldered on at one end of the inner cable, and the other end is clamped in at the brake or gear mechanism. Ferrules are installed at the ends of the cable casing to provide a firm termination at the anchor points. There will be several different cables on your bike, and you should take care to get the right kind. In addition to the different nipple shapes in use by different makers to match particular components, the thickness can also vary. Usually an end cap is crimped (squeezed) around the free end of the inner cable—pull it off with pliers when replacing the cable.

The cables for indexed gearing controls are designed to be rather stiff so that they can take up some compressive, as well as tensile, forces. The inner cables for brake controls must be quite thick to take up the high forces without stretching. Make sure the outer cable has the right diameter for the pertinent inner cable to slide through freely.

Conventional cables for the brakes and derailleurs should be cleaned and

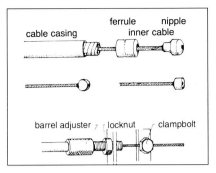

Details of a typical control cable and its adjusting mechanism.

The principle of the quick-release operation. Assemble the unit with the lever set in the *open* position and tighten the connection by twisting the lever into the *closed* position. And check to make sure it's actually tight.

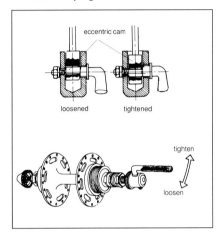

lubricated regularly, although most of them have a nylon liner, or sleeve, between inner and outer cable, which reduces friction and keeps the cables running smoothly longer. Certainly if you live in a dusty climate, use only wax (rather than grease) to lubricate the cable. Put some wax on a cloth and run this cloth over the inner cable.

Many people consider lubricating the rear derailleur cable wrong; invariably these are the ones who ride only in dry, dusty regions and don't know about wax as a cable lubricant. (In most parts of the world you won't find cable lubrication to be a disadvantage if it's done right).

Adjusting the cable tension is often necessary to adjust brakes or gears. To this

purpose, an adjusting mechanism is generally installed somewhere along the length of the cable. Before attempting adjustment, make sure the cable end is clamped in firmly. To adjust, loosen the locknut (usually a round knurled design) while restraining the adjusting barrel. Next, unscrew the adjusting barrel far enough to obtain the desired cable tension, and finally tighten the locknut while holding the adjusting barrel to restrain it.

If the length of the adjusting barrel does not allow enough adjusting range, the inner cable must be clamped in further. To do this, first loosen the locknut all the way while restraining the adjusting barrel, then screw the adjusting barrel in all the way, and clamp the cable in a new location while keeping it pulled taut with the aid of a pair of pliers. Then re-adjust with the barrel adjuster.

QUICK-RELEASES

Quick-release mechanisms are used on the seat clamp and on the wheels to ease adjustment and removal, respectively. The quick-releases for saddle clamp and wheel hubs work on the same principle. Instead of holding the axle or bolt by means of one or two nuts that are screwed down, a toggle lever is used, as shown in the illustration, and the other end is held with a thumbnut.

The thumbnut is not intended to be used for tightening the connection, but merely to adjust it in such a way that twisting the lever tightens the whole connection firmly. Open the lever by twisting it, close it by twisting it back. If the connection does not hold, first place the lever in the *open* position, then tighten the thumbnut perhaps half a turn and try again, until the lever not only holds the part firmly but can also be opened enough to allow removal or adjustment of the part in question.

Quick-release operation on the front wheel is often complicated on account of wheel-retention devices. If the wheel does not come out right away, check what is holding things up, unscrew the thumbnut further and if necessary spread the fork apart or twist a clip out of the way.

To operate a quick-release, shown here on the front wheel hub, do not use the lever merely as a wingnut. Instead, insert the hub with the lever in the open position, and then cock the lever into the closed position once the hub is positioned correctly. If it's too tight or too loose, first unlock the lever, then adjust the nut at the other end, and try again. If your fork ends have prongs or ridges, you will have to unscrew the nut quite far before you can remove or install the wheel—and you'll have to screw it in again before you can use the quick-release lever.

BALL BEARINGS

Virtually all moving parts rely on ball bearings to minimize friction and wear. They all work on the same principle, and their condition has a great effect on the bike's performance. Understanding their operation, maintenance, and adjustment is as important for every home bike mechanic as it is for the occasional cyclist.

Two kinds of bearings are in use: cup-and-cone, or adjustable, bearings and cartridge bearings (often referred to as sealed bearings). Although the latter are generally more accurate when new and can be better sealed against dirt and water, they are not inherently superior. Besides, there is little maintenance you can do on these models: either they run smoothly or they must be replaced, which is best left to a bike mechanic, as it generally requires special tools. Sometimes—but not usually—subsequent lubrication is allowed

for by means of an oil hole or a grease nipple that is integrated in the part in which the bearings are installed. In other cases, the best you can do is to lift off the seal with a pointed object and apply grease using a grease gun.

The conventional cup-and-cone bearing consists of a cone-shaped and a cup-shaped bearing race, one of which is adjustable relative to the other by means of screw threading. The bearing balls lie in the recess between these two parts and are lubricated to minimize friction. Generally, bearing grease is used as a lubricant. Actually, oil—any thickish mineral oil—is even more effective, but can be messy, as it tends to leak out and has to be replenished frequently.

Several manufacturers have grease fittings available, with which grease can be injected into the bearings without disassembly. The most sophisticated of these is the Grease Guard system, which seals off the bearings with chevron-shaped seals, thus retaining the grease directly at the bearing. For after-market installation, you can use the Stein grease fittings, available at many bike shops. Repeat grease injection at least once a month and after every ride in very dusty or wet terrain.

Regular grease lubrication should be repacked once a season. To do it, you have to disassemble the entire bearing. Clean and inspect all parts, replacing anything that appears to be damaged (corroded, pitted, or grooved). Then fill the cup-shaped bearing race with bearing grease and push the bearing balls in, leaving

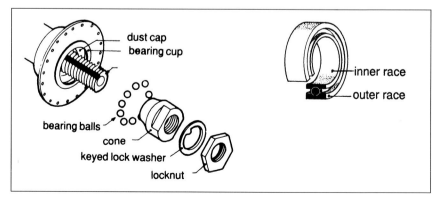

The two types of bearings used on the bike: the cup-and-cone bearing and the cartridge bearing unit. Only the former is adjustable; the latter can be sealed against dirt more effectively.

enough space to allow their free movement, followed by reassembly and subsequent adjustment. The bearing balls are often held in a retainer, and when overhauling a sticky bearing, it may help to replace the retainer with loose balls.

Adjustable bearings must be so adjusted that the moving part is free to rotate with minimal friction, yet has no "play" (looseness). To adjust a cup-and-cone bearing, loosen the locknut or lockring while holding the underlying part (the cone in the case of a hub or a pedal, the cup in the case of a headset or bottom bracket). Next, lift the underlying lock washer, if installed, and tighten or loosen the threaded main bearing part (cone or cup) about a quarter turn at a time. Finally hold that part again, while tightening the locknut or lockring.

PREVENTIVE MAINTENANCE

It is simple to keep the bike in good operating condition so that it is working well whenever you ride it. That will eliminate the vast majority of repairs later on. It is easy enough to spot when a nut or a bearing has come loose, and if corrected immediately, no harm is done. Yet left unchecked, the situation rapidly becomes worse, often leading to an expensive and complicated replacement job after only a week or so of neglect.

Although most of the actual maintenance operations are covered in detail in the chapters that follow, this is the time to get familiar with a systematic schedule to check the bike. It is based on (almost) daily, biweekly, and semiannual checks, proceeding as outlined below.

DAILY INSPECTION

This may seem to be overdoing it a little, but there are a few things you ought to look out for before you take the bike out for a ride. These will be covered in this section.

Tires

Check whether the tires are inflated properly, considering the type of terrain you will ride in: 4 bar (60 psi) for smooth, hard roads; 3 bar (45 psi)

Ball bearing detail, showing the bearing balls embedded in grease on a conventional adjustable cup-and-cone bearing. On cartridge bearing units there's not much visible, and they have to be replaced in their entirety if they don't run smoothly.

Adjusting a ball bearing is a matter of tightening the cone (in the case of a hub) or the bearing cup (on a bottom bracket or a headset).

for moderately rough but hard surfaces; 2 bar (30 psi) for irregular but mainly firm ground; 1 bar (15 psi) for really loose ground or snow.

Handlebars

Make sure the handlebars are straight, at the right height and clamped tightly—both in the head tube and in the stem.

Saddle

Verify that the saddle is straight, level, at the right height, and firmly in place.

Brakes

Check the effectiveness of the brakes by verifying each can block the wheel against your weight pushing the bike forward with the lever depressed, leaving about 2 centimeters (3/4 inch) between brake lever and handlebars.

Gears

Lift the rear wheel and, while turning the cranks, check whether the derailleurs can be shifted to reach all the gears—in other words, every combination of chainring and cog.

BIWEEKLY INSPECTION

At least every other week during the time you use the bike, clean it as explained at the end of this chapter. Then carry out the same checks listed above for the daily inspection, and in addition do the following:

Wheels

Check for broken spokes and wheel wobble: lift the wheel off the ground and turn it relatively slowly, keeping an eye on a fixed point such as the brake pads. If the wheel seems to wobble sideways relative to the fixed point, it should be trued (see Chapter 27).

Brakes

Observe what happens when you pull the brake levers forcefully: the brake pads must touch the side of the rim over their entire surface. Adjust the brake as outlined in Chapter 30 if they don't.

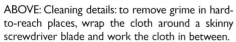

ABOVE: Cleaning details: to remove grime in hard-to-reach places, wrap the cloth around a skinny screwdriver blade and work the cloth in between.

RIGHT: To lubricate correctly, don't spray oil indiscriminately. Instead, lubricate only the parts shown on the list in the text, using the appropriate lubricant, and aim accurately. Wipe off any excess.

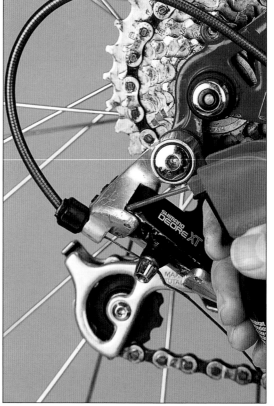

Tires

Check the tires for visible signs of wear, damage, and embedded objects. Remove anything that doesn't belong there (using tweezers) and replace the tire if necessary.

Cranks

Using the wrench part of the crank extractor tool, pull the crank attachment bolts tight, as explained in Chapter 28.

General Check

Check all the other screws, bolts, and nuts to make sure they are tight; verify whether all moving parts turn freely and all adjustments are correct. Repair or replace anything damaged or missing.

Lubrication

Lubricate the parts shown in the illustration, using the lubricants indicated below and wiping any excess off afterwards.

Chain

Use special chain lube in spraycan.

Brake Levers, Pivots, Cable Ends

Use light spray can lubricant, aiming precisely with the little tubular nozzle installed on the spray head.

SEMIANNUAL INSPECTION

If you use your bike all year, the work described below will be necessary twice a year. This is a complete overhauling job, which very nearly returns the bike to its as-bought condition. Treated this way, your mountain bike will literally last a lifetime, unless of course you have a collision that destroys the frame. But even then, on a high-

quality bike, it may be worthwhile to salvage most of the parts, replacing only what was actually damaged.

If you use the bike only in the fair-weather period, carry out this work at the end of the season. Then merely do a biweekly inspection at the beginning of the next season. During the semiannual inspection, proceed as follows:

First carry out all the work described above for the biweekly inspection, noting in particular which parts need special attention because they seem to be loose, worn, damaged, or missing. Subsequently, work down the following list:

Wheels

With the wheels still installed, check for damage of the rim or the tire and for loose or missing spokes then remove the wheels.

Check the hubs for play, wear, and tightness as explained in Chapter 27. Preferably disassemble and lubricate or overhaul the hubs, or inject grease if the hubs are equipped with special grease injection fittings called Grease Guard.

Chain

Remove the chain and measure the length of a 100-link section—replace the entire chain if it measures more than 129.5 centimeters (51 inches). The apparent stretch is a sign of wear that will affect shifting as well as transmission efficiency. In addition, the worn chain will also wear out the chainrings and the cogs. If the chain is not badly worn, merely rinse it out in solvent, after which it should be lubricated immediately (to prevent rust) and reinstalled, following the instructions in Chapter 28.

Bottom Bracket

Check it for play and freedom of rotation. If the bottom

Lubrication points. Refer to the text to determine what kind of lubricant to use in each of the locations marked with an arrow.

bracket is of the adjustable type, remove the crank and disassemble and overhaul the bearings as explained in Chapter 28. If it has cartridge bearings and does not run properly, get it overhauled at a bike shop.

Headset

Try it out and make sure it rotates without play or rough spots. Preferably, disassemble and overhaul the bearings as described in Chapter 31.

Derailleurs

With the chain removed, clean, check, and lubricate both derailleur mechanisms, making sure the pivots work smoothly and the little wheels, or pulleys, of the rear derailleur turn freely. If necessary, overhaul or replace parts as explained in Chapter 29.

CLEANING THE BIKE

Do this job whenever your bike gets dirty—at least once a month in clean terrain and dry weather, much more frequently in dirty terrain and inclement weather.

Cleaning procedure

1. If the bike is dry, wipe it with a soft brush or a cloth to remove any dust and other dry dirt. If the bike—or the dirt that adheres to it—is wet, hose or sponge it down with plenty of clean water. Take care not to get water into the hubs, bottom bracket, or headset bearings, though.

2. Using a damp cloth, clean in all the hard-to-reach nooks and crannies. Wrap the cloth around a pointed object, such as a screwdriver, to get into hidden places, such as between the cogs on the freewheel and the chainrings, underneath the brake arms, or at the derailleur pulleys.

3. Clean and dry the same locations with a clean, soft, dry cloth.

4. With a clean wax-soaked cloth, treat all the bare metal areas very sparingly to inhibit rust and the paintwork to protect it; then rub it out with a clean cloth.

CHAPTER TWENTY-SIX

FRAME MAINTENANCE

The most important thing to know about frame maintenance is how you can judge whether anything is wrong with the frame. This should be done after a serious crash and whenever you get the feeling the bike is not tracking as well as it used to.

FRAME DAMAGE

In case of a head-on collision, the first thing to bend is the front fork (discussed in Chapter 31), but there is a chance of the downtube literally buckling at a point just behind the head tube. Left unchecked, this may lead to the frame's collapse, which can be highly dangerous. It's the kind of damage only a professional frame builder can solve for you and one that's only worthwhile on an expensive frame because the downtube has to be removed and replaced by a new one. Check the appropriate location for damage. If it is buckled, take the bike to a bike shop to find out what can be done about it.

Other kinds of frame damage are less dramatic. A collision, a fall, or other forms of abuse may cause the frame to get out of alignment. You can verify this by trying to line up the front and the rear wheel while looking from behind. If it can't be done, either the frame or the front fork may be misaligned. Finally, it sometimes happens that one of the drop-outs gets bent—usually the one with the derailleur eye, which results in poor gear shifting.

In the following procedures, the checks that can be carried out relatively simply will be described in some detail. See a bike shop about correcting any damage detected.

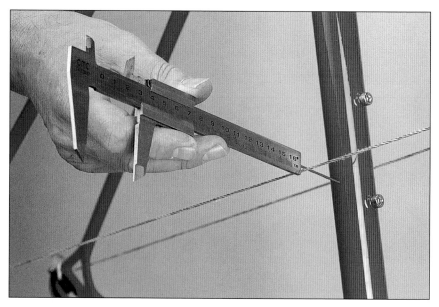

This is how you measure the frame for misalignment if you don't use a special tool Using the caliper's depth gauge (the piece that sticks out the back) measure the distance from the frame tube to the wire pulled taut. The frame is bent if it doesn't measure the same on both sides.

FRAME ALIGNMENT CHECK

Tools and equipment

   3 meters (10 feet) of twine
   Straightedge marked in millimeters or 32nds

Procedure

   1. Remove the rear wheel from the bike, following the description in Chapter 27.
   2. Wrap the twine around the frame as shown in the illustration, pulling it taut at the drop-outs.
   3. Measure and compare the dis-

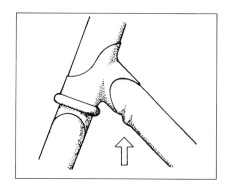

Typical front-impact frame damage. After a frontal crash or collision, check this point for such a bulge. Consult a frame builder if that's what you've got.

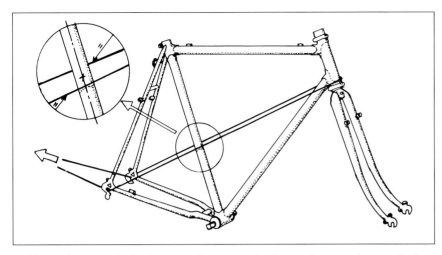

Frame alignment check. Measure and compare the distance between the stretched line and the frame tube on both sides if you have reason to suspect the frame may be bent. Consult a frame builder or experienced bike shop mechanic if the frame does turn out to be bent.

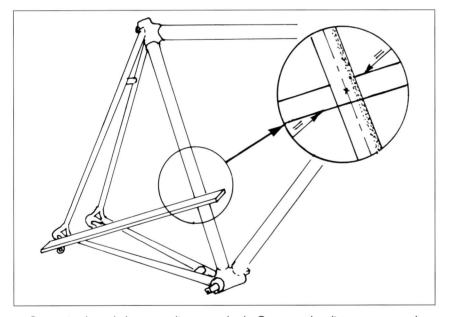

Rear triangle and dropouts alignment check. Compare the distance measured directly between the dropout with the distance measured between the straight-edge and the frame's seat tube on each side, and of these two dimensions added to the seat tube diameter.

tance between seat tube and twine on both sides. If the difference is more than 3 millimeters (1/8 inch), the frame is out of alignment and should be corrected.

REAR TRIANGLE ALIGNMENT

Occasionally, the misalignment is due to a minor deformation of the tubes of the rear triangle. If this is the case the repair can be done, but we suggest you consult an experienced bike mechanic and have him or her do the work for you. This applies especially on light frames and those made of aluminum and titanium. Kevlar- and carbon fiber-reinforced frames just can't be corrected for love or money.

DROP-OUT CHECK

After a fall, the reason for derailleur problems may be that the rear derailleur eye (on the right-hand rear drop-out) is bent. In other cases, the wheel just doesn't want to center, even though it seems to be undamaged. To establish whether the drop-outs are still straight after a fall or rough transportation—this damage is more typically caused by the latter—proceed as follows:

Tools and equipment
    60 centimeters (2 feet) metal straightedge

Procedure
1. Remove the rear wheel from the bike, following the relevant procedure in Chapter 27.
2. Hold the straightedge snug up against the outside of the right-hand drop-out, holding, but not forcing, the other end near the downtube, and measure the distance between the straightedge and the seat tube.
3. Repeat step 2 for the left-hand drop-out.
4. Measure the seat tube diameter at the same point.
5. Compare the distance between the straightedge and the seat tube on both sides.
6. Measure the distance between the drop-outs and compare it with the sum of the seat tube diameter (from step 4) and the two distances measured in steps 2 and 3.
7. If the difference is more than 3 millimeters (1/8 inch), at least one of the drop-outs should be straightened—preferably by a frame builder or experienced bike mechanic, but you may want to try your hand at it yourself. Usually, you can tell by means of a visual inspection which is the one that's bent.

DROP-OUT ALIGNMENT

After the preceding check, you may want to straighten a bent drop-out. However, don't do it if cracks are visible at any point or if the derailleur mounting lug (with its threaded hole) is bent relative to the rest of the drop-out. Leave such problems to a bike mechanic, who has a special tool for this job. The same goes for composite and aluminum frames—the aluminum drop-outs used on those tend to crack, if not when they get bent in the first place, then when you try to straighten them.

Tools and equipment

Vise with soft metal jaw protectors, mounted on a work bench

Procedure

1. Establish whether it is just the derailleur eye or the drop-out itself that is bent. In the latter case, check which drop-out has to be bent in which direction, by checking carefully from behind and from the top when the wheel has been removed from the bike.

2. Clamp the drop-out to be straightened in the vise just below the location of the bend. Alternatively, you can use two 8-inch adjustable wrenches, one on either side of the bend.

3. Force the frame in the appropriate direction, using the bike (or the adjustable wrenches) for leverage.

4. Check again and make any corrections that may be necessary.

TOUCHING UP PAINT DAMAGE

In off-road use, you can't help but scratch up your bike sometimes. At least once a season, it will be worthwhile to touch up any nicks and scratches. Don't do this kind of work if the frame is made either of carbon or Kevlar-reinforced plastic resin or has tubes that are bonded together with resin rather than being welded or brazed, because the solvents used in the paint may not be compatible with the resin.

Tools and equipment

Touch-up paint
Small paintbrush
Cloth
Sandpaper or steel wool
Paint thinner

Procedure

1. Clean the bike thoroughly to uncover any locations that may have to be touched up.

2. Sand down the area of the damage, folding the sandpaper into such a small pad that you remove as little good paint as possible.

3. Clean the area with a dry rag, then with paint thinner, treating only the small area immediately affected, and again with a clean, dry cloth.

4. Dip the paintbrush in the paint very sparingly, and treat only the area where the paint has been removed, minimizing any overlapping of paint that is still intact.

5. Clean the brush in paint thinner immediately after use and allow it to dry suspended with the bristles down but not touching anything.

6. Allow the frame to dry at least overnight before touching it again.

Note

If you can only get paint in a spray can, spray a little in a bottle cap and dip the brush in it.

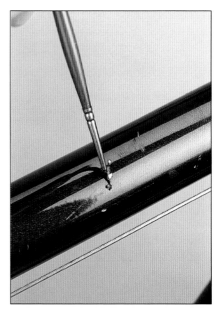

To touch up paint damage on conventional brazed or welded frames, first clean the frame and remove any grease or wax, for example, with paint thinner. Don't fool around with bonded and carbon-fiber frames, because the paint thinner may damage the resin used.

WHEEL MAINTENANCE

In this chapter we'll cover the major maintenance and repair operations required by the wheel. First you will be shown how to remove and replace the wheel, which is often necessary to transport the bike or to carry out other maintenance jobs.

WHEEL REMOVAL AND INSTALLATION

This description is based on a wheel with a quick-release hub.

Tools and equipment

Cloth for rear wheel

Wrench (only needed for wheel without quick-release)

Removal procedure

1. For the rear wheel, first put the chain on the smallest cog and the smallest chainring by means of the derailleur, while turning the cranks with the wheel raised off the ground.
2. Release the brake by squeezing the brake arms against the rim and unhooking one of the cable nipples on the cantilever brake or U-brake, by releasing one side of the V-brake, or by twisting the cam plate out on the roller-cam brake. In the case of an under-the-chainstay U-brake, just push the wheel forward in the drop-outs until it hits the inside of the brake, which will spread the brake arms apart. All this is not necessary if you are removing a wheel with a flat tire, but it will be when you try to reinstall it with an inflated tire.

Before removing or installing the wheel, untension the brake (left). On the rear wheel, place the chain on the smallest cog and a small chainring, then pull back the chain with the derailleur to allow the cogs to pass (right).

3. Twist the lever on the quick-release into the *open* position.
4. On the rear wheel, pull back the derailleur and the chain.
5. Pull out the wheel, guiding it past the brake pads.

Note

If the front wheel doesn't come out after loosening the quick-release, that may be due to the presence of wheel-retention ridges at the end of the fork. If that is the case, unscrew the thumbnut at the end of

the quick-release skewer and don't forget to screw it back in after reinstalling the wheel with the lever still in the *open* position.

Installation procedure

1. On a rear wheel, first put the shifters in the position to engage the gear with the chain on the smallest cog and the smallest chainring (turn the cranks forward if you have to engage another chainring in the front).
2. Make sure the brake is released— if not, squeeze the brake arms

together and unhook the cable nipples (on the cantilever brake, V-brake, or U-brake) or twist the cam plate out (on the roller-cam brake).

3. Twist the lever on the hub's quick-release into the *open* position.

4. On the rear wheel, pull back the derailleur with the chain.

5. Slide the wheel back into position, guiding it past the brake pads.

6. Straighten the wheel between the fork blades or the chainstays and the seat stays.

7. Holding the wheel in the correct position, flip the quick-release lever into the *closed* position and make sure the wheel is locked firmly in place (see note below).

8. Check whether you have installed the wheel perfectly centered, and correct if necessary.

9. Tension the brake or reinstall the cable nipple, then readjust the brake so the brake pads touch the sides of the rim fully when the brake lever is applied.

Notes

1. If the quick-release does not tighten the wheel properly, or conversely, if it does not fit clear of the drop-outs, put the lever in the *open* position and unscrew or tighten the thumbnut by perhaps one turn, then try again.

2. If the wheel is held with axle nuts instead of a quick-release, use a fitting wrench on the nut. It will be best to use two wrenches simultaneously—one on either side of the hub.

PUNCTURE REPAIR

In case of a puncture, you can either patch the tube or replace it. Whether you actually fix the old tube or install a new one is up to you, but you can't carry unlimited spares, so you will be confronted with the need to actually fix the leak yourself sooner or later.

Tools and equipment
Patch kit
Tire levers

Slide the wheel out, or into place, after loosening the quick-release lever. You may have to loosen the thumbnut at the other end before the assembly can clear the wheel-retention prongs that are a feature found on many fork-ends these days.

Tools to remove and reinstall wheel
Sometimes spare tube

Checking procedure
1. Remove the wheel from the bike, following the preceding procedure.
2. Check the valve: try to inflate and check whether air is escaping there. Sometimes a Schrader valve leaks and can be fixed by tightening or

replacing the interior mechanism, using either a special tool or a narrow object such as a small screwdriver.
3. Check the circumference of the tire for signs of damage and mark their location.

Removal procedure
1. If the tire still contains air, push the pin of the valve in; on a Presta valve,

Insert the tire levers carefully so as not to pinch the tube. If the tire seems too tight, work the tire bead toward the center of the rim to loosen it.

first unscrew the small round nut at the end of the pin.

2. Push one side of the tire toward the (deeper) center of the rim around the entire circumference of the wheel to loosen that side enough to ease removal.

3. If it does not come off by hand, place the longer end of a tire lever under the side of the tire and hook the short end around a spoke.

4. Move along the rim by two or three spokes, and insert the second tire lever.

5. If necessary, insert the third tire lever two or three spokes in the opposite direction (if it *is* necessary but you have only two, remove one of the two installed and move it to the new location).

6. Remove the tire levers and pull the rest of that side of the tire off by hand, working around.

7. Remove the tube from under the tire, and push the valve out of the valve hole.

Tube inspection procedure

1. Check the tube, starting at any location you may have marked as an obvious or probable cause of the puncture.

2. If the leak is not easily detected, inflate the tire and check carefully for escaping air, passing the tube by your eye, which is your most sensitive detection device. This takes some practice, but to date we have not encountered a leak that could not be found this way.

3. If you cannot detect escaping air, submerge the inflated tire in water. (If not enough of that precious liquid is available, rub a little water from your water bottle over the inflated tire, systematically working around and reinflating the tire as required to maintain adequate pressure.)

4. Once you have established the location of the leak, mark it.

Patching procedure

1. Take a patch from the patch kit (generally, the smallest size will do, except if you are dealing with several holes close together or with a long tear).

2. If necessary, dry the tube local to the leak. Roughen the area around the leak with sandpaper or scraper and wipe clean.

3. Take a drop of rubber solution from the tube and quickly spread it smoothly and evenly over an area around the leak that is a little larger than the patch.

4. Allow the rubber solution to dry one minute for a normal butyl tube

(or twice that long if you should have a latex tube, recognized by its softness and its color: not black but white or red).

5. Leave the cellophane backing on but remove the plastic or aluminum foil from the adhesive side of the patch without touching the adhesive, and place the patch, centering it over the leak.

6. Push the patch down, then compress, kneed, and flex the patch and the tube together to make sure the patch adheres fully. If it does not, remove the patch and restart at step 1 of this procedure.

7. Leave the cellophane backing on to prevent adhesion between the tube and the inside of the tire.

8. Inflate the tube partly to establish whether air escapes. If it does, there may be another hole, or the first one was not patched properly. Fix or redo until the tube holds air.

9. While waiting to verify whether the tube holds air, check the inside of the tire and remove any embedded objects that may have caused the puncture—or cause subsequent ones. Particularly tricky are thorns, which wear off to be invisible on the outside, yet protrude inside to pierce the tube when the tire is compressed. Take them out with tweezers from your first-aid kit if your fingernails won't do the trick.

10. Also check inside the rim bed to make sure none of the spokes protrudes and that they are covered by rim tape. File off any spoke ends that do protrude, and replace or patch the rim tape if it is broken.

Reinstallation procedure

1. Let most of the air escape from the tube until it is limp but not quite empty.

2. Starting at the valve, put the tube back under the tire over the rim.

3. Starting opposite the valve and working in both directions toward it, pull the side of the tire back over the rim, making sure the tube does not get pinched between the tire bead and the rim.

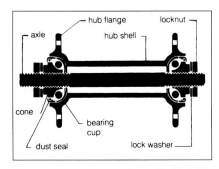 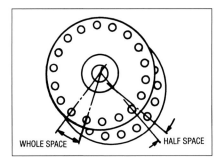

Cross-section through a typical hub. This hub is equipped with cup-and-cone bearings. The details of the quick-release are not shown here.

Angle between adjacent spokes and number of spacings. Refer to the accompanying drawing and the text for an explanation on how to use this table.

No. of spokes in wheel	1-cross angle	spaces	2-cross angle	spaces	3-cross angle	spaces
24	75°	2½	135°	4½	–	–
28	64.3°	2½	115.7°	4½	167.1°	6½
32	56.3°	2½	101.3°	4½	146.3°	6½
36	50°	2½	90°	4½	130°	6½
40	45°	2½	81°	4½	117°	6½
44	40.9°	2½	73.6°	4½	106.4°	6½
48	37.5°	2½	67.5°	4½	97.5°	6½

4. If the tire has a Presta valve, reinstall the knurled locknut. Whatever the valve, make sure it is straight.

5. Partially inflate the tire and check once more to make sure the tube is not pinched. Knead the tire sidewalls from both sides, and make sure the tire is centered. The ridge on the side should be equally far from the rim around the circumference on both sides.

6. Inflate the tire to the desired pressure, preferably checking with a pressure gauge: 4 bar (60 psi) for hard, smooth surfaces; 2 to 3 bar (30 to 45 psi) for rough terrain; 1 to 1.5 bar (15 to 22 psi) for soft, loose soil, mud, or snow.

Note

Even if you choose not to patch a tube while you are out in the field, replacing it with your spare tube instead, fix the puncture once you get home, so you can use the fixed tube as a spare.

Tube replacement procedure

If the puncture cannot be fixed, or if you want to install another tube for any other reason, proceed as described under *Removal procedure* above to remove the tube, then install the new tube and continue as described under the *Reinstallation procedure*.

Replacing the Tire Casing

To replace the tire casing itself, initially proceed as described above to remove the tube, and remove the other side of the tire to the same side. Put one side of the new tire in place and continue as described in the *Reinstallation procedure* above.

THE HUB

You can maximize the life of a hub by means of frequent checks, adjustment, lubrication, and overhauling. To replace a hub, the entire wheel has to be rebuilt, which runs the bill up con-

siderably. Besides, hubs are often only available as pairs, effectively doubling the cost of replacement when only one is worn.

CHECKING THE HUB BEARINGS

This procedure applies to any kind of hub, regardless whether it is the conventional adjustable bearing type or a cartridge bearing model.

Tools and equipment
Usually none required

Procedure

1. To check whether the hub runs freely, lift the wheel off the ground and let it spin slowly. It should rotate several times and then oscillate gradually into the motionless state with the valve at the bottom. (If reflectors are mounted on the spokes, the wheel may come to rest in a different place.) If it does not turn freely, adjust the bearings to loosen them (and they should probably be lubricated).

2. To check whether there is play in the bearings, grab the rim close to the brake, countering at the fork or the stays, and try to push it sideways in both directions. If it moves loosely, tighten the bearings.

ADJUSTING THE HUB BEARINGS

Carry out this work when the preceding test indicates a need for readjustment. It applies to cup-and-cone bearings only. For a rear wheel, first remove the freewheel (see Chapter 28) if it is of the screwed-on type.

Tools and equipment
Cone wrenches
Wrench to fit locknuts
Tools to remove wheel

Procedure

1. Remove the wheel.
2. Loosen the locknut on one side by

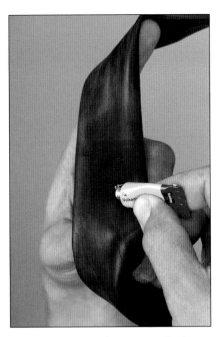

Pull out the tube—all the way if you intend to replace it, or only as far as you need it if you know where the puncture is. But do check the inside of the tire casing to remove any protruding objects that may have caused the puncture.

After cleaning the area, apply the rubber solution over an area slightly bigger than the patch. Let dry until it no longer looks wet and shiny.

Remove the foil backing and place the patch centered on the hole, starting in one corner, making sure it does not wrinkle. Push down over the entire surface to ensure bonding.

After the tube has been very slightly inflated to make sure it does not get caught between the rim and the tire bead, push it on the rim under the tire and pull the tire bead back over the rim, working gradually around the circumference. Use only your bare hands, not a tire lever.

one turn, countering at the cone on the same side of the wheel with the cone wrench.

3. Tighten or loosen the cone by about 1/4 turn at a time until the bearing is just a little loose. To loosen, counter at the cone on the other side with an open-ended wrench. To tighten, counter at the *locknut* on the other side.

4. Hold the cone with the cone wrench and tighten the locknut hard up against it, which will slightly decrease the play, justifying the advice given in step 3 to keep it just a little loose.

5. Check and readjust if necessary.

6. Reinstall the wheel.

OVERHAULING THE HUB

Do this work when the bearings of the hub are no longer running smoothly and cannot be returned to proper working order by means of adjustment.

Tools and equipment

Cone wrenches
Wrenches to fit locknuts
Cloths
Bearing grease

Disassembly procedure

1. Remove the wheel, following the procedure at the beginning of this chapter.
2. Remove the quick-release skewer.
3. Remove the locknut on one side, countering at the cone on the *same* side.
4. Lift off the lock washer.
5. Remove the cone, countering at the cone on the other side and catching the bearing balls as you remove it.
6. Pull the axle (with the other cone, washer, and locknut still installed at the other end) out of the hub shell, again catching the bearing balls and removing the plastic seal (if installed) from the hub shell.

Overhauling procedure

1. Clean and inspect all bearing parts.
2. Replace the bearing balls and any other parts that may be damaged, as evidenced by pitted, grooved, or corroded surfaces.

Reassembly procedure

1. Fill the bearing cups in the hub with bearing grease, then reinstall the plastic dust seals, if applicable.
2. Push the bearing balls into the grease, filling the circumference but leaving just enough space for them to move freely.
3. Insert the axle with one cone, washer, and locknut still installed. On a rear wheel, make sure it goes the same way round as it did originally.
4. Screw the other cone on the free axle end until the bearing seems just a little loose.
5. Install the lock washer with its prong, in the groove in the axle.
6. Screw the locknut on and tighten it against the cone.
7. Check and, if necessary, adjust the bearing as described above until it runs satisfactorily.
8. Reinstall the wheel.

Note

If parts that are screwed onto the axle are replaced, make sure the axle protrudes equally far on both sides—if necessary, reposition both cones and locknuts to achieve this.

RIM AND SPOKES

The way to minimize wheel problems—most typically broken spokes or a bent rim—is to keep the spokes tensioned evenly and adequately. Check the feel and the sound of plucking a well-tensioned new wheel at a bike shop and compare yours. If necessary, increase the tension of all or specific spokes, following the procedure outlined in the following section on Wheel Truing.

WHEEL TRUING CHECK

When a wheel is damaged, the rim is often permanently deformed sideways, resulting in wheel wobble. When riding, you will notice this as lateral oscillations. Check for this by turning the wheel slowly while it is lifted off the ground, observing the distance between the rim and a fixed point on the frame's rear triangle or on the fork, for a rear wheel and a front wheel, respectively. On a properly trued wheel, this distance is the same on both sides of the wheel and does not vary as the wheel is turned.

EMERGENCY REPAIR OF A BUCKLED WHEEL

Sometimes the damage is so serious that it will be obvious—and there is little you can do to solve the problem permanently. Just the same, such a seriously bent wheel can often be straightened enough to ride home—carefully.

Support the wheel at the low point and push down forcefully on the high points. Check frequently and continue until the whole is reasonably round. Then follow the procedure *Wheel Truing* to fine-tune the wheel far enough to be able to ride it home. Have it corrected or replaced as soon as possible.

You gain access to the hub bearing after removing the locknut and the cone on one side, after which you can pull out the axle from the other side with the other cone and locknut still installed.

Use two cone wrenches to adjust the hub, and force the cone and the locknut tightly against one another. Then check to make sure the bearing is not too tight. Redo if necessary.

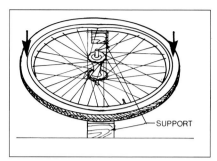

Emergency repair of a buckled rim. Gently but firmly push on the side of the rim that bulges up, supporting it in the areas that are bulged in the other direction.

WHEEL TRUING

This is the work done to get a bent wheel back into shape. It can be carried out in the field—at least well enough to get you home.

Tools and equipment
 Spoke wrench

Procedure
 1. Slowly spin the wheel while watching a fixed reference point on both sides, as described under *Wheel Truing Check*. Mark the locations that have to be moved farther to the left and the right.
 2. Using the spoke wrench, loosen the nipples of the spokes on the high side in the area of a high spot, tighten those on the opposite side, in that area. Turn the ones in the middle of the high spot a half turn, those farther from the center only a quarter turn at a time.
 3. Continue this process for each offset area, checking and correcting frequently, until the wheel is satisfactory.

REPLACING SPOKES

Sometimes a spoke breaks—usually at the head, which is hooked in at the hub flange. Stock a few replacement spokes of the same thickness and length.

Tools and equipment
 Spoke wrench
 Sometimes tools to remove freewheel

Procedure
 1. Unscrew the remaining end from the nipple. If that is not possible, let air out

of the tire, lift tire, tube, and rim tape local to the spoke nipple, and remove it to replace it with a new nipple.
 2. Count four spokes over along the circumference of the rim for a spoke that is routed the same way as your spoke will have to be. Refer to this one to find out just how to run it and how it should cross which other spokes.
 3. Hook the spoke through the hole in the hub.
 4. Route your spoke the same way as suggested by the example.
 5. Screw the nipple onto the threaded end of the spoke, slowly increasing tension until it is about as tight as all other spokes on the same side of the same wheel.
 6. Follow the procedure given under *Wheel Truing* until the wheel is perfectly true.

Note
 If several spokes are broken, figure out which rim hole goes with which hub hole by observing that every fourth spoke along the rim, and every second one on the same hub flange, runs similarly.

EMERGENCY SPOKE INSTALLATION

You can make an emergency spoke from an oversized spoke with the head cut off and

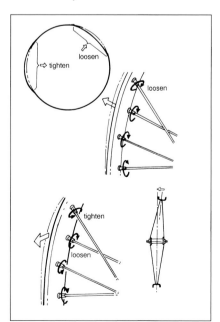

Cartridge bearing hubs, and some models with regular bearings, have a seal that must be carefully replaced.

bent at the unthreaded end in a Z-pattern so it will hook through the spoke hole in the hub flange. This bent spoke can be hooked in without removing the freewheel.

When you get home, replace this temporary repair with a permanent spoke of the right length, a job you can either do yourself or leave to a bike shop.

WHEEL BUILDING

Before you start, take a very close look at the old wheel (or another similar wheel) and the various descriptions and illustrations in this chapter that show spoking details—try to understand what's going on before you start.

Make sure you get the right spoke length—ask at the bike shop, telling them which hub and which rim you will be combining and which spoking pattern and how many spokes you'll be using. Most mountain bike wheels are built with 32 spokes, and for structural reasons we recommend using a three-cross pattern.

Ask at the bike shop what size to use for your rim, hub, and spoking pattern.

The principle of wheel truing. To correct radial misalignment (also called wheel hop), loosen the spokes in the areas where the rim goes in too far, and tighten the spokes in the areas where the rim goes out too far. To correct lateral misalignment (also called wheel wobble), loosen the spokes on the side where the rim is offset to that side, and tighten them on the opposite side in that same area.

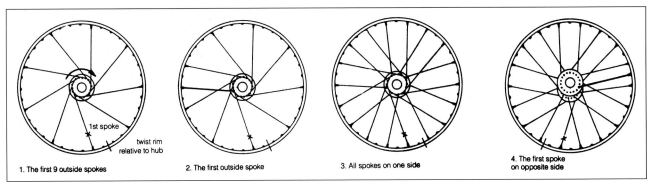

1. The first 9 outside spokes   2. The first outside spoke   3. All spokes on one side   4. The first spoke on opposite side

1st spoke
twist rim relative to hub

Wheel spoking sequence. Although you can leave in place the six spokes you may have used to determine the correct length, it's best to proceed in this sequence when building a new wheel.

The easy way to replace a rim—but only if the new one is identical to the old one—is by taping the two together lined up at the valve hole. Then move one spoke after the other from the old rim to the new one. After that, the wheel still has to be trued and tensioned.

On an off-set rear wheel the spokes on the right-hand side should be about 3 millimeters (1/8 inch) shorter than those on the left-hand side; or, if you can't find the optimum spoke size, deviate a little on the low side for the spokes on the right-hand side, a little on the high side for the left-hand spokes.

If you're rebuilding a wheel using an old hub or an old rim (or both), first cut away all the old spokes and remove them.

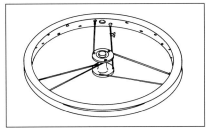

Tools and equipment
   Spoke wrench
   Medium-size screwdriver
   Lubricant
   Cloth

Procedure
   1. Check whether all the spokes have the same length: take them all in your hand and push them ends-down on the table, and compare the heights of the heads. Lubricate the threaded ends and wipe off excess lubricant.
   2. Take 8 spokes (assuming a 32-spoke wheel—more or less for other wheels), and put one through every second hole in one of the hub flanges from the outside to the inside. If holes are alternately countersunk on the inside and the outside of the hub flange, select those holes that are countersunk on the inside.
   3. Putting the hub in front of you, held vertically with the batch of spokes stuck through the upper flange, find the spoke hole in the hub that's immediately next to the valve hole and is off-set upward. Take one spoke and attach it with the nipple to that hole; mark this spoke with adhesive tape. We'll refer to it as *spoke one*. Screw on the nipple about five turns.

Spoke length check. If you can't be sure you have the right spoke length, spoke in just these six spokes first. If they're too loose or too tight, you'll need shorter or longer spokes respectively. If they're right, just continue spoking in the remaining spokes.

   4. Similarly attach the other spokes so far installed in the hub into every fourth hole in the rim.
   5. Check to make sure all these spokes are attached to spoke holes that are offset upward in the rim, and that three free spoke holes remain between each pair of consecutive spokes in the rim, one free hole in the hub.
   6. Turn the wheel over and establish whether the remaining free hole immediately next to the valve hole is oriented clockwise or counterclockwise. Select the spoke holes in the flange now nearest to you that are each off set half a space from the spokes already installed on the far flange in that same direction. Insert the next set of eight (or whatever is the appropriate number) spokes in these holes, leaving a free hole between each set of consecutive spokes.
   7. Locate spoke one (the one on the far flange next to the valve hole) and count out the appropriate number of spaces to determine where the next spoke is, which you'll attach in the free spoke hole on the other side of the valve hole, counting clockwise if the free spoke hole is also clockwise

from the valve hole, counterclockwise if the free hole is counterclockwise from the valve hole.

8. Attach the remaining spokes so far inserted in the hub into every fourth spoke hole in the rim.

9. You should now have sets of two spokes, each set separated by two free holes in the rim and by one free hole in the hub flanges. Make any corrections that may be required.

10. Insert the next batch of spokes from the inside to the outside in one of the hub flanges.

11. Take any one of these spokes and "lace" it to cross the chosen number of spokes on the same hub flange for the crossing pattern selected, always crossing under the last one. If you're building a three-cross wheel, that will be over the first, over the second, and then forced under the third. Attach this spoke in the next free hole in the rim that's offset in the corresponding direction. If it doesn't fit, you either have the wrong spoke length for the pattern selected, have tightened the other spokes too much (rarely the case), or you made a mistake somewhere along the line—check and restart if necessary.

12. Do the same with the last batch of spokes, inserting them in the free holes in the other hub flange from the inside to the outside, making the right crossings; then install them in the remaining spoke holes in the rim.

13. You now have a complete, but loosely spoked, wheel. Once more check to make sure the pattern is correct as you intended, then start tightening the spoke nipples progressively, working around several times, first using the screwdriver, then—when the nipples begin to get tighter—with the spoke wrench. Don't tighten too much, though, it should remain easy to turn the nipples with the spoke wrench.

14. Check whether the wheel is correctly centered between the locknuts at the wheel axle, as outlined in the description *Wheel Truing Check* above and the subsequent note.

15. Install the wheel in the bike, which should be hung up off the ground by saddle and handlebars or placed upside-down (taking care to support it at the handlebars so nothing gets damaged), and make the same kind of corrections as outlined under *Wheel Truing* above, until the wheel is perfectly round and has no lateral deflection.

16. Proceed to tighten the spokes all around equally. Unless you're an experienced piano tuner, it's hard to explain in writing how tight is right. Just compare with another good wheel (ask in the bike shop) to develop a feel for the right tension. Tension is checked by pushing spokes together in crossed pairs at a point between the rim and the last cross. On an off-set rear wheel, the right-hand spokes (chain side) should be considerably tighter than those on the other side. All the spokes on the same side of a wheel must be equally tight.

17. Now take spokes together in sets of four—two nearby sets of crossed spokes on each side of the wheel—at the point of their last crossing and squeeze them together quite forcefully. This is done to bend the spokes into their final shape and to relieve built-up stresses, resulting in some disturbing sounds. Don't be perturbed—if you don't do this now it will happen while you're riding the bike, when it's too late to make the required corrections.

18. After this stress-relieving operation, check the wheel for roundness and tightness once more—you will probably have to tighten several spokes a little more, because they have straightened, and some will have partly "unwound" from their nipples.

19. After about an hour's cycling, check and true the wheel once more. It's a lot of work, but think of the satisfaction.

Wheel builder at work. Follow the instructions in the text to build a sound new wheel—if you don't feel up to it, leave that job to a bike shop mechanic.

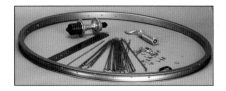

The parts needed to build a new wheel: rim, spokes, nipples, and hub.

The tools needed to build a new wheel: truing stand, spoke wrench, tensiometer, and centering gauge.

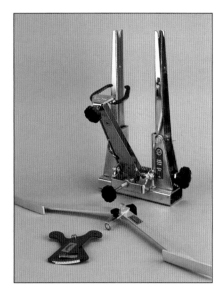

CHAPTER TWENTY-EIGHT

DRIVETRAIN MAINTENANCE

In this chapter we'll go over the maintenance work associated with the bottom bracket, the cranks, the chainrings, the pedals, the chain, and the freewheel with cogs.

THE CRANKS

Usually the first maintenance a new bike needs is to tighten the cranks, because the soft aluminum deforms so much that the connections between the spindle and the cranks come loose frequently until you have covered about 150 to 300 kilometers (100 to 200 miles). This is the reason you should carry the wrench part of the crank tool in your repair kit. Normally the crank only has to be removed when it is damaged or when you have to overhaul the bottom bracket. It is not uncommon in off-road cycling to bend a crank during a fall. Before you replace the entire crank, let a bike mechanic try to straighten it out, which requires a special tool.

TIGHTENING THE CRANKS

Tools and equipment
Depending on model of crank used, either a 6-mm Allen wrench or a matching crank extractor tool and a fitting wrench

Procedure
1. On models with an exposed crank bolt with a hexagonal recess surrounded by a black butyl ring, use the

The cranks are installed on the square, tapered ends of the bottom bracket spindle with bolts (or nuts on low-end bikes).

6 mm Allen wrench and tighten the crank bolts on both cranks, while using the crank arm for leverage. That's all for these models.
2. On models with a separate dustcap, remove it on both cranks.
3. Place the socket part of the crank extractor tool on the bolt inside the recess in the crank and tighten it with a wrench while using the crank for leverage. Do this on both cranks.
4. Replace the dustcap.

REPLACING THE CRANKS

This job is necessary when a crank or an entire crankset has to be replaced. It also has to be done for some bottom bracket maintenance jobs.

Tools and equipment
Crank extractor
Cloth
Grease
Sometimes an Allen wrench

Removal procedure
1. Remove the dustcap (if installed), which can generally be done with a coin or an Allen wrench.
2. Unscrew the bolt or the nut with the wrench part of the crank tool or the Allen wrench, holding the crank firmly.
3. Remove the washer, if one is installed

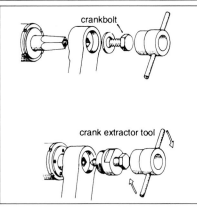

Use of the crank tool. The socket-wrench part of the tool is used to remove the bolt (if your cranks are attached with Allen bolts, use a fitting Allen wrench instead). Remove the bolt and the washer. Then screw the main part of the tool into the threaded recess in the crank and tighten the inner portion of the tool to push the crank off the bottom bracket spindle. Finally, unscrew the tool from the crank.

To remove the crank, once you've removed the dustcap, unscrew and remove the crank bolt. Then screw the crank puller into the crank's threaded recess and tighten the handle to push the crank off the spindle.

under the bolt or the nut. (This is an important step: if you forget to do this, you will not be able to remove the crank, damaging it instead.)

4. Make sure the internal part of the crank extractor is retracted as far as it will go.

5. Screw the crank extractor into the threaded recess in the crank by at least four full turns—preferably more.

6. Holding the crank firmly with one hand, turn the handle of the crank extractor (or the wrench that fits on it instead of a handle on some models) in, which will eventually pull the crank off the spindle.

7. Remove the tool from the crank.

Installation procedure

1. Clean the matching surfaces of the spindle and the crank hole, then apply a thin layer of lubricant to these surfaces.

2. Push the crank onto the spindle, making sure the two cranks are 180 degrees offset and the crank with the attachment for the chainrings goes on the right-hand side.

3. Install the washer, if applicable.

4. Install the bolt or the nut and tighten it fully, then install the dustcap.

Note

At about 40 kilometers (25-mile) intervals during the first 150 to 300 kilometers (100 to 200 miles), firmly retighten the bolt or the nut.

THE BOTTOM BRACKET

The bottom bracket comprises a spindle, or axle, to which the cranks are attached, and two sets of ball bearings that allow it to turn smoothly. Although some bikes have conventional screwed-in, or BSA, models, the trend in recent years has been to install cartridge-type bearings that come as a complete unit. The current crop of cartridge bearings is relatively easy to remove with a simple special tool, and a few can actually be handled with common tools.

ADJUSTING A SCREWED-IN BOTTOM BRACKET

Carry out this work on a conventional bottom bracket when the bearings have developed play or when they are too tight.

Tools and equipment

Bottom bracket wrenches

Procedure

1. Loosen the lockring on the left-hand side by about a half turn.

2. Loosen the adjustable bearing cup by turning it a quarter turn counter-clockwise if the bearing is too tight, clockwise if it is too loose.

3. Restraining the bearing cup, tighten the lockring, then re-adjust if necessary.

Notes

1. Bottom bracket looseness is best detected with the cranks installed, using them for leverage while twisting sideways.

2. Tightness is best established when the cranks are removed, turning the spindle by hand.

REPLACING A CARTRIDGE BOTTOM BRACKET

Tools and equipment

Tools for crank removal and installation
Special tool to match specific cartridge unit and its lockring
Lubricant
Cloth

Removal procedure:

1. Remove the cranks on both sides.

2. Establish the attachment method for the cartridge unit in question. Most commonly, they are screwed in with a special tool from the left side and locked in place with one or two screwed-on lockrings.

3. Remove the lockring or lockrings or other holding device, and then the cartridge unit itself, turning clockwise (left-hand thread) if it is accessed from the left side.

Installation procedure

1. Clean the inside of the bottom bracket and apply a little grease to the screw thread.

2. Carefully align and screw in the unit until the ends of the spindle protrude an equal distance on both sides.

3. Hold the cartridge in place while installing the lockrings (sometimes a lockring on both sides, sometimes only one), tightening up firmly.

OVERHAULING A SCREWED-IN BOTTOM BRACKET

This description applies to BSA, or screwed-in, bottom brackets. Cartridge bearing bottom brackets vary from one model to the next and usually require special tools—refer any problems to a bike shop.

Tools and equipment
Bottom bracket tools
Cloths
Solvent
Bearing grease
Crank tool

Disassembly procedure
1. Remove both cranks as described under *Replacing the Cranks* above.
2. Loosen and remove the lockring on the left side.
3. Loosen and remove the adjustable bearing cup, catching the bearing balls, which are usually held in a retainer.
4. Pull the spindle out, also catching the balls on the other side.

Overhauling procedure
1. Clean and inspect all parts, watching for corrosion, wear, and damage, as evidenced by grooved or pitted bearing surfaces.
2. If there is serious damage or wear, also check the condition of the fixed (right side) bearing cup, which otherwise remains on the bike. On mountain bikes, the fixed cup invariably has left-hand threading, meaning it is removed by turning clockwise, reinstalled by turning counterclockwise.
3. Replace any parts that are visibly corroded, damaged, or worn, taking the old parts to the shop with you to make sure you get matching replacements.

Installation procedure
1. Pack both bearing cups with bearing grease.
2. If the fixed bearing cup had been removed, reinstall it, turning it counterclockwise.
3. Push the bearing ball retainers into the grease-filled bearing cups, making sure they are such a way around that only the balls—not the metal of the retainer—contact the cup.
4. Put the spindle in from the left side—with the longer end first if it is not symmetric, as that'll be where the right-hand crank with the chainrings is installed.
5. Install the adjustable cup with its bearing ball retainer in place.
6. Install the lockring.
7. Adjust the bearing as described in the preceding description until it runs smoothly and without play.

THE CHAINRINGS

Once a month, ascertain that the chainrings are still firmly in place by trying to tighten the little bolts that hold them to each other and to the cranks, countering on the other side. The chainrings are attached with Allen bolts. The bigger chainring is sensitive to damage when it hits obstacles on the ground.

CHAINRING WEAR AND DAMAGE

If you allow the chainrings to wear too far, the teeth become thinner and hooked, with increased spaces in between. Eventually, wear will result in increased resistance and poor shifting. Replace the chainrings if they are obviously worn or when teeth are cracked.

If individual teeth are bent, they can sometimes be straightened, using the procedure described below. When the whole chainring is warped, it can be straightened by carefully using a wedge-shaped block of wood and pushing it between the chainstay and the chainring or between individual chainrings in the location where they are too close. Both these jobs can be done while leaving the chainrings on the bike, but do remove the chain.

REPLACING CHAINRING

This job will be necessary when the chainrings are worn or bent beyond repair—or when you want to change to a different gearing range. To remove, undo the Allen bolts while holding the crank

How to remove a conventional bottom bracket: once the cranks are removed, unscrew first the lockring on the left-hand side, then the right-hand bottom bracket cup, using a notched ring wrench and a pin wrench, respectively. To adjust the bearing, shown here, use both tools simultaneously, holding the lockring while adjusting the bearing cup, and holding the bearing cup while tightening the lockring.

steady. To replace the smaller chainring, the right-hand pedal generally has to be removed first (see below).

If the chainrings have offset tooth patterns, as used to improve shifting, make sure to match their orientation by means of the guide marker, which should be lined up with the crank arm. Tighten the bolts properly and check them again after about 40 km (25 miles).

THE PEDALS

The pedals are screwed into the cranks with a normal right-hand threaded connection on the right, a left-hand one on the left. If they are not marked appropriately, you can tell them apart by holding the threaded end up against the light: the pedal on which the thread seems to go up to the right goes on the right, whereas the one on which the thread seems to go up to the left goes on the left.

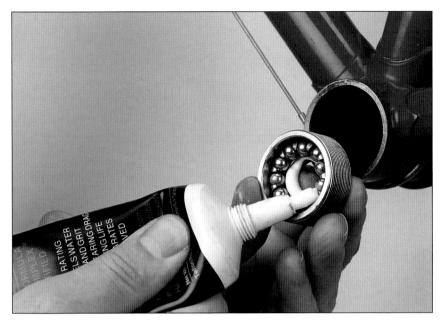

After cleaning all parts, embed the bearings in bearing grease before reassembling the conventional screwed-in bottom bracket.

To remove the biggest chainring, undo the (usually) five screws that hold it to the outside of the crank's "spider." The smaller chainrings are accessed from the back after the crank is removed from the bike.

Pedal maintenance operations are limited to adjustment, overhauling, and replacement.

REPLACING THE PEDALS

This job is done not only when you want to install new pedals but also when transporting the bike on a plane or a bus. The description applies equally to regular and clipless pedals.

Tools and equipment
Allen wrench or pedal wrench
Lubricant

Removal procedure
1. Restrain the crank firmly (for example, with a rod held horizontally just behind the crank and over the top of the chainstays).
2. Unscrew the connection between the pedal and the crank. If the pedal is not too tightly on the crank, and has a hexagonal recess in the end of the threaded stub (reached from behind the crank), use the Allen wrench. If not, use the open-ended wrench.

Note
Turn the left pedal to the right (clockwise) to unscrew, as it has left-hand screw thread.

Installation procedure
1. Clean the threaded hole in the crank and the threaded stub on the pedal, then apply some lubricant to both threaded surfaces.
2. Carefully align the screw thread and screw in the pedal, making sure you turn the right pedal clockwise, the left pedal counterclockwise.

Note
If you remove the pedals frequently (for example, because you often travel with the bike on public transportation), we suggest you place a thin steel washer between the face of the crank and the pedal stub. This will protect the crank and the thread, while making it much easier to loosen and tighten the pedal.

ADJUSTING THE PEDAL BEARINGS

This procedure only applies to pedals with conventional (adjustable) bearings.

Tools and equipment
Dustcap wrench or pliers
Wrench to fit locknut
Small screwdriver

Procedure
1. Remove the dustcap, using either pliers or a special dustcap wrench.
2. Loosen the locknut by one turn.
3. Lift the underlying keyed washer with the tip of the screwdriver to loosen it.
4. Using the screwdriver, turn the cone to the right (clockwise) to tighten the bearing, to the left (counterclockwise) to loosen it. Turn only 1/4 turn at a time.
5. Restraining the cone with the small screwdriver to make sure it does not turn, tighten the locknut.
6. Check and re-adjust if necessary; there should be neither noticeable play nor tightness.
7. Reinstall the dustcap.

OVERHAULING A CONVENTIONAL PEDAL

This is required if adjustment does not have the desired effect. Sometimes the problem will be a bent axle. (If axles are not stocked for the model in question, you'll have to replace the pedals altogether.)

Removing or installing the pedal from the crank with a special pedal wrench. If the pedal is not screwed on with too much force, it can be done with an Allen wrench from the back of the crank. Either way, use the crank for leverage. Put some lubricant on the threaded stub of the pedal spindle to ease removal.

Tools and equipment
  Dustcap wrench
  Wrench
  Small screwdriver

Disassembly procedure
  1. Remove the dustcap, using either pliers or a special dustcap wrench.
  2. Loosen the locknut and remove it.
  3. Lift the underlying keyed washer with the tip of the screwdriver to loosen and then remove it.
  4. Using the screwdriver, turn the cone to the left (counterclockwise) to loosen and remove it, catching the bearing balls as you do so.
  5. Pull the pedal housing off the spindle, also catching the bearing balls on the other side.

Overhauling procedure
  1. Clean and inspect all bearing surfaces and the pedal spindle.
  2. Replace anything that is damaged, corroded, grooved, or pitted, as well as

the pedal spindle if it is bent—or the whole pedal if no spares are available.

Reassembly procedure
  1. Fill both bearing cups with grease and push the bearing balls in this bed of grease, making sure there is just a little room between (one less than the maximum that might seem to fit in a pinch). Be careful not to lose any balls at this stage.
  2. Put the pedal housing on the spindle with the larger side—the end without the dustcap screw threading—first (toward the crank).
  3. After you've made sure you have not lost any bearing balls, install the adjustable cone.
  4. Install the keyed washer with the projecting prong fitting in the groove in the pedal spindle.
  5. Install the locknut, while restraining the cone with the small screwdriver to make sure it does not turn with it.
  6. Adjust the bearing as described above.
  7. Install the dustcap.

CLIPLESS AND OTHER CARTRIDGE BEARING PEDALS

Clipless pedals all run on cartridge bearings, as do some otherwise conventional-looking pedals. These pedals can be replaced following the same instructions that apply to the regular pedal.

The most important maintenance operation is exterior cleaning with water and a fine brush. There is also an Allen bolt on each side to adjust the release force.

To overhaul or adjust the bearings, first remove the pedal and then gain access to the bearing cartridge with the special tool from the manufacturer.

THE CHAIN

The life expectancy of a chain under off-road conditions is limited to about six months—even less if you ride in mud, sand, and dirt a lot. Clean and lubricate the chain as described in the section *Preventive Maintenance* in Chapter 25, at intervals that are consistent with the kind of

Adjusting the tension of the clip on a typical clipless mountain bike pedal. Of course the word *clipless* is a misnomer, because this pedal actually clips to a plate on the shoe, unlike the conventional pedal, which has to be used with separate toeclips to hold the foot in place.

weather and terrain you ride in. To do so, remove the chain to rinse it out in a solvent with five to ten percent motor oil mixed in, and then lubricate it thoroughly. In the following section, we shall cover removal and installation of the chain.

Sometimes, when shifting problems occur after the bike has been in a spill, the reason will be a twisted chain link. This may happen when the derailleur was twisted, trapping the chain in place. Check for this, and replace the twisted chain links.

When selecting a new chain, make sure you get one that is sufficiently narrow if your bike has eight cogs in the back. Contrary to the manufacturer's warning, our experience suggests that setups with Shimano HyperGlide freewheel and SuperGlide chainrings work just as well with other narrow chains as with the same manufacturer's special HyperGlide chain.

REPLACING THE CHAIN

This has to be done if the chain is worn or for a thorough cleaning job. Also,

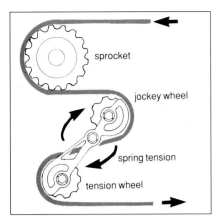

Chain routing at the rear derailleur. This is the way the chain should wrap around the derailleur's pulleys and the cogs on the freewheel.

some derailleur maintenance operations are best done with the chain removed from the bike. The Shimano HyperGlide chain, which is specially designed to match the same company's special tooth shape on the chainrings and cogs, requires special attention; that will be covered in a note at the end of the description.

Tools and equipment
Chain rivet extractor
Cloth

Removal procedure
1. With the aid of the derailleurs, and while turning the cranks with the rear wheel lifted off the ground, put the chain on the smallest chainring in the front and the smallest or second-smallest cog in the back.
2. Put the chain rivet extractor on one of the pins between two links, with the punch firmed up against the pin.
3. Turn in the handle six turns, which pushes the pin toward the opposite side.
4. Turn the handle back until the tool can be removed.
5. Try to separate the chain at this point, twisting it sideways. If it does not work, reinstall the tool and give it another turn until the chain comes apart. Just make sure the pin does not come out altogether, as that makes it very hard to reassemble the chain later.

Installation procedure
1. Make sure the derailleurs are set for the smallest chainring in the front and the second-smallest or smallest cog in the back.
2. Guide the chain around the cog and the derailleur pulleys as shown in the illustration, also passing over the chainring and through the front derailleur cage.
3. Routed this way, there should be just a little spring tension in the rear derailleur, tending to pull it tight.
4. If the chain is too long, remove an *even* numbered set of links, following the same procedure as described above for removal of the chain, but pushing one pin out all the way.
5. Bring the two ends together and fit the outer link plates on the one side around the inner link plates on the other.
6. Using the chain rivet extractor from the side where the pin protrudes, push it back in until it projects equally far on both sides.
7. Twist the chain sideways a few times until it has come loose enough at this point to bend as freely as at the other links. If this can't be done, put the tool on the chain in the other slot (referred to as "spreader position") and turn the handle against the pin just a little until the links are freed.

Note
If you accidentally push the pin out all the way when disassembling, install a section of two new links instead, after removing the two last links on the end with the lost pin—taking care not to lose the pin this time. Make sure you use a section of the same make and type of chain, since different chains make a poor match.

HyperGlide note
The Shimano HyperGlide chain has one slightly oversize chain link pin that can be recognized because the link is black, and should not be separated there. Split it anywhere else instead, and remove the pin all the way, then replace it with a special black link and a special longer pin that are both available with the chain or as a replacement

from the bike shop. Nip off the pointed end of this special link and file it flush.

THE FREEWHEEL
Although cassette-type hubs are now used almost universally, these instructions will be usable for older bikes with screwed-on freewheels as well. If the freewheel doesn't work, get a new one. Here you'll learn how to lubricate the mechanism, how to exchange cogs for those of a different size, and how to remove a complete freewheel.

FREEWHEEL LUBRICATION
Do this job if the freewheel is running roughly yet is not so old that it seems reasonable to replace it (do that after about a year's heavy use, or two years of regular riding).

Tools and equipment
SAE 60 oil
Cleaning materials
Old can or similar receptacle

Procedure
1. Before you lubricate the mechanism, clean the cogs, the spaces between them, and the visible end of the freewheel block, preferably with the wheel removed from the bike.
2. On freewheels with an oil hole, enter oil through it until it oozes out at the other end.
3. On freewheels without an oil hole, put the wheel on its side, the freewheel facing up, with a receptacle under the hub to catch excess oil. Turn the freewheel relative to the wheel, and enter oil through the gap that is visible between stationary and turning parts of the freewheel mechanism—until the oil comes out clean on the other side.
4. Let drip until no more oil comes out, then clean off excess oil.

REPLACING THE CASSETTE FREEWHEEL
The cassette freewheel is held to the rear hub with an internal hollow Allen bolt.

Tools and equipment

9- or 10-mm Allen wrench (depending on make)
Freewheel tool
Chain whip

Removal procedure

1. Remove the smallest cog with the sprocket remover, then lift off the other cogs.
2. Disassemble the hub bearing on one side and remove the axle.
3. Hold the wheel firmly and unscrew the freewheel off with the big Allen wrench.

Installation procedure

1. Clean and lightly lubricate the surfaces of the freewheel and the hole in the hub.
2. Accurately place the freewheel in the hub.
3. Tighten the internal hollow Allen bolt.

REPLACING THE COGS ON A CASSETTE FREEWHEEL

On these units, the cogs are held in splines on the freewheel body, held together with a lockring or the smallest cog. On Shimano HyperGlide cogs, which owe their easy shifting to subtle alignment of specially shaped teeth, one of the splines is wider, to preclude incorrect alignment.

Tools and equipment

Chain whip
Freewheel tool or special cassette tool

Disassembly procedure

1. Remove the wheel from the bike.
2. Place the wheel horizontally with the freewheel facing up.
3. Using the appropriate tool, remove the smallest cog (or a separate lockring on some models).

4. Remove the cogs and the spacers that lie on the splined end that is connected to the rest of the hub and contains the built-in freewheel mechanism, marking the sequence of the cogs and spacers.

Installation procedure

1. Clean all parts and coat them with a thin layer of grease.
2. Install the cogs and the spacers in the same sequence.
3. Screw on the last cog or the notched ring, while holding the freewheel firmly.
4. Reinstall the wheel.

REPLACING A SCREWED-ON FREEWHEEL

If your rear hub has a small diameter that is the same over its entire width between the flanges, you have the conventional ("old-fashioned") screwed-on model. You can usually tell once the wheel is removed from the bike, because on these models there will be internal splines or notches into which a freewheel removal tool fits.

Tools and equipment

Freewheel tool
Vise or large crescent wrench

Removal procedure

1. Remove the rear wheel from the bike.
2. Remove the quick-release or the right-hand axle nut and washer.
3. Place the freewheel tool on the freewheel with the ribs or prongs on the tool exactly matching the splines or notches in the freewheel body.
4. Install the quick-release or the right-hand axle nut, leaving about 2 millimeter (3/32 inch) of space between tool and nut.

5. If you have a vise available, clamp the tool in with the side matching the freewheel facing up; if not, place the wrench on the flat faces of the tool and clamp the wheel securely, for example, with the tire pushed against the floor and one wall of the room.
6. Turning counterclockwise to loosen the screw thread between hub and freewheel, forcefully turn either the wheel relative to the vise, or the wrench relative to the wheel—about one turn, until the space between the tool and the nut is taken up.
7. Loosen the nut another two turns and repeat this process until the freewheel can be removed by hand, holding the tool.

Installation procedure

1. Clean the threaded surfaces of the freewheel (inside) and the hub (outside), and coat these surfaces with lubricant to prevent corrosion and to ease subsequent removal.
2. Put the wheel down horizontally with the threaded end facing up.
3. Carefully screw the freewheel on by hand until it cannot be tightened further that way.
4. Install the wheel, and allow the driving force to "automatically" tighten it as you ride.

REPLACING THE COGS ON A SCREWED-ON FREEWHEEL

On these units, the cogs are generally either all or partly screwed onto the freewheel. You will need two chain whips—one wrapped around the smallest cog, the other around one of the bigger cogs. When you have finished reassembly, put the chain on the smallest cog and stand on the pedals to tighten it while pulling the brake lever to apply resistance.

On the cassette freewheel, the individual cogs can be replaced once the ring on top (or on some models the special smallest cog itself) has been removed with a matching freewheel tool. The other cogs are held onto the freewheel body with splines that are shaped so that they can only be installed as intended.

The entire freewheel body can be removed from the rest of the cassette hub to which it is held with a hollow Allen bolt.

To remove the chain, push out one of the pins—but not all the way—with the chain rivet tool. To reinstall the chain, push the pin back in. On the Shimano HyperGlide chain, use the special pin supplied with the chain, and twist off the end of the pin.

The guts of a cartridge-bearing pedal (that can be either a clipless model or a conventional one). It is retracted from the pedal by unscrewing it from the body, working from the side where the threaded stud is.

GEARING SYSTEM MAINTENANCE

This chapter describes the maintenance operations necessary to maintain and adjust the gearing system and its individual components. For the maintenance of cogs and chainrings, you are referred to the preceding Chapter 28, which is devoted to the drivetrain.

ADJUSTING THE DERAILLEUR RANGE

The most common derailleur problem is that one of the derailleurs either exceeds or fails to reach its full range. In the first case, called over-shifting, the chain is pushed sideways too far, so it drops off the innermost or outermost chainring or cog. In the latter case, referred to as undershifting, it doesn't move far enough, so it fails to reach the last cog or chainring. It is easy enough to correct either of these problems.

Tools and equipment
Small screwdriver
Sometimes a cloth

Procedure
1. Establish what the nature of your problem is:
front or rear derailleur?
too far or not far enough?
left or right?
2. If necessary, back off on the shifter and put the chain back on chainring or cog.

The left-hand illustration shows tightening the derailleur cablel. If the derailleur shifts beyond the biggest or smallest cog or chainring, or does not quite reach, adjust the range of travel limit on the rear and front derailleurs respectively, using the set-stop screws.

3. Observe how each derailleur is equipped with two set-stop screws, usually equipped with a little spring under the head, and usually marked with "H" and "L" for high and low gear, respectively.
4. Tightening one of these screws limits the range of the derailleur in the corresponding direction, while loosening that screw expands it.
5. If the chain came off on the right-hand side (outside, or high gear) on the front, tighten the screw marked

H of the front derailleur by perhaps one turn. If it did not quite reach the last gear on that side, loosen the screw by about that much.
6. Check all the gears, turning the cranks with the rear wheel lifted off the ground. Readjust as necessary.

Note
If problems persist, adjust the relevant derailleur system completely, as described for front and rear derailleurs separately below.

ADJUSTING THE REAR DERAILLEUR

Many gearing problems can be eliminated by some form of derailleur adjustment using the cable adjusters on the shifter and the derailleur mechanism.

Tools and equipment

Small screwdriver
Sometimes pliers and an Allen wrench to fit the cable clamp bolt

Procedure

1. To get by until you can do a more thorough job (if you have top-mounted shifters), select the friction mode (*F*) on the right-hand shifter and continue riding.

2. To adjust the derailleur, first carry out the adjustment as described above under *Adjusting the Derailleur Range*.

3. If the gears still do not engage properly, adjust the cable tension, using the built-in adjusting barrel at the derailleur or the shifter.

4. Set the derailleur in the position for the outside (small) cog, lifting the rear wheel and turning the cranks for this and all subsequently described gear changes while adjusting, until the chain engages that gear (or the one next to it, if this can't be achieved).

5. Holding the adjusting barrel, loosen the locknut, then tighten or loosen the barrel either to release or to increase tension on the cable.

6. If the range of the adjusting barrel is inadequate, the cable must be clamped in at a different point: screw the adjusting barrel in all the way, loosen the eye bolt or clamp nut that holds the cable at the derailleur, pull the cable taut (but not under tension) from the end, and tighten the clamp nut or eye bolt again.

7. Try out all the gears and re-adjust the range if that should be necessary, following the description above.

8. Now the derailleur operates correctly in friction mode. The next step will be to fine-tune the indexing. To do that, first with the shifter still set in the *F* position, select the lowest

Depending on the configuration, the rear derailleur is adjusted either with a cable adjuster at the derailleur itself (shown here) or at the shifter. If major adjustments are necessary, the cable may have to be clamped in at a different point.

Clean and lubricate the moving parts of the derailleur, aiming carefully and removing any excess lubricant.

gear (the biggest cog in the rear, combined with the smallest chainring in the front) and make sure it achieves this gear correctly.

9. Select the highest gear again (largest chainring, smallest cog), then put the shifter in index mode, marked *I*.

10. Adjust the cable tension until the chain runs smoothly without scraping against the derailleur cage or the next larger cog.

11. Move the shifter one notch for the next lower gear in the back, engaging the second smallest cog if it is adjusted correctly.

12. If the derailleur does not move the chain to the next cog, tighten the cable by about 1/2 turn of the adjusting barrel.

13. If the derailleur shifts past this second smallest cog, loosen the cable tension with the adjusting barrel by about 1/2 turn.

14. Repeat steps 10 through 13 until the mechanism works smoothly in these two gears.

15. With the derailleur set for the second smallest cog, tighten the cable with the adjusting barrel just so far that the chain runs noisily, scraping against the third-smallest cog.

16. Loosen the cable tension just so far that the noises subdue to achieve the optimal setting.

17. Verify that the derailleur selects all gears with the shifter set in the appropriate position and re-adjust if necessary.

Notes

1. If adjusting does not solve the problem, first check the alignment of the derailleur hanger—the threaded lug on the right-hand drop-out to which the derailleur is attached. If it is bent, get it straightened at a bike shop first.

2. If the cable does not move smoothly, replace it. Replace the shifter if this does not solve the problem either.

3. Most rear derailleurs have a third adjusting screw, with which the angle of the mechanism can be var-

Overhauling the rear derailleur amounts to disassembling the cage with the pulleys (tension and jockey wheels) to clean and lubricate. In cases of serious wear, replace them.

Install the front derailleur on the seat tube with the cage parallel to the chainrings and just high enough to clear the teeth of the biggest chainring.

ied. Select the gear in which the chain runs on the biggest cog, and adjust the cable tension so that the chain comes close to the cog without the cog scraping the pulley.

OVERHAULING THE REAR DERAILLEUR

This work will be necessary when so much dirt has built up that operation of the mechanism has become unreliable and cannot be solved by adjusting. The pulleys and the cage can be removed easily for this work, or you can take the whole derailleur off the bike by loosening the mounting bolt.

Tools and equipment

Wrench to fit bolts through pulleys
(guide wheel and tension wheel)

Solvent
Cloth
Lubricants

Procedure

1. Remove the bolts at the little pulleys over which the chain runs, catching the pulleys, the bearing bushings, and the various other parts.
2. Clean the pulleys and the bushings inside, as well as any other parts of the derailleur mechanism that are more easily accessible now. Replace if badly worn.
3. Lubricate the bushings in the pulleys with grease and all pivots with light spray can oil.
4. Reassemble the chain cage with the little pulleys, guiding the chain as shown in the illustrations.

5. Try out all the gears and adjust the derailleur if necessary.

REPLACING THE REAR DERAILLEUR

This may have to be done when the derailleur's operation cannot be restored by adjusting or overhauling.

Tools and equipment

Wrench to fit derailleur pulley bolt
(or chain rivet extractor)
Allen wrench
Small screwdriver
Cloth

Removal procedure

1. If you prefer to leave the chain intact, remove the bolts at the little

pulleys over which the chain runs, catching the pulleys, the bearing bushings, and the other parts.

2. Otherwise, separate the chain, as described in Chapter 28.

3. Undo the cable attachment and catch the pieces of cable casing.

4. Undo the derailleur mounting bolt and remove the derailleur.

Installation procedure

1. When you get a new derailleur, make sure that it is compatible with the shifter and the cogs installed on the bike.

2. Put the new derailleur in the same position as the old one was, checking to make sure it pivots freely around the mounting bolt.

3. Attach the cable.

4. Either install the chain (if it had been removed) or open up the cage at the guide wheel in the cage to put the chain in place, then reinstall the guide wheel so that the chain runs around it.

5. Try out all the gears and adjust the derailleur and the cable tension if necessary.

ADJUSTING THE FRONT DERAILLEUR

This job must be done when the front derailleur does not shift properly, "dumps" the chain by the side of the chainrings, or when one chainring cannot be reached.

Tools and equipment
    Small screwdriver
    Wrench to fit cable clamp bolt

Procedure

1. First carry out any adjustment of the set-stop screws that may be necessary, following the description *Adjusting the Derailleur Range* above.

2. Set the shifter in the position for the highest gear with the chain on the large outside chainring.

3. In this position, the cable should be just taut, but not under tension.

4. If necessary, tension or loosen it by clamping the cable in at a different

point: loosen the eye bolt or clamp nut, pull the cable taut, and tighten the eye bolt or clamp nut again.

5. Check all gears and make any other adjustments that may be necessary.

REPLACING THE FRONT DERAILLEUR

This may become necessary if the mechanism is bent or damaged—usually the result of a fall. Follow these same procedures to straighten out a front derailleur on which the chain scrapes along the derailleur cage or does not shift properly despite proper cable and set-stop screw adjustments.

Tools and equipment
    Allen wrench
    Wrench
    Small screwdriver
    Sometimes a chain rivet extractor

Removal procedure

1. Loosen the cable attachment by unscrewing the eye bolt or the clamp nut, and pull the cable end out.

2. Either remove the chain with the chain rivet extractor or open up the derailleur's chain guide cage by removing the little bolt through the bushing that connects the two sides in the back of the cage of some models.

3. Undo the mounting bolt.

Installation procedure

1. Install the derailleur on the seat tube, above the chainrings and with the outer cage plate parallel to the chainrings. Don't tighten it fully yet.

2. Fine-tune the position, leaving a distance of 2- to 4-mm (3/32- to 3/16-inch) clearance between the largest chainring and the bottom of the cage, making sure it is aligned. Now tighten the attachment bolt fully.

3. Feed the cable through the mechanism and attach it in the eye bolt or under the clamp nut.

4. Adjust the cable tension so that it is just taut, but not under tension, with the shifter set for the highest gear and the chain on the largest chainring.

5. Check all the gears and adjust the set-stop screws and the cable tension if necessary.

DERAILLEUR CONTROLS

Whatever type of shifter is used on your bike, if it does not give satisfactory service, as evidenced by the derailleur's jumping out of the selected gear, the reason may be a damaged or corroded derailleur cable. So first check that, and lubricate or replace it if necessary.

If the cable and the derailleur themselves are working properly, the problem may be due either to insufficient tension on the spring inside the mechanism, to dirt or corrosion, or to wear of the notched ring inside. Only in the latter case will it be necessary to replace the shifter.

First try cleaning and tensioning the shifter. Unfortunately, most modern shifters are not designed to be overhauled. But if it is an older one, you can probably take it apart carefully and note where the various bits and pieces go. Then clean and lightly lubricate all parts. Finally reassemble, and if necessary turn the screw that holds it all together a little tighter.

REPLACING A CONVENTIONAL SHIFTER

If the shifter cannot be made to work by means of adjustment and cable replacement, the whole unit can easily be replaced, as described here. For twistgrip type shifters, see *Replacing Twistgrip Shifter* below.

Tools and equipment
    Screwdriver
    Allen wrench

Removal procedure

1. Undo the cable at the derailleur.

2. Remove the shifter attachment screw.

3. Pull the cable out and catch the cable casing and any loose items.

Installation procedure

1. Attach the shifter in place.

2. Feed the cable through the shifter with the nipple in the recess.

3. Guide the cable through the

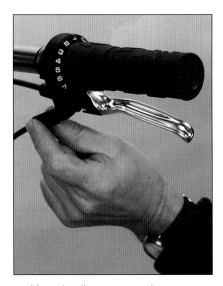

Most derailleur system adjustments are handled with the cable tension adjuster at the point where the cable comes out of the shifter. Only if the adjustment range is insufficient (or when you have to replace the cable) does it become necessary to change the clamping position of the cable at the derailleur itself.

various cable stops and the cable casing, and attach the end at the derailleur.
4. Adjust the derailleur cable tension as described above for front and rear derailleurs separately.

Note

On Shimano STI models, the brake levers and gear shifters form one unit that cannot be separated. So you'll be faced with buying the whole integrated unit if you can't get the old shifter to work.

REPLACING A TWISTGRIP SHIFTER

These shifters are installed instead of regular handgrips over the ends of the handlebars and clamped on with an Allen bolt. If you want to replace your existing shifters with a twistgrip, see *Replacing a Conventional Shifter* for instructions on removing the existing conventional shifter and cable, then follow the *Installation procedure* below.

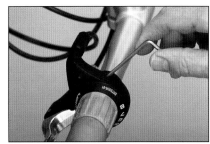

Twistgrip shifters are installed, or repositioned, with the little clamp screw by means of an Allen wrench.

Tools and equipment
Allen wrench

Removal procedure
1. Loosen the cable at the derailleur and push it free at the shifter.
2. Turn the shifter into the position for the highest gear and pull the cable out.
3. Undo the Allen bolt and pull the shifter off.

Installation procedure
1. Slide the shifter into position with the cable guide at the bottom.
2. Feed the cable through the cable stops and the casing, and attach it at the derailleur.
3. Adjust the derailleur operation.

REPLACING THE DERAILLEUR CABLE

This work is necessary if the cable is pinched or otherwise damaged, or if the inner cable shows signs of corrosion or frayed strands. Especially in the case of under-the-bar shifters, the cable must match the shifter, because some manufacturers use different nipple shapes.

Indexed shifters use relatively stiff stainless steel inner cables and a nylon sleeve between inner cable and cable casing. These same cables can of course also be used on non-indexed systems. They have to be cleaned from time to time and checked to make sure they are not pinched or damaged anywhere.

Lubrication is best done by removing the inner cable from the housing and smearing wax over the inner cable. If you can't disassemble the cable, you may get by just squirting a few drops of oil between the inner cable and the cable casing where the casing ends.

Tools and equipment
Screwdriver
Wrench to fit cable clamp bolt
Wax
Cloth

Removal procedure
1. Undo the cable at the derailleur by loosening the cable clamp nut or the eye bolt that holds the cable to the derailleur.
2. Put the shifter in the position for the highest gear.
3. On under-the-bar shifters, open up the mechanism only to the point where the cable and the nipple are exposed.
4. Push the cable free at the shifter.
5. Pull the cable out and catch the cable casing and any other loose items.

Installation procedure
1. Put a dab of wax on the cloth and run the new inner cable through the wax-soaked cloth.
2. Feed the cable through the shifter with the nipple in the recess. On a SunTour under-the-bar shifter, pay attention to the orientation of the eccentric nipple.
3. Guide the cable through the various guides and the cable casing, and attach the end at the derailleur.
4. Adjust the derailleur cable tension as described separately for front and rear derailleurs.

BRAKE MAINTENANCE

Refer to Chapter 25 for the brake performance test. If you establish that the brakes fail this test, adjust the brake according to the specific instructions for the type of brake in question. But before you do, clean the rims and check whether the brake pads touch the rim over their full width when the lever is applied. If they do not, adjust the brake pads, following the description below.

ADJUSTING OR REPLACING BRAKE PADS

If the brake pads do not lie flat on the side of the rim over their full width and length when the lever is engaged, they should be repositioned. There are two general types of brake pad attachments: bolt-mounted and stud-mounted. In the latter case, the brake pad is not held in the brake arm directly but has a stud that in turn is clamped in an eye bolt on the brake arm. Brake pads work best, and usually squeal least, if they are adjusted with about 1 millimeter (1/32 to 1/16 inch) of "toe-in," meaning that the front end of the pad should touch the rim just before the rear does.

Tools and equipment

Wrench to fit brake pad attachment bolt

Procedure

1. Loosen the bolt that holds the brake pad to the brake arm about one turn.

2. While applying the brake lever with modest hand force, move the brake pads into the position to con-

Testing the brake's operation amounts to making sure the brake is applied firmly when the lever is pulled in with 2 centimeters (3/4 inch) of clearance between lever and handlebars (right). Testing can be done statically (below), but it is better to ride the bike in a safe place at low speed and apply each brake separately.

Adjust the brake pads so that they make contact with the rim over their entire length and width. To minimize squealing and rumbling, adjust them so that the front of the pad—the leading edge—touches the rim just before the rest of the pad.

The brake cable tension is adjusted at the point where the cable comes out of the lever.

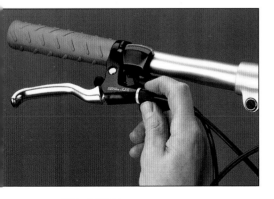

tact the rim over their entire length and width, then increase lever force. You may have to twist the brake pad and the underlying spherical and cupped washers, or whatever other device is provided for angular adjustment, to achieve this position.

3. Adjust for toe-in to prevent vibrations and squealing, by placing a piece of cardboard under the rear section of the pad.

4. Pushing the brake pad against the side of the rim firmly with one hand, while making sure it does not shift from its correct position, tighten the bolt fully.

5. Check to make sure the brake works correctly, and fine-tune the adjustment if necessary.

Note

If toeing in does not silence the brake, you can sometimes achieve it by doing what seems counter to logic: adjust for "toe-out" by making the rear end of the pad touch the rim first. If it works, good; if it increases vibrations and noise, re-adjust it for toe-in as described above.

ADJUSTING THE BRAKES

The most common type of brake adjustment is that required to tighten the cable a little in order to compensate for brake pad wear. This operation is about the same regardless what type of brake you have. First carry out the brake pad adjustment described above.

Tools and equipment

Sometimes wrenches to fit the cable clamp bolt
Sometimes pliers

Procedure

1. Loosen the tension on the cable. This is generally done by squeezing the brake arms against the rim and unhooking either the cable casing attachment (V-brake), the connecting cable (cantilever brake, U-brake), or the cam plate (roller-cam brake).

2. To increase cable tension with the cable adjuster (usually installed at the

brake lever), loosen the locknut, screw the barrel adjuster out, and finally retighten the locknut, while holding the barrel adjuster.

3. Check operation of the brake and re-adjust if necessary.

Notes

If the adjusting range is inadequate, first screw in the barrel all the way, then pull the cable tauter and clamp the cable in at a different point at the brake. Finally use the barrel adjuster to fine-tune.

To make sure low-profile cantilever brakes are optimally effective, keep the two sides of the straddle cable equally long and the angle between them at 120 to 130 degrees when the brake lever is not applied.

CENTERING A CANTILEVER BRAKE

This work is necessary if one brake shoe is markedly closer to the side of the rim than the other, though the wheel is properly centered. First try adjusting the position of the pad in the brake arm. Most models have a limit screw in one of the brake arms that is screwed in or out to achieve the desired effect. If that does not solve the problem, remove the mounting bolts and place the end of one of the springs in a different hole in the pivot boss. If there is only one hole, bend the spring in the appropriate direction using two pairs of pliers. Reassemble and repeat if necessary.

CENTERING A V-BRAKE

Follow essentially the same procedure as for cantilever brakes. The only difference lies in the fact that there is no straddle cable to worry about. Instead, the outer cable stops at one brake arm, and the inner cable continues on across the top to the other brake arm. Either one or two brake arms will have an adjustment screw that can be adjusted with a 2-mm Allen wrench.

CENTERING A U-BRAKE

The U-brake is centered by means of a tiny Allen screw installed vertically just below one of the brake pivots. Tighten or loosen this screw by one or two turns to

bring the brake arm on the same side closer to or farther from the side of the rim. Adjust the brake pads close enough to the rim so they contact the rim fully when applied.

OVERHAULING OR REPLACING BRAKES

This work is recommended once a year or whenever the brake gives unsatisfactory performance and adjustment does not solve the problem.

Although there are slight differences in the procedure as it applies to different brakes, you will find a general description here, including comments for specific models. Most comments apply to all brakes, though.

This work is most easily carried out while the wheel is removed. For easy wheel removal, push the brake pads together just enough to unhook the cable (V-brake, cantilever, or U-brake). On the roller-cam, remove the cam plate, then loosen the tip of one spring and spread the brake arms asymmetrically.

Tools and equipment

Cone wrench or other flat open-ended wrench
Allen wrench
Open-ended wrench
Needle-nose pliers

Removal procedure

1. Pull the brake arms together at the brake pads and release the cable—on the roller-cam brake, twist the cam plate out from between the rollers.
2. Check the condition of the cable and replace it if necessary: remove the cable anchor clamp using a wrench on the nut and an Allen wrench on

the bolt part. Pull the cable out and later insert the new one. If an end cap is installed on the end of the cable, it must be pulled off with needle-nose pliers—we recommend soldering the end of the cable to prevent fraying, following the instructions under *Replacing Brake Cables.*

3. Unscrew the fixing nut or bolt on top of the brake arm pivot bolt of each brake arm.

4. Using the needle-nose pliers, remove the upper end of the spring of each brake arm from its seating, then pull the brake arm, the spring, and the bushing off the pivot stud.

5. Clean, inspect, and if necessary repair or replace any damaged parts. In particular, remove any rust from the pivot stud of the pivot boss, then apply some grease to this location. On the roller-cam, disassemble the rollers from the brake arms, and install them again after inspection, cleaning, and lubrication.

6. If appropriate, disassemble the brake pads and their fixing bolts, in order to clean and if necessary replace them (if the brake pads are badly worn). Reinstall, following the instructions in the adjusting procedures for the brake in question or those under *Adjusting or Replacing Brake Pads.*

Installation procedure

1. After ascertaining that all parts are functional, clean and, where appropriate, lightly greased, first put the springs on the pivot studs, with the long arms of the spring pointing up and to the inside. On newer cantilever brakes, the spring is integrated in the brake arm unit. You can still take it apart if you really need to, but you usually don't.

2. Install the adjusting bushing over the top of the spring around the stud of each mounting boss, with the cylindrical bushing part protruding.

3. Install the brake arms on the adjusting bushings, followed by the washer and the nut or the bolt.

4. In the case of a roller-cam brake,

hook the end of the spring into its seating at the end of the roller pin of each brake arm.

5. Push the brake pads together and reinstall the cam plate between the rollers (on the roller-cam) or the connecting cable (on other models). If appropriate, readjust the cable tension by adjusting at the brake lever or—if the deviation is significant—by clamping the anchor plate (U-brake or cantilever brake) or the cam plate (roller-cam brake) at a different point on the cable.

6. Carry out the adjustments outlined in the adjusting instruction for the particular brake.

BRAKE CONTROLS

The brakes are operated by means of levers mounted on the handlebars via control cables, which are partly enclosed in sections of cable casing that run between the lever and cable stops on the frame. Usually, adjusting the brake, as described in the various sections above, actually amounts to tightening or loosening the control cable tension.

Make sure the lever is suitable for your brake. V-brakes can only be used with levers with two cable nipple recesses inside—one marked V for V-brakes, the other marked C.

This is how the V-brake is adjusted. Pictured is the first successful mountain bike brake without a straddle cable and without need for an external outer cable anchor point.

On many brakes there are three locator holes for the end of the brake arm return spring. Choose the one that balances the two brake arms best.

The brake lever must be installed so that it can be easily reached and pulled in so far that the brake is fully applied when about 20 millimeters (3/4 inch) remains between the brake lever and the handlebars at the tightest point. Thus, there are three forms of adjustment of the brake lever: mounting location, reach, and cable tension.

Tools and equipment:
Often Allen wrench
Sometimes open-ended wrench

Location adjustment procedure
1. Determine in which direction, or directions, the brake lever should be moved or rotated to provide adequate and comfortable operation.
2. Establish whether any other parts installed on the handlebars (such as the shift levers) may have to be moved in order to allow moving the brake lever to the desired location. Loosen these parts so they can be easily moved.
3. Loosen the Allen bolt of the clamp that holds the lever to the handlebars by one or two turns, then twist or slide the lever into the desired location and tighten the clamping bolt again. Whatever you do, make sure the lever does not extend beyond the end of the handlebars, to avoid accidental brake application while closely passing any objects where the brake levers might get caught.
4. Retighten any other components that may have been moved to new locations; make sure all parts are in their most convenient location and are properly tightened.

Reach adjustment procedure
1. Most mountain bike brake levers are equipped with a set-screw to adjust

how far away from the handlebars the lever sits when not pulled. This screw can be turned in or out in order to limit the range of travel of the brake lever as appropriate to the reach of your hand.
2. Check the distance between the handlebars and the brake lever in the released position compared to the maximum comfortable reach of your hand. In generally, it should be opened as far as possible commensurate with the size of your hand, as a larger reach allows the most effective brake application and the most accurate adjustment of the brake cable.
3. If adjustment is necessary, tighten the reach-adjusting set-screw to reduce the range (the maximum opening position), or loosen it to increase the range.
4. Check to make sure the brake can be applied properly, and adjust the brake cable, following the appropriate instruction below, if necessary.

Cable attachment procedure
1. Feed the cable through the slot and the adjuster and hook the nipple into the appropriate recess. If you have a V-brake, use the notch marked V, otherwise the one marked C. If the lever has only one recess for the nipple, it is not suitable for use with V-brakes.

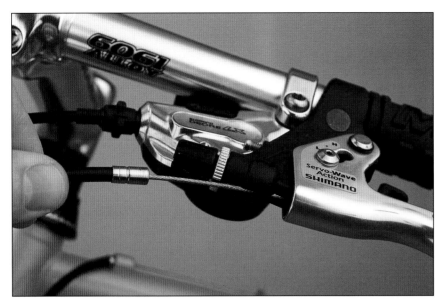

When replacing the brake cable or the brake lever, install the inner cable's nipple in the handle and then guide the inner cable from the lever through the slot in the lever housing. Next, insert the cable casing into place.

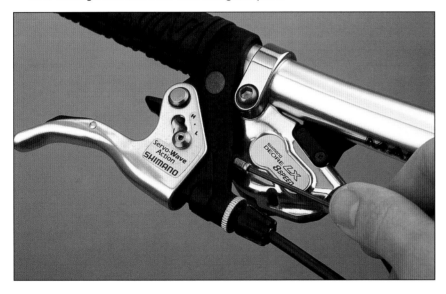

The amount of reach of many brake levers can be adjusted with the screw shown here—screw it out to get the lever farther from the handlebars, in to keep it closer.

2. Pull the cable taut and attach it at the brake.

3. Follow the adjustment steps outlined in the procedure *Adjusting the Brakes*.

REPLACING THE BRAKE CABLES

This should be done about once a year—or whenever the cable is pinched, corroded, or damaged, especially if signs of broken strands are in evidence.

Tools and equipment:

Wrench to fit cable clamp bolt
Cable cutters
Lubricant
Possibly soldering equipment

Removal procedure

1. Release tension on the brake by squeezing the brake arms against the rim, then unhook the cable-casing attachment (V-brake), the connecting cable (U-brake or cantilever brake), or the cam plate (roller-cam brake).

2. Unscrew the eye bolt or clamp nut that holds the cable to the connecting plate, the cam plate, or the brake itself (depending on the type of brake), making sure not to lose the various parts.

3. Push the cable through toward the lever, then pull it out once enough slack is generated, catching any pieces of cable casing and end pieces.

4. Screw the adjuster and the locknut at the lever in and leave them in such a position that their slots are aligned with the slot in the lever housing, so the cable can be lifted out.

5. Remove the cable, dislodging the nipple from the lever.

Installation procedure

1. Establish whether the cable casing is still intact, and replace it if necessary, cutting it to length in such a way that no hook is formed at the end—if necessary, bend the end of the spiral back or file it flush.

2. Lubricate the inner cable with grease or wax.

3. Place the nipple in the lever and guide the cable through the slot in the lever, the various guides and stops, and the sections of casing.

4. Attach the end in the eye bolt or clamp nut at the brake.

5. Adjust the cable tension as described above.

6. If you have the equipment to do it, solder the strands of the inner cable together before you cut it off, leaving about 2.5 centimeters (1 inch) projecting beyond the point where it is clamped in.

7. Cut off the excess cable length. This is best done with a special cable-cutting tool, though it can be done with other sharp and strong pliers, such as diagonal cutters. If you did not solder the cable strands together, install a cable-end cap and crimp it on with pliers.

THIRTY-ONE

STEERING SYSTEM MAINTENANCE

I n this chapter, we'll cover maintenance work on the parts of the steering system: front fork, headset bearings, stem, and handlebars. Some of these procedures will vary depending on the type of headset used—threaded or threadless. On the threaded headset the upper bearing is screwed onto the fork's steerer tube. Many bikes built since about 1994 have the threadless headset, on which the fork's steerer tube is not threaded, and the bearing is adjusted by means of a bolt in the top of the handlebar stem.

HANDLEBARS AND STEM

The jobs most typically required are adjusting the height, straightening the bars, and replacing either part. Most mountain bike handlebars have a diameter of 22.2 mm (7/8 inch), with a bulge in the middle that may be 25.4 mm (1 inch) or sometimes 26.6 mm (1 1/8 inch) in diameter where it is clamped into the stem. Make sure stem and handlebars match when replacing either one. If the handlebars are too close to, or too far from, the rider, the stem must be replaced by a longer or shorter model.

ADJUSTING AND TIGHTENING THE HANDLEBARS

This is required when the bike is set up for a different rider, when the position proves uncomfortable, or when the handlebars are not firmly in place. This description assumes a conventional threaded headset.

Most work on the steering system is most easily performed like this, with the bike on the ground and the front wheel held between your legs.

To adjust the handlebars on a bike with a conventional (threaded) headset, loosen the expander bolt at the top of the stem with an Allen wrench.

Tools and equipment

Allen wrench
Sometimes a mallet or a hammer

Procedure

1. If the front brake cable is anchored at the stem, first loosen the brake to relax the cable.

2. If appropriate (if it has to be adjusted), loosen the attachment of the stem by unscrewing the expander bolt two to three turns.

3. Straddle the front wheel, keeping it straight relative to the bike's frame, and put the handlebars in the required position as regards height and orientation, holding it steady there with one hand.

4. If the stem doesn't budge, unscrew the expander bolt another four to six turns, lift the wheel off the ground, supporting the bike from the handlebars, then tap on the expander bolt with the mallet, after which it will usually come loose. If it doesn't, enter some spray lubricant between the stem and the collar or locknut at the top of the headset and try again.

5. Still holding firmly, tighten the expander bolt.

6. Verify whether the handlebars are now in the right position and make any corrections that may be necessary.

7. If the brake's adjustment was affected (see step 1 above), tension the cable and adjust the brake as outlined in Chapter 30.

Threadless headset note

The handlebar height on a bike with a threadless headset can be varied only by means of a different stem, one with more or less rise.

TIGHTENING THE HANDLEBARS IN THE STEM

The connection between the handlebars and the stem should be firm, so the handlebars don't twist out of their proper orientation. Do this by simply tightening the bolts that clamp the stem collar around the bars, using a matching Allen wrench.

REPLACING THE HANDLEBARS AND THE STEM

This has to be done when the bars are bent or otherwise damaged, when you want to install a different design, or in the context of a general overhauling operation of the bike.

Tools and equipment

Allen wrench
Cloth
Lubricant

Removal procedure

1. Loosen all cables leading to items installed on the handlebars (gear and brake levers), as explained in Chapters 29 and 30.

2. Using the Allen wrench, loosen the expander bolt three to four turns, or until the stem is obviously loose.

3. If the stem won't come loose, unscrew the expander bolt four to six more turns, lift the wheel off the ground, holding the bike by the handlebars, then tap on the expander bolt with the mallet, after which it will usually come loose. If it doesn't, enter some spray lubricant between the stem and the collar or locknut at

To reorient the handlebars on a bike with a threadless headset (no height adjustment possible here), loosen the clamp bolts that hold the stem around the fork's steerer tube extension.

the top of the headset and try again.

4. Remove the handlebars complete with the stem.

Installation procedure

1. Clean the stem and the inside of the fork's steerer tube with a clean rag, then put some grease on the wedge (or the cone) and the part of the stem that will go inside the steerer tube, in order to prevent rust and to ease subsequent adjustment or replacement.

2. Tighten the expander bolt so far that the wedge is snug up to the stem's slanted end in the right orientation, still allowing free movement of the stem in the steerer tube.

3. If a cone-shape device is used

The handlebars themselves are attached to the stem with one or more binder bolts that clamp the stem collar around the handlebars.

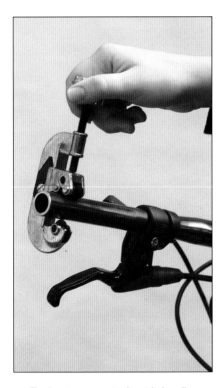

To shorten excessively wide handlebars (that is, those obviously designed for bigger riders than you are), you can use a pipe cutter.

instead of a wedge, align the ribs on the cone with the slots in the end of the stem.

4. Install the stem and position it in the correct orientation.

5. Straddle the front wheel, keeping it straight relative to the bike's frame, and put the handlebars in the required position as regards height and orientation, holding it steady there with one hand.

6. Still holding the handlebars firmly in place, tighten the expander bolt.

7. Verify whether the handlebars are now in the right position and make any corrections that may be necessary.

8. If the brake's adjustment was affected (see step 1 above), tension the cable and adjust the brake as described in Chapter 30.

REPLACING THE HANDLEBARS OR THE STEM INDIVIDUALLY

This must be done when the handlebars are seriously damaged or when you want to install another model. First check whether the new handlebars have the same diameter as the old ones—if not, also replace the stem.

Tools and equipment
Allen wrench
Large screwdriver
Tools to replace items installed on the handlebars

Removal procedure
1. Remove any components installed on the handlebars: handgrips, brake levers, and gear shifters—after first releasing tension in the cables.
2. Loosen and remove the binder bolts clamping the stem collar around the handlebars.
3. Using the big screwdriver, spread open the collar and pull the thicker section of the handlebars out of the collar; then release the screwdriver and pull the handlebars out.

Installation procedure:
1. Push the handlebars through the collar, twisting if necessary, until the thicker section is reached, then open up the collar with the big screwdriver and insert the handlebars all the way.
2. Bring the handlebars to the correct location.
3. Install the bolts and tighten them partway.
4. Adjust the bars in the exact location desired and hold them there firmly while tightening the bolts.
5. Install all the components on the handlebars.
6. Check the position and orientation again, making any adjustments that may be necessary.

REPLACING THE HANDGRIPS

You will have to remove the handgrips to remove the handlebars from the stem, or you may want to replace the grips themselves, either because they are damaged or because you've found a more comfortable model.

Tools and equipment
Small screwdriver
Cloth
Dishwashing liquid
Hot water
Hairspray

Procedure
1. Lift the ends of the grips off the handlebars a little with the small screwdriver and enter some dishwashing liquid if they won't come off easily.
2. Before reinstalling the handgrips, remove all traces of dishwashing liquid, so they won't slide off.
3. To make installation easier, dip the handgrips in hot water to soften them. Then treat the inside with hairspray so they don't slide off.

INSTALLING BAR-ENDS

First cut back the ends of the handgrips and then install the bar-ends by tightening the Allen bolt that pulls them tight around the handlebar ends—firmly enough so they don't slip under load. An alternative is to replace the handlebars with a model with integrated bar-ends.

THE HEADSET

The headset is the double set of ball bearings with which the steering system is pivoted in the frame. For regular maintenance, the headset should occasionally be lubricated and perhaps overhauled, or it may have to be replaced.

The threaded headset is screwed onto a threaded fork steerer tube.

The threadless headset fits on a fork with a smooth steerer tube. It is adjusted via a bolt that is reached from the top of the stem.

Both models are available in a variety of sizes—regular 1-inch and both 1 1/8-inch and 1 1/4-inch oversize types. Use tools and parts that match the model in question.

ADJUSTING A THREADED HEADSET

At least once a season, and whenever the steering is rough or loose, adjust the bearings as follows:

Tools and equipment
Headset wrenches or large crescent wrenches

Procedure
1. Loosen the collar or locknut on the upper headset by about one turn (after loosening a set screw on some models).
2. Lift the washer under this nut enough to release the underlying part, which is the adjustable bearing cup.
3. Tighten or loosen the adjustable bearing cup by turning it to the right or the left, respectively.
4. Put the washer in place and tighten the collar or locknut, holding the adjustable cup in place.
5. Check to make sure the adjustment is correct (not too loose and not too tight). Re-adjust if necessary, following the same procedure.

Note
If adjusting does not solve your problem, the headset must be overhauled according to the following description.

OVERHAULING A THREADED HEADSET

Follow these same disassembly and installation procedures when either the headset or the fork is to be replaced.

Tools and equipment
Headset wrenches or large crescent wrenches
Tools to remove handlebars and brake.
Bearing grease
Cloths

Disassembly procedure
1. Remove the handlebars with the stem as described above and loosen the front brake cable; then remove the front wheel, after unhooking or relaxing tension on the front brake cable.
2. Loosen and remove the collar or locknut on top of the headset.
3. Remove the lock washer by lifting it straight off.
4. Unscrew the adjustable bearing cup, while holding the fork to the frame.
5. Remove the bearing balls, which are usually held in a bearing ball retainer.
6. Pull the fork out from the frame, also catching the lower bearing balls, again usually held in a retainer.

Inspection and overhauling procedure
1. Inspect all parts for wear, corrosion, and damage, evidenced as pitting or grooves.
2. Replace the entire headset if significant damage is apparent; always use new bearing balls, either loose or in a retainer to match the particular size of headset installed.
3. If the headset has to be replaced, it will be preferable to get the fixed cups and the fork race removed (and new ones installed) with special tools at the bike shop.

Installation procedure
1. If the fixed cups and the fork race are intact—or once they have been replaced—fill the bearing cups with bearing grease.
2. Hold the frame upside-down and embed one of the bearing retainers in the grease-filled lower fixed-bearing race (which is now facing up). The retainer must be installed in such a way that the bearing balls—not the metal ring—contact the inside of the cup.
3. Hold the fork upside-down and put it through the head tube.
4. Turn the frame the right way around again, while holding the fork in place.
5. Embed the other bearing retainer in the grease-filled upper fixed-bearing cup.
6. Screw the adjustable bearing cup onto the threaded end of the fork's steerer tube by hand.
7. Place the lock washer on top of the adjustable cup, and do the same with any part that may be installed to serve as a brake cable anchor or a spacer.
8. Screw the collar or locknut onto the threaded end of the steerer tube, without tightening it completely.
9. Install the front wheel.
10. Adjust the bearing as outlined above.
11. Check and, if necessary, correct any adjustments involved (handlebars and front brake).

MAINTENANCE OF A THREADLESS HEADSET

The bearings are adjusted by means of an Allen bolt on top of the special stem used with these headsets, after loosening the stem clamp and any other clamped parts. To tighten the headset, turn the bolt to the right; to loosen it, turn the bolt to the left—about 1/8 of a turn at a time until it feels right.

Tools and equipment
Allen wrenches
Cloths
Grease

Disassembly and overhauling procedure
1. Remove the bolt and the cap from the top of the stem.

On a conventional headset, adjustment is achieved with the upper bearing cup. It is secured in place by a lockring with a keyed flat part (either the part that serves to anchor the front brake's outer cable or a separate lock washer) in between. Use matching headset tools to adjust, remove, or install. If you're merely adjusting the headset, there's no need to remove the handlebars and the stem.

To adjust a threadless headset, use the bolt in the plastic washer on top of the stem.

2. Remove the stem by undoing the Allen bolts that clamp it around the top of the fork's steerer tube.

3. Remove any spacers and brake cable hanger that may be installed between the stem and the upper headset bearing.

4. Hold the fork to the frame, and pull the conical compression ring off toward the top of the steerer tube, followed by the upper headset bearing.

5. Pull the fork out from the frame and remove the lower headset bearing.

6. Clean, lubricate, and overhaul the bearings just as you would a regular headset.

Installation procedure

1. Follow steps 1 through 5 of the general procedures for bearing installation under *Overhauling a Threaded Headset* above.

2. Hold the fork in place and install the upper bearing race, then the conical compression ring with the skinny end first.

3. Install the stem around the top end of the steerer tube, but do not tighten the stem clamping bolts yet.

4. Install the cap and the Allen bolt in the top of the stem so that the bolt's threading engages the thread in the threaded insert inside the steerer tube, and *gently* tighten the bolt until the bearing feels right.

5. Hold the handlebars straight and tighten the stem's clamp bolts.

Note

The special fork with a threadless steerer tube is equipped with a star-shaped threaded insert in the steerer tube. It may have to be replaced if you accidentally force it out. Install it from the top, using a piece of pipe or conduit that just fits inside the steerer tube and hammer it into position.

THE FRONT FORK

The majority of production mountain bikes use either the unicrown design front fork or a suspension type. But there are differences, primarily on account of the headset bearing used: threaded or unthreaded, and both types come in several different steerer tube diameters: 1 inch, 1 1/8 inches, and 1 1/4 inches.

If the steering gets sticky when turning the bars, even though it seems fine when going straight, it will be due to a bent head tube, usually as a result of a collision. When replacing a fork that is bent, make sure the bosses installed for the brakes are in the right location for the kind of brakes used, and check the length of the steerer tube, which must also be the same as the old one—assuming it was correct. To determine the required steerer tube length, deduct 2 millimeters (3/32 inch) from the sum of the stacking height of the headset (given by the manufacturer) and the length of the head tube.

FRONT FORK INSPECTION

This will be necessary whenever you have had a serious crash or when the bike does not seem to steer the way it should. Generally, a visual check is adequate, referring to the illustration for the typical kinds of damage possible.

REPLACING THE FRONT FORK

Although it may sometimes be possible to straighten a bent fork, it's best to replace the entire fork, giving

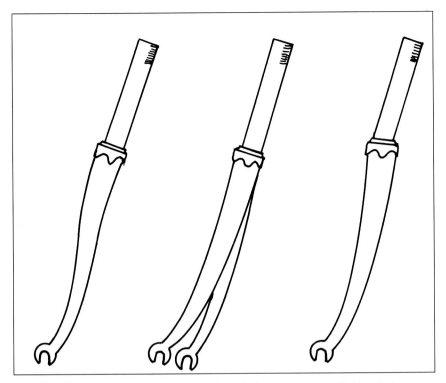

Fork damage. In a crash or collision, the front fork may get damaged either by bending both blades together, one blade relative to the other, or the steerer tube itself. In addition, a side impact may cause damage to minor parts such as the fork-ends or the brake pivot bosses.

yourself a sorely needed margin of safety that may prevent a bad crash later on. Sometimes the fork's steerer tube has to be cut shorter to fit the frame. It is preferable to get that done at a bike shop, as the screw thread often has to be recut too. If you do decide to do it yourself, first screw the locknut on as a guide so you'll cut straight. File any burrs off the end before installing the fork.

Tools and equipment

Headset wrenches or large crescent wrenches

Tools to remove handlebars and front brake

Procedure

1. Untension the cable for the front brake and remove the entire front brake as explained in Chapter 30; then remove the front wheel follow-ing the appropriate procedure in Chapter 27.

2. Remove the handlebars with the stem, following the description under *Replacing the Handlebars and the Stem*.

3. Disassemble the upper headset as outlined in the relevant description above.

4. Remove the fork, following the same description.

5. If necessary, use the fork as a reference to buy the new one, taking it to the bike shop with you.

6. Install the fork and the headset as described for the installation of the headset.

7. Install the handlebars as described above.

8. Install the front brake and hook up the cable.

9. Check and, if necessary, adjust all parts affected: headset, handlebars, and front brake.

SADDLE AND SEATPOST MAINTENANCE

CHAPTER THIRTY-TWO

Although these are not among the most trouble-prone components on the mountain bike, they do justify some attention. The jobs described here will be adjustment of the position of the saddle, replacement of saddle and seatpost, and any maintenance needed on a leather saddle.

ADJUSTING THE SADDLE HEIGHT

The saddle position should be adjusted whenever the bike is set up for another rider or when the position is uncomfortably high or low for the present rider. Chapters 3 and 5 explain how the correct height is determined. Here you'll just be shown how to go about it.

Tools and equipment

Usually none required (sometimes lubricant)

Procedure

1. Flip the lever of the quick-release binder bolt into the *open* position in order to loosen the seatpost.
2. The seatpost with the saddle should now be free to move up and down. If it is not, hold the lever and unscrew the thumbnut on the other side by about one turn. If it still isn't free, enter some penetrating lubricant between the seatpost and the seat lug, wait a minute or two and try again, if necessary twist the saddle with the seatpost relative to the frame.
3. Place the saddle in the desired

location. If lubrication was needed, first remove the seatpost all the way, then clean the seatpost and the interior of the seat tube and apply some grease to the outside of the seatpost before inserting it again.
4. Holding the saddle at the correct height and aligned perfectly straight forward, flip the quick-release lever to the *closed* position.
5. Check that the saddle is now installed firmly. If not, loosen the quick-release lever, tighten the thumbnut perhaps one turn, and try again.
6. Try out and re-adjust if necessary until the location is satisfactory.

Note

If your bike has a Hite-Rite spring adjuster, apply just enough downward force on the saddle to achieve the desired location when installing it. If the range of the Hite-Rite is incorrect for the required saddle position, undo the clamp around the seatpost and attach it higher or lower as required.

ADJUSTING THE SADDLE ANGLE AND POSITION

Generally, both of these adjustments are carried out with the same bolts that hold the saddle to the seatpost, which can be reached from under the saddle (except on some special seatposts, such as the old Campagnolo Euclid model, which has an adjustment by means of a large knurled button and an additional quick-release—a case of adjustability overkill).

The saddle height is adjusted by sliding the seatpost in or out after the quick-release binder bolt is opened. To tighten the quick-release, pull the lever against the seatstays.

Tools and equipment

Allen wrench or other wrench to fit seatpost adjusting bolts

Procedure

1. If the saddle must be moved forward or backward, loosen both bolts by about one or two turns each.
2. Holding the clamp on top of the seatpost with one hand and the saddle with the other, move the latter into the correct position.
3. If the saddle merely has to be tipped (that is, the front raised or lowered relative to the rear portion), loosen the nuts and then move the saddle into the desired orientation.

4. Holding the saddle in the correct location and orientation, tighten the bolts, while preventing the saddle from moving.

5. Check and re-adjust if necessary.

REPLACING THE SADDLE AND THE SEATPOST

It is usually easier to remove the combination of saddle and seatpost than to remove the saddle alone. This is also the first step in removing the seatpost.

Tools and Equipment:
Cloth
Grease
Wrench if a Hite-Rite is installed

Removal procedure
1. Loosen the quick-release binder bolt until the seatpost can be moved up or down freely, as described under *Adjusting the Saddle Height*.
2. Pull the saddle with the seatpost out of the frame's seat tube.

Installation procedure
1. Clean the outside of the seatpost and the inside of the seat tube, then smear grease on the seatpost to prevent corrosion and to ease subsequent adjustments.
2. Install the seatpost with the saddle installed, and adjust it at the correct height.
3. In case you are installing the seatpost with a Hite-Rite, clamp the Hite-Rite around the seatpost when it is perfectly aligned and at the maximum height you will ever want the saddle to be.
4. Tighten the quick-release binder bolt as described under *Adjusting Saddle Height*.

Note
If adjustment problems persist, especially if the seatpost won't come loose, it may be necessary to drill out the hole at the bottom of the slot in the rear of the seat lug to about 3 millimeters (1/8 inch)—or drill such a hole there if there isn't one, as it prevents the formation of cracks and eases clamping or unclamping the lug around the seatpost.

REPLACING THE SEATPOST OR THE SADDLE INDIVIDUALLY

Not exactly a job that is often necessary, except if a new saddle or seatpost has to be installed—or to get water out of the frame. Just the same, here's how to go about it.

Tools and equipment
Allen wrench or other wrench to fit bolts that hold saddle to seatpost
Sometimes wrench for Hite-Rite nut

Removal procedure
1. For the time being, leave the saddle installed on the seatpost and remove the seatpost complete with the saddle as described under *Replacing the Saddle and the Seatpost*, loosening the Hite-Rite clamp around the seatpost if installed.
2. Separate the saddle from the seatpost by unscrewing the bolts that hold the saddle's wires to the seatpost clamp.

Installation procedure
1. Install the saddle on the seatpost.
2. Install the seatpost with the saddle as described under *Replacing Saddle and Seatpost*.
3. In case you are installing the seatpost with a Hite-Rite, clamp the Hite-Rite around the seatpost when it is about as high as you will ever want the saddle to be.
4. Adjust the height, the forward position, and the angle of the saddle as described in the relevant sections above.
5. Check and re-adjust if necessary.

LEATHER SADDLES

If you use a leather saddle, make sure it does not get wet. Wrap a plastic bag around the saddle when transporting the bike or leaving it outside when there is the slightest chance of rain. If it does get wet, don't sit on it until it is thoroughly dried out, because otherwise it will deform permanently. To keep it water-resistant and slightly flexible, treat it with leather treatment such as Brooks Proofide at least twice a year.

To adjust the saddle's angle and forward position, first loosen the bolt or bolts holding the seatpost's clip around the saddle wires.

Tightening the cover of a leather saddle. Tighten the nut under the end of the saddle by one or more turns until the saddle cover feels firm.

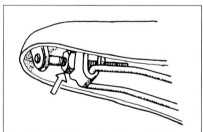

The tension of a leather saddle can be adjusted with the nut under the "nose" of the saddle.

Adjust the tension of a leather saddle no more than once a year and only when it is noticeably sagged, tightening the bolt shown in the illustration perhaps one turn at the most. Don't overdo this adjustment, as it often causes the saddle to be pulled into an uncomfortable shape.

THIRTY-THREE

SUSPENSION MAINTENANCE

I n this chapter we'll look at the maintenance jobs suitable for the home mechanic on the various suspension components: suspension forks, flexible stems, suspension seatposts, and rear suspension systems. Major overhauls are best left to an experienced bike mechanic.

SUSPENSION FORK MAINTENANCE

The most common problem with any suspension fork is dirt on the stanchion tubes, which tends to enter between the bearing surfaces, resulting in wear and erratic response. Rubber boots around the stanchions, covering up the seals where the stanchion tubes disappear into the slider tubes, are designed to prevent that as much as possible. Make sure they are installed properly and replace them if they are split.

To check the front suspension fork's operation, lock up the front brake and push in the bike's front end under your weight and let go again. Pay attention to smoothness of depression and return. If the response is erratic, you have a problem that's going to get worse when riding the bike. Also check all screws, nuts, and bolts, making sure they are tightened properly at least once a month.

Cleaning procedure

Clean the outside of the fork and the rubber boot with plenty of water, heeding the following warnings:

1. Don't push down and let go of the fork while cleaning it, because that may suck dirt and water under the boots or the seals, aggravating any problems you may already have or causing a problem where there wasn't one to start with.

2. Wash and wipe with a motion directed away from the seals.

3. Once the outside is clean, loosen the boots and carefully clean the stanchion tube, again working away from the seals.

4. If the seals can be lifted, do so with a small screwdriver and blow out any dirt with an air compressor or a bicycle pump, then wipe off any remaining dirt with a dry cloth.

OVERHAULING AN ELASTOMER SUSPENSION FORK

Before embarking on this project, check to make sure the stanchion and slider tubes are not bent—if they are, you'll have to replace the whole unit, because no amount of overhauling will correct the situation. To overhaul the fork, first remove the front wheel and the brake arms.

Tools and equipment

Allen wrenches (a special long one for some models)
Teflon or silicone lubricant
Cloth
Screwdriver

Disassembly procedure:

1. Check to see which side allows access to the fork's guts—from the top or the bottom, as evidenced by a plastic cap covering an opening in the slider tube or

On some telescoping forks, the spring elements can be reached by unscrewing an Allen bolt accessible from the bottom of the stanchion tube.

the stanchion tube. Turn the bike upside down if access is from the bottom.

2. If access is from the bottom, remove the brake bridge. If access is from the top, it can be left in place.

3. Remove the plastic caps covering the openings.

4. Using a matching Allen wrench, loosen and remove the retainer bolts inside. On some models, you'll need to hold the preload adjuster on the other end to stop it from turning as you turn the bolt.

The guts of a typical low-end telescoping suspension fork. The stiffness can be varied as a function of rider weight and terrain by choosing different pads, which are usually color-coded.

5. On some models, the elastomer pads come out with the bolt; on other models, turn the bike around so that they drop out.

6. Pull the slider tubes out from the stanchions, which may require some force before they pop off.

Overhauling and assembly procedure

1. Clean all the parts inside and outside, then inspect them for damage.

2. If required (for example, to get a softer or a firmer ride, or if there is obvious damage), replace the pads, making sure not to forget to reinstall any washers originally used between the pads.

3. Apply silicone or Teflon-based grease to all sliding surfaces, inside and out.

4. Reinsert the elastomers, followed by the slider tube and the bolt.

5. If you notice things don't fit, check to find out what's holding them up. Usually it's a split bushing that merely needs to be compressed as you slide it into place.

6. Compress slider tube and stanchion tube until you can tell you're compressing the elastomer; then screw in the bolt.

You can adjust the damping effect on a sophisticated suspension stem by tightening the pivot bushing with a matching Allen wrench.

7. If necessary, replace the brake bridge.

8. Fine-tune the bolt tension (and the preload adjuster if installed) until both legs of the fork feel equally tensioned; then reinstall the end caps.

MAINTENANCE OF AIR-OIL SUSPENSION FORKS

Although these are more complicated, you'll get a shorter description here: Do all the cleaning and checking described above, but don't fool around with the mechanisms yourself if there is a problem. A cop-out? Not really. These are sensitive devices and it's more important to know when they require maintenance or replacement than just how it's done. If you notice a problem you can either take it to a bike shop that has a mechanic who has worked on these things before, and don't let anyone else touch them; or you can call the manufacturer's service hotline and ask them to send you maintenance instructions.

Note

Make sure you have another bike to ride while you're working on the air-suspension forks. Don't give up until you're satisfied—and be smart enough to take it to the shop if you find you've tried to bite off more than you can chew.

This is the way to adjust the preload, or stiffness, on this simple elastomer-pad suspension stem.

SUSPENSION STEMS

To install an after-market suspension stem, make sure you order the one that matches the type and size of head tube and headset on your bike (threaded or unthreaded, regular or oversize steerer tube diameter). Follow the instructions in Chapter 31 for the stem installation.

If you need to adjust the preload and damping, there is an adjuster in the form of an Allen bolt on some models. Simple elastomer-sprung models just have a preload bolt, but even that will help to give you the kind of feel that matches your weight and riding style.

REAR SUSPENSION SYSTEMS

Rear suspension systems differ so much from one another that comprehensive instructions for their maintenance can't be given that do any of them justice.

In general, it will be enough to keep all sliding and pivoting surfaces meticulously clean, slightly lubricated with silicone or Teflon lubricant. Tighten the various screws, nuts, and bolts about once a month.

Be alert to the way the bike rides. If you notice erratic operation or a sudden change in response, check the whole system out carefully, paying attention to both the spring unit and the various pivots. If you have a problem that can't be solved with cleaning, adjusting, and tightening, take the bike to a shop.

ACCESSORY MAINTENANCE

I n this chapter, we'll just cover installation and removal of some of the various mounttain bike accessories, and give simple suggestions for maintenance of accessories in general.

LOCK MAINTENANCE

Lubricate the lock very sparingly after it has been cleaned: one or two drops of oil at the point where the shackle goes into the body of the lock, and one drop on the key—then insert the key to lock and unlock it a few times. Finally wipe off any excess lubricant.

PUMP MAINTENANCE

If the pump doesn't work properly, the leak is usually at the head of the pump (the part that is put on the valve) or at the plunger inside the pump.

Tools and equipment
Wrench
Lubricant
Cloth

Procedure
1. Tighten the screwed bushing that holds down the grommet, or rubber sealing washer, in the head of the pump.
2. If this doesn't solve the problem, unscrew it and check the grommet, replacing it if necessary (for instance, if it's inflexible, cut, frayed or has an enlarged hole); then screw the bushing back on.
3. If still no luck, unscrew the other end of the pump and check the condition of the plunger. If it is no longer

Sophisticated rechargeable-battery-powered lights have industrial-quality connectors so that the individual components can be removed separately.

flexible, impregnate it with any kind of vegetable fat (don't use mineral grease if it's rubber) and make sure it is screwed down tight. If necessary, replace the leather or plastic plunger.

INSTALLING LIGHTS

Most of these units come with some kind of instructions. In case you don't have any, follow these very general instructions as a guideline.

Tools and equipment
Varies between different makes and models, but usually screwdriver, pliers, wrench, and electric insulating tape or handlebar tape

Most simple battery lights available in the United States, which may give enough light only for road use, run on either two C-cells or on four AAA-cells. Replace them when they start getting dim, rather than waiting until they go out altogether. The lights most readily available in Great Britain (conforming to the applicable British Standard requirement) run on two larger D-cells and last about three times as long at the same brightness.

Procedure
1. Get the appropriate mounting hardware, and install the lights and reflectors in such a way that they do not protrude beyond the bike more than necessary.
2. For lights, the highest mounting position is generally the best, as it does not throw such confusing shadows and is more readily visible to others.

Luggage rack installation detail. If there is enough room between the eyelet and the chain when the chain is on the smallest cog, it's best to use a slightly longer bolt secured with a locknut from the back.

3. For reflectors, the lowest position is best. Make sure they are mounted with their reflective surface exactly vertical.

4. Attach each part by means of at least two bolts, to prevent it from vibrating loose.

5. If the battery fits in a pouch, hold the pouch with three straps wedged in one of the frame's junctions; if it is contained in a water bottle, don't choose a flimsy plastic bottle cage but a sturdy steel one.

LIGHT MAINTENANCE

Tools and equipment
Spare batteries
Spare bulb
Sandpaper or steel wool
Battery terminal grease
Electrical insulating tape

Procedure

1. Usually, when a battery light lets you down, it's a matter of a dead or dying battery. Check that first by trying the light with other batteries installed.

2. If that does not solve the problem, check whether the bulb makes proper contact with the terminal—

Fenders can only be installed if the bike has adequate clearance between the tire and the fork; this one is marginal at best.

scrape the contacts of bulb, battery, and terminals to remove dirt or corrosion, and screw in the bulb fully.

3. If still no luck, check the bulb and replace it if the filament is broken.

4. To prevent corrosion of the contacts, lightly coat the terminals of battery, bulb, switch, and any other parts that carry electricity with battery terminal grease, available in auto part stores.

RECHARGEABLE BATTERIES

On lighting systems with rechargeable batteries and wiring connections, occasionally check the connections and recharge the NiCad batteries at least once a week, as these have a limited shelf life, which means they drain even when not in use. Lead-acid gel batteries, on the other hand, have a much longer shelf life, but they too must be recharged and they should never be fully discharged.

LUGGAGE RACK INSTALLATION

Usually, the luggage rack is attached to bosses welded or brazed onto the bike's frame and front fork.

If your bike does not have the requisite bosses, you can use clips, providing you first wrap the frame or fork-tube local to these clips with a large rubber patch,

installed with rubber solution just as you would do for a flat tire. This protects the paint and prevents slipping of the clip under the effect of load and vibrations.

FENDER INSTALLATION

Fenders are mounted by means of stays that run to the eyelets at the drop-outs and a clip attached to the fork or the brake bridge. If your bike is lacking one or even both of the holes needed for the attachment bolts, you'll have to drill your own. If you want to make the fenders easily removable, use homemade wing bolts, made by soldering a washer in the saw cut of a slotted-head screw.

To straighten out the position of the fenders, simply clamp the stays in at a different point. Cut off the excess length, so there are no dangerous protrusions on the bike.

CHAINRING PROTECTOR (ROCKRING)

This device is installed in the same holes as the chainrings, so make sure you get the right version to match your equipment. Use the special (longer) mounting bolts provided. Check the attachments from time to time, and tighten the bolts if necessary.

GENERAL ACCESSORY INSTALLATION AND MAINTENANCE

Follow these points for any accessories in general if you can't locate more precise and specific instructions:

1. Use stainless steel nuts and bolts wherever possible.

2. Install the accessory in a location where it does not hinder your movement and does not get in the way.

3. Attachment must be at a minimum of two points, preferably offset relative to one another.

4. If it is meant to be fixed but comes loose, don't just retighten it: find a better attachment method.

5. If it is a moving part, check whether it moves freely without resistance, and lubricate or adjust it if necessary.

6. If it gets damaged, remove, repair, or replace it immediately.

7. If it doesn't do the job you had hoped it would, remove and discard it.

APPENDIX

leg length		recommended seat tube height				recommended straddle height	
		A center to top of lug		B center-to-center		ground to top tube	
cm	in	cm	in	cm	in	cm	in
73	29	35	14	34		65	26
74		36		35		66	
75		37		35	14	67	
76	30	38	15	36		68	27
77		39		37		69	
78		40		38	15	70	
79	31	41	16	39		71	28
80		42		40	16	72	
81	32	43	17	41		73	29
82		44		42		74	
83		45		43	17	75	
84	33	46	18	44		76	30
85		47		45	18	77	
86	34	48	19	46		78	31
87		49		47		79	
88		50		48	19	80	
89	35	51	20	49		81	32
90		52		50	20	82	
91	36	53	21	51		83	33
92		54		52		84	
93		55		53	21	85	
94	37	56	22	54		86	34
95		57		56		87	

Remarks:
The seat tube lengths shown in this table are recommended values. The maximum size is about one inch (2.5 cm) more, the minimum about one inch (2.5 cm) less.

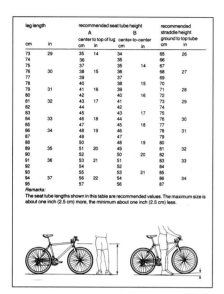

ABOVE
Frame sizing.
This table gives suggested nominal frame sizes as a function of your leg length, measured as shown in the accompanying detail illustration.

ABOVE RIGHT
Gear table: gear in inches for 26-inch wheel bicycle.
Gear is the equivalent wheel diameter of a directly driven bicycle and is always measured in inches.

BOTTOM
Gear table: development in meters for 26-inch wheel bicycle.
Development is the distance traveled per crank revolution and is always measured in meters.

NUMBER OF TEETH ON CHAINRING

COG	24	26	28	30	32	34	36	38	39	40	41	42	43	44	45	46	47	48	49	50	51	52	53	
13	48	52	56	60	64	68	72	76	78	80	82	84	86	88	90	92	94	96	98	100	102	104	106	13
14	45	48	52	56	60	63	67	70	72	74	76	78	80	82	84	85	87	89	91	93	95	97	98	14
15	42	45	49	52	55	59	62	66	68	69	71	73	75	76	78	80	81	83	85	87	88	90	92	15
16	39	42	45	49	52	55	58	61	63	65	67	68	70	72	73	75	76	78	80	81	83	85	86	16
17	37	40	43	46	49	52	55	58	60	61	63	64	66	67	69	70	72	73	75	76	78	80	81	17
18	35	38	40	43	46	49	52	55	56	58	59	61	62	64	65	66	68	69	71	72	74	75	77	18
19	33	36	38	41	44	47	49	52	53	55	56	57	59	60	62	63	64	66	67	68	70	71	73	19
20	31	34	36	39	42	44	47	49	51	52	53	55	56	57	59	60	61	62	64	65	66	68	69	20
21	30	32	35	37	40	42	45	47	48	50	51	52	53	54	56	57	58	59	61	62	63	64	66	21
22	28	31	33	35	38	40	43	45	46	47	48	50	51	52	53	54	56	57	58	59	60	61	63	22
23	27	29	32	34	36	38	41	43	44	45	46	47	49	50	51	52	53	54	55	57	58	59	60	23
24	26	28	30	32	35	37	39	41	42	43	44	45	47	48	49	50	51	52	53	54	55	56	57	24
25	25	27	29	31	33	35	37	39	41	42	43	44	45	46	47	48	49	50	51	52	53	54	55	25
26	24	26	28	30	32	34	36	38	39	40	41	42	43	44	45	46	47	48	49	50	51	52	53	26
27	23	25	27	29	31	33	35	37	38	39	39	40	41	42	43	44	45	46	47	48	49	50	51	27
28	22	24	26	28	30	32	33	35	36	37	38	39	40	41	42	43	44	45	46	47	48	49		28
30	21	23	24	26	28	29	31	33	34	35	36	36	37	38	39	40	41	42	43	44	45	46		30
32	20	21	23	24	26	28	29	31	32	33	33	34	35	35	37	37	38	39	40	41	41	42	43	32
34	18	20	21	23	24	26	28	29	30	31	31	32	33	33	34	35	36	37	37	38	39	40	41	34
38	16	18	19	21	22	23	25	26	27	27	28	29	29	30	31	31	32	32	33	34	35	36	36	38
	24	26	28	30	32	34	36	38	39	40	41	42	43	44	45	46	47	48	49	50	51	52	53	

NUMBER OF TEETH ON CHAINRING

COG	24	26	28	30	32	34	36	38	39	40	41	42	43	44	45	46	47	48	49	50	51	52	53	
13	3.80	4.10	4.50	4.80	5.10	5.40	5.70	6.10	6.20	6.40	6.50	6.70	6.90	7.00	7.20	7.30	7.50	7.70	7.80	8.00	8.10	8.30	8.50	13
14	3.60	3.90	4.10	4.40	4.70	5.00	5.30	5.60	5.80	5.90	6.10	6.20	6.40	6.50	6.70	6.80	7.00	7.10	7.30	7.40	7.60	7.70	7.90	14
15	3.30	3.60	3.90	4.10	4.40	4.70	5.00	5.30	5.40	5.50	5.70	5.80	5.90	6.10	6.20	6.40	6.60	6.80	6.90	7.10	7.20	7.30		15
16	3.10	3.40	3.60	3.90	4.10	4.40	4.70	4.90	5.10	5.20	5.30	5.40	5.60	5.70	5.80	6.00	6.10	6.20	6.40	6.50	6.60	6.70	6.90	16
17	2.90	3.20	3.40	3.70	3.90	4.10	4.40	4.60	4.80	4.90	5.00	5.10	5.20	5.40	5.50	5.60	5.70	5.90	6.00	6.10	6.20	6.30	6.50	17
18	2.80	3.00	3.20	3.50	3.70	3.90	4.10	4.40	4.50	4.60	4.70	4.80	5.00	5.10	5.20	5.30	5.40	5.50	5.60	5.80	5.90	6.00	6.10	18
19	2.60	2.80	3.10	3.30	3.50	3.70	3.90	4.10	4.30	4.40	4.50	4.60	4.70	4.80	4.90	5.00	5.10	5.20	5.40	5.50	5.60	5.80		19
20	2.50	2.70	2.90	3.10	3.30	3.50	3.70	3.90	4.00	4.10	4.30	4.40	4.50	4.70	4.80	4.90	4.90	5.00	5.10	5.20	5.30	5.40	5.50	20
21	2.40	2.60	2.80	3.00	3.20	3.40	3.60	3.80	3.90	4.00	4.10	4.20	4.20	4.30	4.40	4.50	4.60	4.70	4.80	4.90	5.00	5.10	5.15	21
22	2.30	2.50	2.70	2.80	3.00	3.20	3.40	3.60	3.70	3.80	3.90	4.00	4.10	4.15	4.20	4.30	4.40	4.50	4.60	4.70	4.80	4.90	4.95	22
23	2.20	2.30	2.50	2.70	2.90	3.10	3.20	3.40	3.50	3.60	3.70	3.80	3.90	4.00	4.10	4.15	4.20	4.30	4.40	4.50	4.60	4.70	4.80	23
24	2.10	2.20	2.40	2.60	2.80	2.90	3.10	3.30	3.40	3.50	3.50	3.60	3.70	3.80	3.90	4.00	4.10	4.15	4.20	4.30	4.40	4.50	4.60	24
25	2.00	2.20	2.30	2.50	2.70	2.80	3.00	3.20	3.25	3.30	3.40	3.50	3.60	3.70	3.70	3.80	3.90	4.00	4.10	4.15	4.20	4.30	4.40	25
26	1.90	2.10	2.20	2.40	2.60	2.70	3.00	3.10	3.20	3.30	3.40	3.50	3.60	3.85	3.90	4.00	4.10	4.15	4.20					26
27	1.85	2.00	2.20	2.30	2.50	2.60	2.80	2.90	3.00	3.10	3.20	3.25	3.30	3.40	3.50	3.55	3.60	3.70	3.80	3.80	3.90	4.00	4.10	27
28	1.80	1.90	2.10	2.20	2.40	2.50	2.70	2.80	2.90	3.00	3.05	3.10	3.20	3.30	3.35	3.40	3.50	3.60	3.65	3.70	3.80	3.90	3.90	28
30	1.70	1.80	1.90	2.10	2.20	2.40	2.50	2.60	2.70	2.80	2.90	2.95	3.00	3.05	3.10	3.20	3.30	3.35	3.40	3.50	3.55	3.60	3.70	30
32	1.60	1.70	1.80	1.90	2.10	2.20	2.30	2.50	2.55	2.60	2.70	2.75	2.80	2.90	2.95	3.00	3.05	3.10	3.20	3.25	3.30	3.40	3.45	32
34	1.50	1.60	1.70	1.80	2.00	2.10	2.20	2.30	2.40	2.45	2.50	2.60	2.60	2.70	2.75	2.80	2.90	2.95	3.00	3.10	3.15	3.20	3.25	34
38	1.40	1.50	1.60	1.70	1.80	2.00	2.10	2.20	2.25	2.30	2.40	2.45	2.50	2.55	2.60	2.70	2.75	2.80	2.85	2.90	2.95	3.00	3.10	38
	24	26	28	30	32	34	36	38	39	40	41	42	43	44	45	46	47	48	49	50	51	52	53	

ADDRESSES

Adventure Cycling Association, Box 8308, Missoula, MT 59807, USA

Australian Cycling Council, 153 The Kingsway, Cronulla, Sydney 2230, Australia

Bicycle Federation of America, 1818 R Street NW, Washington, DC 20009, U.S.A.

Bicycle Federation of Australia, 399 Pitt Street, Sydney 2000, Australia

British Cycling Federation, 70 Brompton Road, London SW3 1EN, Great Britain

British Cycling Federation, Touring Bureau, 3 Moor Lane, Lancaster, Great Britain

British Cyclo-Cross Association, 208 Ecclesall Road, Sheffield 511 8JD, Great Britain

Bureau of Land Management, U.S. Department of the Interior, 18th and C Streets, NW, Room 1013, Washington, DC 20240, USA

Canadian Cycling Association, Touring Department, 333 River Road, Vanier, Ontario KlL 8B9, Canada

Canadian Mountain Bike Association, 27 Cornerbrook Drive, Don Mills, Ontario M3A 1H5, Canada

Cross-Country Cycling Club, 5 Old Station Cottages, Ford, Arundel, West Sussex BNl8 OBJ, Great Britain

Countryside Commission, John Dower House, Crescent Place, Cheltenham GL50 3RA, Great Britain

Cyclists' Touring Club, 69 Meadrow, Godalming, Surrey GU7 3HS, Great Britain

International Mountain Bike Association, P. O. Box 7578, Boulder, CO 80306, USA, IMBA@aol.com

League of American Wheelmen, 6707 Whitestone Road, Suite 209, Baltimore, MD 21207, USA

Mountain Bike Club, 3 The Shrubbery, Albert Street, Telford TF2 9AS, Great Britain

National Park Foundation, P.O. Box 57473, Washington, DC 20037, USA

National Park Service, U.S. Department of the Interior, 18th and C Streets NW, Room 1013, Washington, DC 20240, USA

NORBA (National Off-Road Bicycle Association), P.O. Box 1901, Chandler, AZ 85244, USA

ADDRESSES CONT.

Rough Stuff Fellowship, 9 Liverpool Avenue, Southport, Merseyside PR8 3NE, Great Britain

Sierra Club, 730 Polk Street, San Francisco, CA 94109, USA

United States Forest Service, U.S. Department of Agriculture, P.O. Box 2417, Washington, DC 20013, USA

US Geological Survey, 1200 Eads Street South, Arlington, VA 22202, USA, (map distribution for states east of Mississippi River)

U.S. Geological Survey, P.O. Box 25286, Denver, CO 80225, USA, (map distribution for states west of Mississippi River)

PERIODICALS

Bicycle Action, 136/138 New Cavendish Street, London W1M 7FG, Great Britain

Bicycle Guide, 6420 Wilshire Boulevard, Los Angeles, CA 90048, USA

Bicycle Magazine, P.O. Box 381, Mill Harbour, London E14 9TW, Great Britain

Bicycle USA, 190 Ostend Sreet, Suite 120, Baltimore, MD 21230, USA, (LAW members' magazine)

Bicycling, 135 N. 6th Street, Emmaus, PA 18104, USA

Bike, 333046 Calle Aviador, Dana Point, CA 92675, USA

Cycletouring, 69 Meadrow, Godalming, Surrey GU7 3HS, Great Britain, (CTC members' magazine)

Dirt Rag, 181 Saxonburg Road, Pittsburgh. PA 15238, USA

Making Tracks, 5 Old Station Cottages, Ford, Arundel, West Sussex, BN18 0BJ, Great Britain

Mountain Bike, 2101 Rosecrans Avenue, Suite 6200, El Segundo, CA 90245, USA

Mountain Bike Action, 25233 Anza Drive, Valencia, CA 91355, USA

Mountain Biker, 6420 Wilshire Boulevard, Los Angeles, CA 90048, USA

Mountain Biking, 7950 Deering Avenue, Canoga Park, CA 91304, USA

Mountain Biking UK, Woodstock House, Luton Road, Faversham, Kent ME13 8HQ, Great Britain

New Cyclist, 14 St. Clement's Grove, York YO2 1JZ, Great Britain

Rough Stuff Journal, A. J. Matthews, 9 Liverpool Avenue, Southport, Merseyside PR8 3NE, Great Britain

BIBLIOGRAPHY

Advanced First Aid. New York: Doubleday/American National Red Cross, 1973.

American Youth Hostels Handbook. Delaplane, VT: American Youth Hostel Association, (annual).

Ballantine, R., and R. Grant. *Richard's Ultimate Bicycle Book*. London: Dorling Kindersley, 1993.

Barnett, J. *Barnett's Manual: Analysis and Procedures for Bicycle Mechanics*. 2nd ed. Boulder, CO: VeloPress, 1996.

Berto, F. J. *Bicycling Magazine's Complete Guide to Upgrading Your Bike*. Emmaus, PA: Rodale Press, 1988.

Bicycling magazine, eds. *Bicycling Magazine. Best Bicycle Tours*. Emmaus, PA: Rodale Press, 1981.

Bicycle Touring Atlas. New York: American Youth Hostel Association, 1969.

Brandt, J. *The Bicycle Wheel*. 3rd ed. Palo Alto, CA: Avocet, 1993.

Bridge, R. *Freewheeling: The Bicycle Camping Book*. Harrisonburg, PA: Stackpole Books, 1974.

———. *Bike Touring*. San Francisco: Sierra Club Books, 1979.

Bunelle, H., and S. Sarvis. *Cooking for Camp and Trail*. San Francisco: Sierra Club Books, 1984.

Burney, S., and T. Gould. *Mountain Bike Racing*. 2nd ed. London: A&C Black; New York: Lyons & Burford. 1995.

Campground and Trailer Park Guide. Chicago: Rand McNally, (annual).

Clark, J. *Mountain Biking the National Parks*. San Francisco: Bicycle Books, 1995.

Climates of the States. Port Washington, NY: United States National Oceanic and Atmospheric Administration, 1974.

Coello, D. *The Mountain Bike Manual*. Salt Lake City: Dream Garden Press, 1985.

———. *Mountain Bike Repair Handbook: Technique, Equipment, Repair*. New York: Lyons & Burford, 1990.

Coles, C. W., H. T. Glenn, and J. S. Allen. *Glenn's New Complete Bicycle Manual: Selection, Maintenance, Repair*. 2nd ed. New York: Crown Publishers, 1989.

The Complete Guide to America's National Parks. Washington DC: National Park Foundation, 1984.

The CTC Handbook. Godalming, Surrey (G. B.): Cyclist's Touring Club, (annual).

Cuthberson, T. *Anybody's Bike Book*. Berkeley, CA: Ten Speed Press, 1984.

———. *Bike Tripping*. Berkeley, CA: Ten Speed Press, 1984.

DeLong, F. *DeLong's Guide to Bicycles and Bicycling*. Radnor, PA: Chilton Books, 1978.

Eastman, P. F. *Advanced First Aid for All Outdoors*. Centerville, MD: Cornell Maritime Press, 1976.

Faria, I. E. *Cycling Physiology for the Serious Cyclist*. Springfield, MS: Thomas, 1978.

Fletcher, C. *The New Complete Walker*. New York: Knopf, 1974.

Food and Nutrition Board. *Recommended Dietary Allowances*. Washington, DC: National Academy of Sciences, 1974.

Forester, J. *Effective Cycling*. Cambridge, MA: MIT Press, 1984.

Gatty, H. *Finding Your Way on Land and Sea*. Brattleboro, VT: Stephen Green Press, 1983.

Gordis, K., and G. LeMond. *Greg LeMond's Complete Book of Bicycling*. New York: Putnam, 1989.

———. *Greg LeMond's Pocket Guide to Bicycle Maintenance and Repair*. New York: Putnam, 1989.

Greenhood, D. *Mapping*. Chicago: University of Chicago Press, 1964.

Hefferson, L. *Cycle Food*. Berkeley, CA: Ten Speed Press, 1976.

Howard, J. *The Cyclist's Companion*. Brattleboro, VT: Stephen Green Press, 1984.

Inside the Cyclist. Brattleboro, VT: Velo-News, 1984.

International Bicycle Touring. Mountain View, CA: World Publications, 1976.

Janssen, P.G.J.M. *Training, Lactate, Pulse-Rate*. Oulu, Finland: Polar Electro Oy, 1987.

Kals, W. S. *Land Navigation Handbook*. San Francisco: Sierra Club Books, 1971.

Keefe, M. *The Ten-Speed Commandments*. Garden City, NY: Doubleday, 1987.

Kellstrom, G. *Map and Compass*. New York: Charles Scribner's Sons, 1973.

Kelly, C., and N. Crane. *Richard's Mountain Bike Book*. New York: Ballantine Books; Oxford: Oxford Illustrated Press, 1988.

Kennedy, M. J., M. Kloser, and P. Y. Samer. *Fat Tire Rider*. Brattleboro, VT: Vitesse Press, 1993.

Lynn, L., et al. *The Off-Road Bicycle Book*. Butterset (Great Britain): Leading Edge, 1987.

Marr, D. *Bicycle Gearing*. Seattle: The Mountaineers, 1989.

Nasr, K. *Bicycle Touring International*. San Francisco: Bicycle Books, 1992.

National Atlas of the United States. Washington DC: U.S. Department of the Interior, Geological Survey, 1970.

Nealy, W. *The Mountain Biking Way of Knowledge*. Birmingham, AL: Menasha Ridge Press, 1991.

———. *Mountain Bike!* Birmingham, AL: Menasha Ridge Press, 1992.

Nye, P. *The Cyclist's Source Book*. New York: Putnam Publishing, 1991.

Olson, J. *Mountain Biking*. London: Salamander Books; Harrisburg, PA: Stackpole Books, 1989.

Perry, D. B. *Bike Cult*. New York: Four Walls Eight Windows, 1995.

Rafoth, R. *Bicycling Fuel*. 3rd ed. San Francisco: Bicycle Books, 1993.

Seidl, H. *Mountain Bikes: Maintaining, Repairing and Upgrading*. New York: Sterling, 1993.

Sloane, E. *Sloane's Complete Book of All Terrain Biking*. New York: Simon & Schuster, 1991.

———. *Sloane's Handy Pocket Guide to Bicycle Repair*. New York: Simon & Schuster, 1993.

———. *The New Complete Book of Bicycling*. 2nd ed. New York: Simon & Schuster, 1992.

Stevenson, J., and B. Richards. *Mountain Bikes: Maintenance and Repair*. (2nd ed.) Huddersfield (Great Britain): Springfield Books; San Francisco: Bicycle Books, 1994.

Stuart, R. and C. Jensen. *Mountain Biking for Women*. Waverly, NY: Acorn Publishing, 1994.

Sutherland, H., J. S. Allen, E. Colaianni, and J. P. Hart. *Sutherland's Handbook for Bicycle Mechanics*. 4th ed. Berkeley, CA: Sutherland's Publications, 1991.

Thomas, D. *Roughing It Easy*. Provo, UT: Brigham Young University Press, 1974.

Van der Plas, R. *The Bicycle Repair Book*. 2nd ed. San Francisco: Bicycle Books, 1993.

———. *Bicycle Repair Step by Step*. San Francisco: Bicycle Books: Huddersfield (Great Britain): Springfield Books, 1994.

———. *Bicycle Technology*. San Francisco: Bicycle Books, 1991.

———. *The Bicycle Touring Manual*. 2nd ed. San Francisco: Bicycle Books, 1993.

———. *Mountain Bike Magic*. San Francisco: Bicycle Books, 1991.

———. *Mountain Bike Maintenance: Repairing and Maintaining the Off-Road Bicycle*. 3rd ed. San Francisco: Bicycle Books, 1994.

———. *The Penguin Bicycle Handbook*. Harmondsworth (G. B.): Penguin Books, 1983.

———. *Roadside Bicycle Repair: The Simple Guide to Fixing Your Bike*. 3rd ed. San Francisco: Bicycle Books, 1995.

Watts, A. *Instant Weather Forecasting*. New York: Dodd Mead & Co, 1968.

Whitt, F. R., and D. G. Wilson. *Bicycling Science*. 2nd ed. Cambridge, MA: MIT Press, 1982.

Zarka, J. *All Terrain Biking*. San Francisco: Bicycle Books, 1991.

Zinn, L. *Zinn and the Art of Mountain Bike Maintenance*. Boulder, CO: VeloPress, 1996.

INDEX